DATE DUE		

Also available from ASQ Quality Press

Measuring Customer Satisfaction: Survey Design, Use, and StatisticalAnalysis Methods
Second Edition
Bob E. Hayes

Improving Your Measurement of Customer Satisfaction: A Guide To Creating,
Conducting, Analyzing, and Reporting Customer Satisfaction Measurement Programs
Terry G. Vavra

Mapping Work Processes
Dianne Galloway

Quality Quotes
Hélio Gomes

Measuring and Managing Customer Satisfaction: Going For The Gold
Sheila Kessler

Total Quality Service: A Simplified Approach To Using The Baldrige Award Criteria
Sheila Kessler

Customer Retention: An Integrated Process For Keeping Your Best Customers
Michael W. Lowenstein

The Change Agents' Handbook: A Survival Guide for Quality Improvement
Champions
David W. Hutton

Creating a Customer-Centered Culture: Leadership In Quality, Innovation, and Speed
Robin L. Lawton

Understanding and Applying Value-Added Assessment: Eliminating Business
Process Waste
William E. Trischler

To request a complimentary catalog of ASQ Quality Press publications,
call 800-248-1946.

Online Customer Care

Strategies
for
Call Center
Excellence

by

Michael Cusack

ASQ Quality Press
Milwaukee, Wisconsin

Online Customer Care: Strategies for Call Center Excellence
Michael Cusack

Library of Congress Cataloging-in-Publication Data
Cusack, Michael, 1955–
    Online customer care : applying today's technology to achieve
world-class customer interaction / by Michael Cusack.
        p. cm.
    Includes bibliographical references and index.
    ISBN 0-87389-383-2 (alk. paper)
    1. Customer services—Management.   2. Teleshopping.   3. Customer
relations.   4. Internet marketing.   5. Internet advertising.
6. Business enterprises—Computer networks.   7. Consumer
satisfaction.   I. Title.
HF5415.5C83   1998
658.8′12—dc21   97-46441
                                                                    CIP

10 9 8 7 6 5 4 3

ISBN 0-87389-383-2

Acquisitions Editor: Roger Holloway
Project Editor: Jeanne Bohn

ASQ Mission: To facilitate continuous improvement and increase customer
satisfaction by identifying, communicating, and promoting the use of quality
principles, concepts, and technologies; and thereby be recognized throughout
the world as the leading authority on, and champion for, quality.

Attention: Schools and Corporations
ASQ Quality Press books, audiotapes, videotapes, and software are available at
quantity discounts with bulk purchases for business, educational, or instructional use. For information, please contact ASQ Quality Press at 800-248-1946,
or write to ASQ Quality Press, P.O. Box 3005, Milwaukee, WI 53201-3005.

For a free copy of the ASQ Quality Press Publications Catalog, including ASQ
membership information, call 800-248-1946, or access http://www.asq.org.

Printed in the United States of America   #37966371

♾ Printed on acid-free paper   72196
                                             HF
                                             5415 5
                                             ·C83
                                             1998

American Society for Quality

Quality Press
611 East Wisconsin Avenue
Milwaukee, Wisconsin 53202

Contents

List of Figures

List of Tables

Preface

Many contemporary customer care environments focus on two major elements. First, the use of technologies that promise to *minimize contact time* with the customer (such as automatic call distribution, computer-telephony integration, and interactive voice response), and secondly the use of voice-to-voice *contact handling techniques,* which enable agents to efficiently and effectively handle every type of customer inquiry or problem with a minimum of difficulty. Both of these elements, while proven contributors to cost reduction and customer satisfaction, nevertheless fall short of fulfilling the premise that every customer contact, however trite or complex, is an opportunity not only to gather valuable *market intelligence,* but also to actually *resolve* the customer's problem on the first point of contact. In other words, while getting through to a courteous, sympathetic agent within ten seconds may initially be highly satisfying, that satisfaction is unlikely to persist if the customer is forced to call back several times in order to resolve a problem.

It is critical, therefore, that processes be in place to facilitate the timely and satisfactory resolution of every customer contact, whether it is via an inbound call center, a company's World Wide Web site, or some other medium. Regardless of whether a customer calls to complain about a product feature, request information about the latest promotional offerings, ask for directions to the nearest branch, inquire about the status of a repair, or request instructions on how to perform a certain task, the agent needs to be able to retrieve relevant information instantaneously and convey it to the customer, while also ensuring that the context of that transaction with the customer is adequately captured for root cause analysis and contact history purposes. Knowledge retrieval and data gathering, therefore, are considered the key elements in the quest for world-class customer interaction.

In the context of this book, customer *care* is defined not only as the provisioning of presale and postsale customer service support, but also as the ability of a business to dynamically gather and *leverage* customer information in a way that is mutually beneficial to both the customer and the business itself. In other words, it is the fostering of an end-to-end relationship with the customer. *Online* customer care is further defined as the provisioning and maintenance of systems and information that enable both *agents* (most often referred to as customer service representatives or CSRs) and customers to quickly find satisfactory answers to inquiries, problems, and complaints through a variety of media. Online customer care may be augmented by business operations support for established customer care environments (i.e., facilities, staffing, scheduling, training, empowerment, and incentives), or may exist as a nonmediated service to customers via utilities such as the World Wide Web. The business case for online customer care minimizes costs and maximizes customer satisfaction, while effectively gathering critical market intelligence data. In order to realize this outcome, a company must focus on the three critical areas of process, technology and content. This book explains how process-driven systems design, user interaction, content provisioning, and data gathering can result in world-class customer interaction.

Traditionally, one of the biggest problems for customer care executives has been how to balance agent productivity with customer satisfaction. By implementing information retrieval systems that facilitate a timely and relevant response to a customer's inquiry or problem, management can realize a significant return on investment through both renewed customer loyalty and direct access to useful market intelligence.

Clearly, there are three major business needs that continue to drive the evolution of online customer care. These are customer satisfaction, cost reduction, and market intelligence. Specific goals may be attributed to these needs, such as resolving a customer inquiry or problem on the first contact, maximizing customer access to agents or databases, gathering customer data, and providing tools for preventive analysis. These goals translate into business requirements, including the provisioning of online information sources, improving training, empowering users, improving agent scheduling, minimizing turnover, conducting customer satisfaction surveys, and providing contact tracking facilities.

Companies are embracing information technologies in order to provide "on the spot" assistance to agents and customers alike. Intelligent troubleshooting systems, online documentation, store locators, referral and escalation systems, call trackers, automated notations, and outbound correspondence templates have been added to demographic, billing, and ordering databases. As computers and telephones become increasingly integrated, companies are offering their customers alternatives to voice-to-voice telephone services. Other media have also emerged as value-added components of customer care. In the three decades since the first call center was opened, however, many companies who have embraced technology as a facilitator of outstanding customer care have found it difficult to quantify the return on investment. This situation often arises because the technology essentially fails to deliver the type of productivity gains being sought.

In summary, this is not a book about workforce management techniques, customer handling skills, or call routing technologies. Those disciplines are already the focal point for a plethora of publications and conferences. Instead, *this book focuses on the existent and emerging processes and technologies that facilitate the realization of business requirements as they pertain to system design, user interaction, knowledge man-*

agement, and data gathering. The availability of online information through outstanding system selection, integration, release, and maintenance processes, combined with task analysis, rapid prototyping, and usability testing, and allied with carefully defined knowledge acquisition and engineering, represent the essential elements of "best in class" customer care. By examining primarily how traditional voice-to-voice communications can be used to facilitate these goals, coupled with considerations of alternative media—particularly electronic mail, the World Wide Web, and interactive voice response—this book strives to present an innovative view of world-class customer interaction.

Overview of the Chapters

While customer care managers, system developers, process engineers, and human factors specialists will be most interested in the discussions of alternative media, information retrieval, process improvement, and technological considerations found in the later chapters of the book, this work in general is designed to be read by any individual who has anything to do with customer interaction, from the business executive to the newly recruited customer care agent. The case study described in Chapter 5, for example, is intended to present a "real world" situation which, in combination with the model for "online customer care," acts as an introduction to the implementation techniques described in the remainder of the book, whereas the first four chapters present a more generalized view of world-class customer interaction.

In many ways, the case study is a turning point from the strategic to the tactical, as the management concepts expressed in "Fundamentals," "Media," and "Business Drivers" are translated into contemporary approaches to customer care. As such, it is recommended that the reader keep both this case study and several other "cases in point" in mind while perusing these chapters. Executive readers will also be interested in the discussion of market intelligence gathering and analysis that is presented in the final chapter.

Chapter 1 "Introduction" explores the evolution of what has become a multibillion dollar industry. This chapter also describes the relationship between measures and contingencies, with particular emphasis on the "customer-facing" contingencies that provide a foundation for the entire book. This section examines the critical issues that confront customer care today, and how online mechanisms can ensure high levels of customer satisfaction.

Chapter 2 "Fundamentals" introduces the role of process as it pertains to the implementation of technology and content in a customer care environment.

Chapter 3 "Media" describes the various facilities contributing to the development of online customer care, particularly electronic mail, the World Wide Web and interactive voice response.

Chapter 4 "Business Drivers" examines the three business drivers behind every successful customer care operation—customer satisfaction, cost reduction, and market intelligence. By elaborating on each of these drivers, a framework for process-driven online customer care is described. This framework uses specific business goals such as resolution on first contact and the gathering of customer data as drivers of business requirements.

Chapter 5 "A Case Study" uses a hypothetical scenario involving a new inbound call center that appears to have prepared adequately for centralized customer care, yet whose performance is far below expectations. This chapter is used to introduce the detailed investigation of online customer care (i.e., chapters on systems design, information retrieval systems, market intelligence, etc.), thus giving the book a practical ("How to...") approach to implementation.

Chapter 6 "Process Considerations" considers those processes that are most relevant to the customer care environment, including a detailed overview of the quality improvement, data gathering, escalations, and follow-up work processes.

Chapter 7 "Systems Design and Development" focuses on the essential elements of systems design and integration as these pertain to customer care. This chapter also takes a critical look at the traditional role of systems development in call centers, and suggests a methodology for user-driven design.

Chapter 8 "Information Retrieval Systems" examines the differences between online documentation and intelligent troubleshooting systems, and how these systems can be used in a customer care environment. This chapter also uses a cost/benefit analysis approach to demonstrate the potential productivity gains that can be engendered by information retrieval systems.

Chapter 9 "Knowledge Management" considers the roles of documentation and knowledge engineers in ensuring that information retrieval systems are most beneficial to the user population. The critical features of relevance, clarity, integrity, completeness, and accuracy are examined in detail.

Chapter 10 "Electronic Mail" presents a step-by-step methodology for ensuring that this medium is used appropriately in a customer care environment. By detailing the creation and delivery of the electronic mail message, to the integration, interpretation, routing, and response process, this chapter considers the practical application of increasingly sophisticated electronic mail functions.

Chapter 11 "The World Wide Web" examines the role of this medium in facilitating "self-service" customer care. This chapter focuses on both user interaction and content development for the Web, and considers the contingencies surrounding the integration of the Web with call centers.

Chapter 12 "High Technology at the Call Center" presents a practical overview of the tools that are most often expected to enhance productivity at the call center. The importance of user-focused interactive voice response unit scripting is considered, as well as the evolving role of computer-telephony integration. Other technologies, such as automatic call distribution and facsimile, are also addressed.

Chapter 13 "Market Intelligence" focuses on customer care as an integral contributor to business planning by describing data gathering, and analysis and information sharing functions and processes.

The author wishes to thank those individuals who inspired this study of online customer care, including Darren Bryden, Logical Design Solutions; Anne Mele, AT&T; Rohit Ramaswamy, Service Design Solutions; and Ron Bass, Lucent Technologies. The author would also like to thank Michael Jeske, Syntelligence Inc., for contributions to the chapter on electronic mail. I also wish to acknowledge Jeanne W. Bohn for her advice and encouragement during the preparation of the manuscript, and most importantly, my wife Christine for her patience and understanding throughout this endeavor. Comments and questions from readers are welcomed and may be directed to the author via **www.olccine.com**.

1

Introduction

Overview

A popular business philosophy is that, in an age of commodities, the differentiating factor between competitive companies is the augmentative support provided after the sale of a product or service. The perception of high cost and intangible benefits engendered by the provisioning of outstanding customer care, however, also ensures that most companies are advocates, rather than practitioners, of this belief. Contemporary customer care organizations are being asked to create and preserve customer loyalty, as well as gather and feed back market data, with a decreasing pool of resources. To augment the diminishing workforce, companies are deploying new technologies that promise significant short-term cost reductions while maintaining a consistent level of customer support.

Customer care today is often shaped by the perceived abilities and limitations of modern technology—a situation that guarantees that the endeavor will be characterized by rapid and continuous change. The evolving capabilities of the computer and telecommunications equipment will provide turn-of-the-century companies with greater opportunities to differentiate themselves from the competition by deploying technologies that *quickly* and *effectively* handle a customer inquiry or complaint either through a human medium (e.g., voice-to-voice, as well as agent-facilitated e-mail, fax, or postal contact), or directly from the computer (e.g., augmented interactive voice response or World Wide Web contact) while also gathering frontline market intelligence data. A critical driver of these technological advances is the notion of *empowering* the user by providing rapid access to information. Yet even the most advanced and costly technologies may be rendered ineffective by suboptimal processes. In order to take advantage of contemporary facilities for online customer care, an ongoing commitment to continuous process improvement, integrated system design, and rigorous content maintenance is required.

A company that bases its business success on outstanding customer care must be willing to demonstrate a commitment to building and maintaining resources that give the customer the needed response through what the customer considers to be the most appropriate medium. For example, a company that produces business software and has identified its customers as professionals in the 25–40 age bracket may decide to provide primary customer care via the World Wide Web, thereby enabling direct access and exploration of database files rather than waiting in queue for a customer care agent. A small-goods manufacturer dealing principally with customer complaints and product returns, on the other hand, might depend upon affable agents to answer the telephone and placate irate callers, and may not even consider alternative media.

Today, it is widely recognized that customer loyalty is at a premium and consumers are likely to take their business elsewhere if they do not receive outstanding postsale support. In an age of increasingly complex commodities, therefore, the provisioning of customer care is recognized as an integral part of the purchase of a product or service. Yet for all the talk of competitive differentiation and "best in class" customer care, attempts to achieve a balance between cost-cutting technologies and personalized support are often dismal failures. In addition to the common complaint of sub-standard agent-customer interaction, there are several other root causes for this situation, including

- Supporting systems that are so poorly designed, integrated, and maintained that agents don't want to use them
- Supporting materials that are so cryptic, irrelevant, or outdated that nobody can locate or interpret the correct response in a timely manner
- Augmentative technologies, such as interactive voice response (IVR), that are implemented in a way that is more detrimental than helpful to customers
- Customer care environments that are unable to gather, analyze, respond, and react to useful market intelligence data

Each of these problems, together with staffing, scheduling, training, and empowerment issues, indicates a breakdown in one or more of the essential elements of process, technology, and content which, in concert, can constitute outstanding customer interaction.

A company that perceives customer care to be a competitive advantage will also focus on creating a reputation for postsale support that exceeds its customers expectations, thus encouraging greater customer loyalty. In an age where *time* for those with purchasing power is at a premium, it can be surmised that many disgruntled toll-free service callers might forgo the warmth of a human response if it meant that they could quickly find the answer they were seeking through some other medium.

Customer care has become a fundamental survival tool for many companies. Yet in many cases, overworked and understaffed customer care environments are struggling to keep up with the plethora of contacts to traditional toll-free service lines—a scenario that can cost the largest companies hundreds of millions of dollars each year. The increasing complexity of modern products and services, coupled with rising customer demands for quality service, both contribute to escalated contact between the customer and the company. This trend has made the provisioning of customer care a high-technology focal point. The best companies are taking advantage of systems development in order to augment and even supersede their agents' efforts to deliver outstanding support.

Today, the majority of contacts with customer care environments are conducted via voice. However, with the home-based proliferation of online service media, customer care utilities will continue to evolve on computer networks like the Internet. Undoubtedly, customers who are predisposed to using online media for research, business, and entertainment purposes will embrace electronic communications far more quickly than the rest of the population. There is little doubt that the use of media like the World Wide Web will increase significantly, particularly if senders are confident that their communication can be created easily, will be answered in a timely manner, and will engender a relevant and understandable response. In order to achieve this goal, it is necessary to focus on processes that many customer care managers have only just begun to explore, such as the efficient handling and response to electronic messages, maintenance processes for online content, and user-driven technological enhancements.

Historical Perspective

According to the *Century Dictionary*, the word "customer" can mean "any one with whom a person has to deal, especially one with whom dealing is difficult or disagreeable." While many agents would agree with that definition, it is interesting to note that the emergence of the telephone as an anonymous means of relaying complaints to a company did not really formalize until the late nineteen sixties. It was then that the American Telephone & Telegraph (AT&T) company helped to initiate what has become a multibillion dollar industry by persuading companies that they needed to support customers by offering toll-free telephone access to centralized *call centers*. Initially, many companies perceived these facilities as expensive gimmicks with limited technological capabilities. As demands from smaller businesses for lower-cost call centers were met, the industry recognized their potential as direct points of sales and service contact with the customer. Soon toll-free numbers were recognized as an indicator of company commitment to customer care. By the early seventies, technologies such as the automatic call distributor (ACD) were being embraced, further enhancing the reputation of the call center as a proficient medium for customer care.

Today, call center agents may perform multiple tasks, sometimes with the same agent being asked to handle both inbound customer care and outbound telemarketing calls (a process often referred to as call blending). These customer contacts, which can typically include presales support, store location requests, order processing, general inquiries, account maintenance, and billing and technical support also involve complaint handling and market intelligence data gathering. The last of these functions can become the critical links between a call center and the remainder of the company. Customer information gathered by customer care facilities can embrace a process sometimes referred to as *database marketing*, whereby the company uses available market intelligence to understand the needs and expectations of its customers.

Toll-free numbers are so commonplace in the United States today that they are no longer viewed as a competitive advantage. Customers consider the facility of toll-free calling as a commodity, rather than as an icon of commitment to customer care. As a result, customer tolerance for long hold times and incompetent call handling has plummeted. In an effort to satisfy demands, companies have financed the development of the sophisticated tools found in contemporary call centers, such as automatic number identification (ANI), dialed number identification service (DNIS), interactive voice response (IVR), computer-telephony integration (CTI), intelligent call routing, and contact tracking systems. Ironically, the cost of these innovations and the need to demonstrate a quick return on investment is often used as an excuse to reduce agent head count.

Despite the power of contemporary technological solutions, achieving "best in class" customer care clearly requires ongoing senior management recognition of its role as an integral part of the company's value chain, not just an investment in a conglomeration of binary configurations and a group of poorly paid and undertrained frontline agents who will supposedly appease the customer. Whether indirectly via the Internet, directly via voice, or through some other media, it is motivated humans who provide outstanding customer care. Technology, together with and driven by constantly crafted processes and rigorous content engineering, enables customer care professionals to delight the customer by providing timely, accurate, clear, and complete solutions to inquiries and problems. Yet this scenario illustrates the challenge that continues to create difficulties for the majority of customer care operations—lack of decision-making authority and upper management support.

In this age of increasing demands and decreasing budgets, the burgeoning information technology industry is often perceived by management as the elixir for reducing customer churn. Few would doubt that telecommunications and computer systems can help to realize outstanding levels of service and thereby nurture customer retention, but it is an unfortunate fact that many companies appear to view technological implementation as a solution by itself, rather than as an integrated endeavor that embraces people-driven process and content considerations. As a result, many call centers find it more satisfactory (and cost justifying) to measure their effectiveness based solely on metrics such as the quantity of calls answered, calls abandoned, and the average speed of answer, rather than on more involved factors such as the number of calls resolved on first contact versus the average talk time, levels of customer satisfaction, cost/benefit and root cause analysis, integrity of online information, average percentage of customer base contacting customer care, and the timeliness of customer callbacks. Those customer care environments who manage to define the value of their existence through these and other key measurements tend to be viewed as viable profit centers that augment the company's marketing strategies, rather than as isolated and expensive satellites.

While there are good reasons to believe that modern technology will achieve the desired effect, poorly designed and maintained applications can actually have a detrimental influence on customer satisfaction. The technology-driven customer care environment is still relatively new, and the chasm between process and technology is self-evident. Call center managers, for example, may be expert in the process of dealing with people, while system developers may see the opportunity for automating many tasks without necessarily considering the optimal customer interaction. The poor relation in this scenario is process. There is a tremendous amount of planning required in order to automate successfully, and automating broken processes can only result in discordant customer contacts. Yet this is a common occurrence as senior managers seek short-term results by implementing the latest technologies in order to justify diminishing the workforce.

Best in class customer care systems can radically improve levels of customer satisfaction by increasing the number of resolutions on first contact, reducing costs by lowering contact times, and providing useful market intelligence. Accomplishing these goals can realize a rapid and significant return on investment, as well as establishing customer care as a true competitive differentiator. By reducing customer-agent contact time (as well as after-contact work, such as notations, etc.) in addition to giving customers direct access to online databases through media like the Internet, companies can realize significant cost reductions while maintaining outstanding levels of customer care.

Regardless of its failures and successes, online customer care would not exist at all were it not for the telecommunications industry. The network is the common denominator of every customer care environment—the conduit for voice, data, and image transactions, and often the only direct link between a company and its customers. The integration of computers with telecommunications continues to transform customer care into a potentially powerful and cost-effective enterprise.

Telecommunications Support

The massive growth of customer care in the late 20th century is facilitated by the extraordinary reach and power of the telecommunications industry. A plethora of emerging services continue to transform what is referred as POTS (plain old telephone service). Forced multiple-call handling, for example, provides managers with the option of delivering an emergency call when an agent is already handling a customer. Voice mail is a common feature of the interactive voice response unit that enables a customer to leave a detailed message without waiting for an agent. Call center networking capabilities also provide managers with the ability to route calls based on the number dialed by the customer (dialed number identification service or DNIS), time in queue, number of calls in queue, and the number of available agents.

Additionally, one of the most far-reaching developments in telecommunications for customer care is the capacity for remote agents to handle customer calls directly from the home or satellite business locations. Agents log into the switch through the IVR and calls are routed to their locations as if they were sitting at a workstation in the call center. Supervisors can then monitor the performance of these agents through the call management system. Using, for example, the integrated services digital network (ISDN), which facilitates the simultaneous transferal of any available customer data to the agent's terminal with the arrival of the call, or even technologies like asymmetric digital subscriber line (ADSL), which carries data over existing copper telephone lines at up to six megabits a second, agents can interact with the call center's host computers in order to log customer contacts, retrieve information, and conduct transactions. The narrowing gap between these technologies means that computer telephony integration is becoming more commonplace and less expensive—a trend that will have a significant effect on customer care in the near future.

Contemporary Customer Care

For three decades, company managers who may have been aware of the existence of call centers, but unaware of their potential benefits, have often been removed from the realities of dealing with customers on a daily basis. Today, technology is making it possible for managers to get in direct contact with the customers who make their jobs exist in the first place. It is not inconceivable that every management employee, from the CEO to the first-level management trainee, will augment the role of the customer care agent by regularly interacting with callers and discovering their needs and suggestions. It is a technologically enabled concept that can bring customer care out of geographical and tactical isolation and into the forefront of every business decision, making root cause analysis and market intelligence driving forces for marketing and product management strategies. Instead of being perceived as an insignificant postsale operation, therefore, best in class customer care can become an integral part of the entire company.

Several leading-edge companies use customer care as a training ground for new managers. The problem with this approach from the call center perspective is the high turnover rate, which can negatively impact talk times. Once the management trainee leaves the center, it is quite possible that he or she will never deal directly with the customer again. Conversely, the prospect of answering a customer's inquiry or problem is extremely confronting to those managers who have never even visited a call center, much less interacted with disgruntled customers. The ideal, of course, is that anyone who responds to a customer contact will have a timely and accurate answer. Online customer care systems can supplement basic training by providing the necessary tools to present information in a way that is meaningful to both the agent and the customer. In this regard, the prospect of company-wide customer care promises to *augment* the work of the trained agent by not only reducing hold times, but also bringing a universal awareness of real-life customers into the company. One certainty of this approach is that any innate problems with customer care processes, technologies, or content would quickly come to the attention of decision makers, most likely making world-class customer care a realistic part of company policy. Just as important, it would also ensure the inclusion of the customer in the design and delivery of products and services.

A company that wants to create best in class customer care must first understand the processes that are essential to its business strategy. All processes should be a natural reflection of customer needs. By evolving existing processes to provide maximum customer satisfaction, inherent cross-organizational flaws will be identified rapidly.

There are several different ways, of course, to effect change. For some customer care environments it can mean long-term and financially robust efforts to redesign service processes and implement technological change. For most, however, it means convincing senior management that an independent assessment of the relationships between the call center and the rest of the organization would reveal significant shortcomings. Perhaps the biggest challenge for any customer care manager is finding supporters within the company who understand the financial and operational issues of managing what appears to many to be a cost center.

Trends

A new medium for customer care emerged from the integration of telecommunications and the computer. The Internet and its graphical offspring, the World Wide Web, are currently the principal drivers of this phenomenon. The two simple reasons for the success of the Web and other emerging online networks as tools for customer care are *cost* and *convenience*. Companies are anxious to find an alternative to the high cost of voice-to-voice customer care, and the graphical Web is the ideal medium to give the customer *direct* access to nonproprietary problem-solving information. Both of these goals are easily achievable through the readily available network of Internet servers. Customer care practitioners might think of the Web as a graphically enhanced interactive voice response facility. However, instead of wading through the often interminable menus and monotone inflexibility of voice response, the customer embraces the intuitive graphical interface and information availability which is potentially thousands of times greater than even the most sophisticated interactive voice response unit. Added to the "click of a button" availability of e-mail and online forums, the potential for offloading customer contacts from overwrought call centers is significant. The emergence of high-speed cable modems and fiber optic lines into the home will continue to augment the business case for conducting customer care via these online facilities. Ultimately, online transactions will probably be as acceptable and ubiquitous as interacting with automatic teller machines (and considerably more convenient). Many customers, particularly the new class of computer literate buyers, may choose to link to customer care agents through the network only on an "as needed" basis.

Given that online access from the home will continue to proliferate as a result of the widespread presence of the personal computer as well as the availability of low-cost Internet access devices, and that media such as e-mail will continue to become more commonplace (further facilitating distributed "work-at-home" customer care), the viability of centralized call centers as they exist today will eventually be brought into question. It seems likely that cost-cutting companies will downsize and disperse these high-expense operations using evolving technologies like CTI, while still touting "world class" customer care through alternative media.

Over the next decade, the proliferation of high-speed transmission facilities to the home will certainly encourage a huge increase in online services. It is also fashionable to suggest that the television will be transformed into a media terminal, with users being able to choose what they want to do directly from the screen. The Internet and similar networks are likely to become powerful interactive media provisioners, with video-on-demand, pay-by-the-hour software, teleconferencing, technical support, ordering, live connections to customer care agents, and so forth, in addition to normal television facilities. Controlled by wireless keyboards and other devices from a comfortable chair, these media will epitomize the integration of the telephone, computer, and television for increasingly sophisticated audiences. An extreme view would be that those who rely solely on the telephone to communicate with customer care facilities may ultimately find themselves with a level of service response akin to the gradual decline of the postal service and the public library. In this regard, companies are most interested in providing premium customer care to those customers who contribute most to the bottom line. In the not so distant future, those are the "most valued" customers who will be able to afford the coming wave of interactive services.

The availability of technologies like residential ISDN and computer-telephony integration are encouraging a growing focus on *dispersed* customer care. From an economic viewpoint, the decreasing cost associated with working at home while staying in constant communication with centralized operations is making telecommuting a serious consideration for many high-cost customer care environments. Given that the agent population is highly trained and competent, the automatic call distributor is primed for integration, security issues have been overcome, and online systems are rigorously maintained to ensure that the most up-to-date information on company policies and procedures and problem-solving scenarios is available to agents, then the biggest hurdle to overcome may well be the loss of direct supervisory influence as practiced in a centralized call center environment. This latter issue requires a significant paradigm shift in many companies. Telecommuting agreements must be developed, remote management ground rules established, and effective communication policies described. Monitoring capabilities for telecommuting agents are perhaps not as sophisticated as those found in centralized operations, but it is possible to monitor performance remotely on an individual basis. Using computer-telephony integration and skills-based routing, customer care management can continue to ensure that the most qualified agents receive appropriate customer calls.

While the American Midwest has enjoyed a boon in centralized call center operations due to its promise of low-cost facilities and readily available workforce, the evolution of telecommuting means that a company can route a call to an agent just about anywhere without having to worry about excessive costs. The advantages of telecommuting are clearly manifold—no more parking and commuting delays (thus resulting in a reduction in absenteeism and agent turnover), absence of facility costs, improved scheduling flexibility and disaster recovery, maintenance of service levels during peak periods, and increased access to highly motivated agents, such as professionals who have given up office work to raise a child or take care of a sick family member, physically handicapped individuals, retired managers, and the like. Given that high-speed network costs will continue to plummet, it seems apparent that those companies who hire highly reliable and conscientious agents will reap the benefits of this growing practice.

Although telecommuting has been commonplace for several years at some companies, the sheer scale of evolving a telecommuting practice for even moderate-volume call centers has discouraged many companies from taking that leap forward. Those who have attempted this endeavor in the past have often been stymied by unexpected costs and technology issues. The rapid emergence of the World Wide Web, coupled with ongoing efforts to realize high-speed networking even to suburban environments, however, has revolutionized the telecommunications industry and thus made telecommuting a plausible endeavor for those companies who are looking beyond the "normal" model of customer care. The best candidates for telecommuting are those companies who are seriously concerned about agent turnover, absenteeism or tardiness due to environment problems, and exorbitant facility costs. While telecommunications costs are clearly going to rise as a result of telecommuting, the cost/benefits described previously may augment a plausible business case for many contemporary companies.

As stated, telecommuting engenders the loss of direct management supervision (historically the biggest stumbling block for call center managers), loss of agent-to-agent information sharing, and the loss of easy-to-access subject matter experts. By starting with a small number of work-at-home agents, however, a company can examine the potential pitfalls of wider-scale telecommuting operations.

Several telecommunications vendors have developed "work at home" software that takes advantage of the same call center technology that is available at a centralized site. This allows overflow calls during unexpected "spikes" in call volume to be routed to agents who would not normally be available to handle customer inquiries. When call volumes exceed a certain threshold, the call center system automatically dials available telecommuting agents, alerting them to log on to answer calls. In terms of equipment and facilities, telecommuting agents may require a headset that screens out background noise, an ISDN modem-equipped desktop terminal or personal computer, TCP/IP data connections, and a residential ISDN telephone line. It is, of course, possible but less than optimal to operate with two analog telephone lines and a modem.

It is often said that the ideal way to predict the future is to invent it. For visionary companies, that means identifying key uncertainties that are likely to have a big impact on business in the future. These uncertainties can then be developed into internally consistent visions of possible futures, giving the company a jump start into the strategic changes that will ultimately affect the business environment.

Industry Perspective

While it is well known that so-called best in class companies achieve higher levels of customer satisfaction at a lower cost, it is also interesting to note that there is a direct correlation between both these elements in terms of postsale customer care. In other words, those contingencies that apply to customer satisfaction, such as *access* (minimal queue time and low rates of abandonment) and *resolution on first contact,* also contribute directly to lower costs. However, while actual *contact time* and *after contact work* are not of direct concern to most customers, these elements, which combine to measure individual productivity, are the greatest drivers of *low-cost* customer care. Together, high productivity and a high rate of resolution on first contact will obviously lower *access* time.

Yet increasing productivity <u>and</u> increasing resolution on first contact remain an enigma for most customer care environments. The two rarely go together. Today, call centers are employing many kinds of technologies in an effort to reduce contact time, coupled with training geared toward increasing resolution on first contact. Many call centers, however, suffer from extremely low rates of worker compensation, often creating a vicious cycle of high turnover and consequently no choice but to rush inadequately trained agents "out to the line" as soon as possible. Call center managers, reluctantly or otherwise, who are driven solely by productivity levels can inadvertently

Senior Management Strategy

Provide customer care at the lowest possible cost while gathering optimal market intelligence data in addition to critical product or service feedback.

APPROACH

Implement a state-of-the art online customer care system that will provide a rapid return on investment through decreased contact time and sophisticated reporting capabilities, thus enabling agent workforce reduction.

IMPLEMENTATION

Significant short-term investment in system design and development, usually motivated by high-level prototypes and substantial end-user involvement. Process and technology development normally independent efforts. Large volume of content material produced in parallel, but not usually in conjunction, with the training effort.

Overall Strategy

Resolve the customer inquiry or problem on the first point of contact in the least possible time while gathering market intelligence in a courteous and professional manner.

Process Development	Process Improvement
System Design	System Maintenance
Knowledge Engineering	Knowledge Maintenance

Initial Research & Development

Ongoing Initiatives

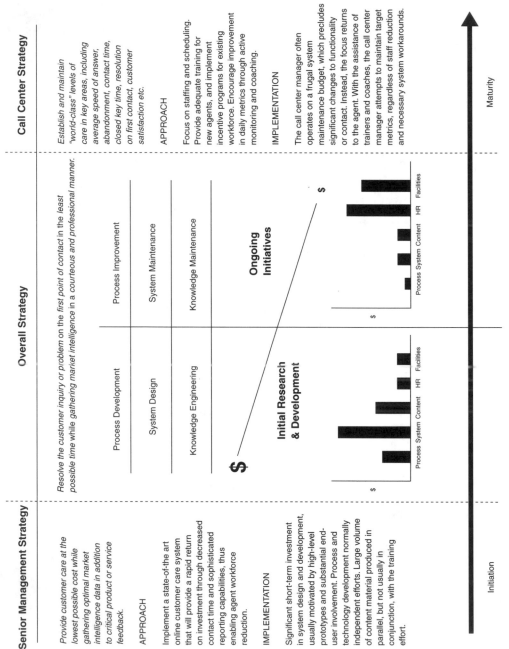

Process System Content HR Facilities

Call Center Strategy

Establish and maintain "world-class" levels of care in key areas, including average speed of answer, abandonment, contact time, closed key time, resolution on first contact, customer satisfaction etc.

APPROACH

Focus on staffing and scheduling. Provide adequate training for new agents, and implement incentive programs for existing workforce. Encourage improvement in daily metrics through active monitoring and coaching.

IMPLEMENTATION

The call center manager often operates on a frugal system maintenance budget, which precludes significant changes to functionality or contact. Instead, the focus returns to the agent. With the assistance of trainers and coaches, the call center manager attempts to maintain target metrics, regardless of staff reduction and necessary system workarounds.

Initiation   Maturity

FIGURE 1.1 The typical customer care life cycle

encourage customer dissatisfaction and multiple callbacks by rewarding those agents who minimize contact time with the customer.

There is no question that technology can alleviate many of these difficulties, but for most companies that premise translates to a one-time extravagant expense, rather than a progressive partnership between people, process, and technology. As is evidenced by the Traditional Customer Care Life Cycle (see Figure 1.1), the decision to implement new technology may mean an initial investment that in some cases exceeds the normal customer care budget for an entire year. After deployment, however, the technology budget dwindles to less than 1 per cent, while worker compensation takes the lion's share of operating costs. What this means is that failure to get the technology right first time can have irreversible consequences. It is easier to implement readily available hardware and software solutions that technologically attempt to lower contact times with the customer than to focus on the more work-intensive processes and technologies that will actually assist the agent in resolving the customer's inquiry or problem.

The greatest challenge of customer care occurs at the human level, where agents can spend countless minutes on tasks that beg for automated solutions. Immediate access to information and the generation of useful market intelligence data remain rare commodities, even in contemporary customer care environments. These are difficult problems which, because of product or service-driven differences and the need for seamless integration, do not lend themselves easily to off-the-shelf solutions. Instead, the solutions are often expensive and require a tremendous amount of planning and maintenance in order to succeed. Yet the benefits of a well-designed and maintained customer contact system can be staggering, in many cases taking minutes off routine calls while decreasing agent stress (and consequently reducing turnover) and increasing customer satisfaction. Technology, like process and content, demands constant evaluation and improvement. Failure to allocate an adequate system maintenance budget, for example, is to presume a perfection that simply doesn't exist. Many systems are designed without adequate end-user participation, for example. The common approach is that as long as the system functions correctly when it is deployed, then it has met all of the necessary requirements. The fact is that a company where unilateral or "one-step" system design and development is practiced tends to place more emphasis on the time, budgetary, and skill limitations of the programming team than on the needs of the user, making integrated and intuitive customer care systems an unlikely goal.

2

Fundamentals

The Quest for Personalized Care

Unlike the owner of the village store, the average call center agent is rarely knowledgeable about the particular needs of certain customers, their personal likes and dislikes, or trials and tribulations in their everyday lives. Impersonal, often sharing its secrets reluctantly, the agent's computer does not innately care whether Judy just lost her job, or that Jack went to school with the store owner's father, or that Allison prefers the village store atmosphere to the cheaper and better-stocked supermarket. The call center computer system was not built to consider human circumstance, but merely to process, store, and retrieve information. Long-standing customers, however, particularly those used to localized care, do not like the sense of becoming just another name in a corporate database. After all, village store businesses flourished long before the first call center, and often enjoy far more customer loyalty than the most technologically enabled corporations.

A fundamental question for every call center manager, therefore, is how to empower agents by providing them not just with contact tracking systems, but with the sort of information and authority that will make every worthy customer feel as though the company cares about him or her personally. This goal is clearly a nontrivial task that involves a multitude of processes and, depending on the size of the customer base, significant technological support. For reasons that are explored in this book, many customer care environments fall short of this lofty goal and settle for providing customers with a form of "commodity care" that does not remotely approach the village store philosophy.

World-class customer interaction may mean that the agent is supported by tools that analyze the customers' previous buying history and provide advice accordingly, such as the latest special offer, advice on how to save money on their current service, why one product is more appropriate to their needs than another, and so on. It may also mean that the agent is given tools that enable the rapid resolution of an installation problem, or given step-by-step instructions on how to perform a certain function. It may also allow the agent to consolidate bills, perform credit adjustments, or investigate a fraudulent charge. Or perhaps it means being able to fax or e-mail the customer directions to the nearest store from the desktop, or add new service features while the customer is still on the telephone, and so on.

Fulfillment of these examples depends upon a robust process framework, often supported by primary system functions. This could involve the systematic provisioning of algorithms for nearest service center location (including hours of operation, and special instructions), search engines for online documentation (including user instructions, policies and procedures, promotional information, competitive activity tracking, and dynamic updating), rules for problem solving, integrated billing systems, and automatically generated notations and correspondence templates. It may also mean providing agents with a decision support system for cross-selling, an escalation and commitment tracking tool, and integrated multimedia (i.e., voice-to-voice, e-mail, fax, World Wide Web, interactive voice response, and postal) contact tracking facilities (see Figure 2.1, Supporting multichannel customer care).

In the context of human interaction, outstanding customer care in a centralized environment invites comparison with the successful village store owner. For just as the owner is adept at giving advice on how to care for paint brushes, for example, so too must the system database rapidly retrieve expert information and present it to the call center agent in a way that is instantly understandable. Or just as the village store owner knows the cost, quantity, and location of virtually every item in stock, so too must the system facilitate the agent by providing an integrated view of the entire business. And just as the village store owner knows his or her regular customers by name and background, so too must the system be populated with information that can tell the agent at a glance exactly who the customers are and why they have contacted the company in the past. Also akin to the village store owner, the call center agent must be able to recognize and act upon opportunities to embrace new business by presenting tangible options to the customer in a timely manner. Finally, recognizing that agents, unlike the village store owner, are not decision makers, the system must also enable company management to extract meaningful reports, which in turn may be profitably used to drive key business initiatives.

Best in class companies rely on rigorous process evaluation and improvement techniques to retain their competitive advantage. Service design and delivery in general invokes a series of steps that impact every facet of customer care. For example, *process* dictates every action that a company takes in order to satisfy the customer, reduce costs, and gather market intelligence. *Technology* can help to facilitate these processes through user-driven systems development and maintenance. From the *content* perspective, the focus is on identifying the boundaries of customer care by acquiring, engineering, and maintaining knowledge, and using technology to distribute the information through various customer care media. The following pages examine these fundamental elements of process, technology, and content as each pertains to the provisioning of customer care.

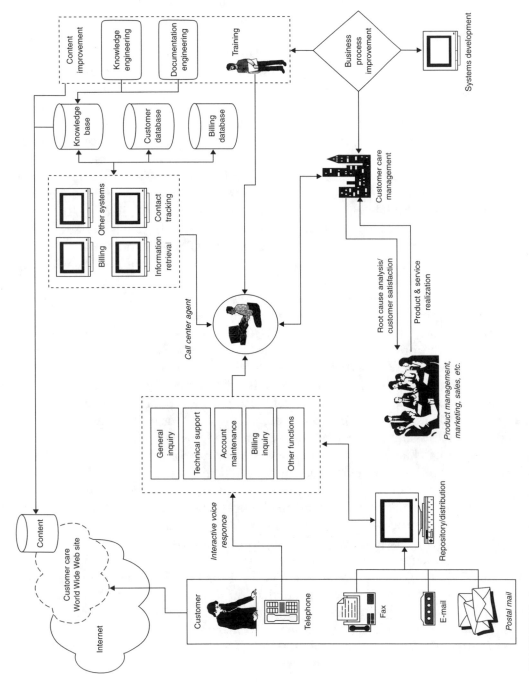

FIGURE 2.1 Supporting multichannel customer care

15

Process Considerations

It stands to reason that all processes must be driven by customer needs. Yet it is surprisingly common for non–customer-facing organizations within a company to design systems and processes that demonstrate little or no understanding of the customer care environment. Technology, for example, should be a powerful process enabler, yet all too often processes have to adapt to the limitations of the computer system rather than the converse. A common scenario is the existence of disparate contact tracking, trouble ticketing, troubleshooting, follow-up, online documentation, and outbound correspondence applications. These systems are often designed without studying the ways in which agents or customers might optimally interact with an *integrated* system in a real-world situation. The result is usually convoluted processes and work-arounds, which have a detrimental effect on customer relations.

Today, few companies offer such exclusive products and services that they do not have to worry about what happens after the customer has made the purchase. Yet customer care is rarely thought of as a critical source for market intelligence. In effect, even if the customer care environment embraces the most elaborate processes, it may not enjoy the support of the organization in general. This situation results in customer suggestions for product and service improvement being ignored and an absence of rigorous analysis for customer complaints.

It is only when customer retention levels begin to plunge that many companies pay attention to the postsale support environment, and then only to complain that the agents are not doing enough to identify the reason why the customer is complaining about the product or canceling the service. For example, one marketing manager dictated no less than thirty-two reasons why a customer might cancel a contract, and added these reasons to an existing list of *two hundred and ten* contact categorizations. Needless to say, the agents, who were being primarily measured on talk-time, put the majority of disgruntled customers into the "Other" category.

Business process improvement initiatives must originate at the executive level—trying to promote change from within the customer care organization rarely attracts the serious attention of product management, marketing, and systems development groups. Failure to secure an early buy-in to this strategy will result in resistance to change later on. In fact, no matter how much effort customer care management may put into making its processes as efficient as possible, these external suppliers can easily cause havoc by failing to deliver relevant information or effect requested changes. For example, marketing often neglects to advise customer care of a particular promotion, leaving the Web site bereft of relevant information and the agent perplexed when the customer calls in to complain that the "free gizmo I got in the mail" doesn't work. Similarly, product management may decide to shorten the new feature introduction cycle by three weeks, leaving customer care without any troubleshooting information because the knowledge engineers didn't have time to develop it. Process-driven customer care in a multichannel environment (i.e., involving several media facilitators, such as e-mail, fax, and interactive voice response) presents a unique set of challenges in terms of increased customer satisfaction, reduced costs, and market intelligence data gathering.

Case in Point: Perception vs. Reality

A Director of Customer Care once boasted that, as a result of unprecedented customer demands resulting from the launch of a new service, the customer care environment had grown from two hundred agents in January to more than a thousand three months later. His ability to manage such a massive growth in workforce augured well for his future in the company. After all, everybody knew that the customer response to the new service offering had been overwhelming. Clearly, an increase in the workforce was justified, but a closer examination of this situation revealed that the decision to quadruple resources had been driven not only by call volume, but by the fact that agents were taking more than three times as long as predicted to resolve customer inquiries and problems, if these issues were resolved at all. There were no well-understood processes in place to handle e-mail, or postal or fax contacts, resulting in a plethora of calls to the toll-free number from frustrated customers. The much touted and extremely expensive online documentation system had a six-week turnaround on any new information, simply because no consideration had been given to content maintenance after the system was initially deployed. Processes had been documented for escalated contacts, but there were no service contracts in place to ensure that other departments had understood and agreed with the time frames being given to customers. Agent turnover within the first month of service had reached 25 percent, resulting in a reduction in training for new agents from four weeks to five days. Despite these glaring problems, the director was recognized for his ability to lead a large workforce during a crisis and subsequently promoted. The manager of the call center, on the other hand, was ostracized for his apparent inability to schedule agents appropriately for peak calling times.

The moral of this not so absurd parable is that failure to implement integrated processes as key drivers of customer care can result in reactive management practices that doom the environment to be perceived as a cost center whose function is purely to placate irate customers. As such, the call center ceases to be perceived as a viable part of the marketing process. The emphasis on getting the customer off the phone as quickly as possible results in diluted market intelligence and often a tremendous backlog of customer commitments. Efforts to redress this situation are purely reactive and piecemeal, and senior managers often take steps to distance themselves from what is perceived as an operational nightmare.

Approaches to Business Process Improvement

There are many suggested approaches to business process improvement. Total quality management (TQM) and business process reengineering (BPR) are certainly at the forefront of contemporary endeavors that have evolved from the manufacturing model and the legacy of people like W. Edwards Deming. Regardless of the preferred methodology, one of the first steps that must be taken is to identify and define a candidate process, and assign it to a process owner. Subsequent iterations to the process should be prioritized based on customer requirements or perceived competitive advantage, and appropriate measures should be established for that process. As the process is implemented, these measures should assess conformance to customer expectations, and the process should be improved accordingly. Most companies are trying to take this model a step further by understanding their customers so well that they can deliver a product or service that *exceeds* all known expectations, thereby creating a new competitive edge and increased customer loyalty.

It is not unusual to find reams of carefully contrived flowcharts in obscure call center locations, such as storerooms or beneath empty desks. These documents probably represent the efforts of a small group of individuals whose task long ago was to brainstorm how to handle various types of customer contact. Depending upon the mix of people and time constraints, this may typically have resulted in detailed descriptions of internal technical support and billing inquiry processes, a relative absence of cross-organizational processes, and a cursory mention of content and knowledge maintenance processes. Even in large organizations that may have dozens of call centers for various purposes, it is standard practice to use a totally different process-modeling methodology and content classification for each one, depending upon the motivation and personalities of the engineering team. The sentiment expressed might be that "it doesn't matter what anyone has done before, we're going to do it this way and it's up to them if they want to rework their process flows and bring everything into line." In other words, everyone has a personalized idea about the optimal way to describe processes, and unless there is a company-wide imposed standard, cross-organizational processes can resemble a contemporary "Tower of Babel."

Normally, process owners are assigned to specific areas of concern, such as billing inquiry, credit and collections, troubleshooting, reservations, and so forth. While the most elaborate processes may be designed for these areas, it is not unusual for key customer care operations processes to be overlooked until such incidents arise. Take, for example, the customer who insists on calling the call center back before the deadline for their commitment is scheduled to be met. In the ideal world, of course, this should never happen, and it may well be that the customer contact process owner may have only created a process that visits this contingency at a very high level. Failure to fully describe the repeat customer callback process, however, can create a debilitating situation in which agents may take several courses of action, such as erroneously calling a supervisor, creating a secondary commitment, or transferring the call to the originating agent. This is just one example of several processes that are more difficult to define after operations have commenced, if only because the original process owners have been deployed elsewhere and no one else has the time to fully investigate the situation. Here are some of the other processes that are typically overlooked in the foundation of a new customer care environment:

- Twenty-four-hour online content maintenance
- Knowledge acquisition and engineering
- Customer contact categorization

- Interactive voice response unit scripting and functional support
- Online and offline escalations
- Agent feedback and response
- Root cause analysis of inbound contacts
- E-mail and fax support
- Online help maintenance
- Online scripting
- Service realization
- Postal mail logging and routing

Several of these processes may seem obvious, but it is surprising how many can be overlooked in the dynamic and often frantic atmosphere that surrounds the opening of any new call center. Even in long-established centers, these processes often exist only as unspoken agreements and understandings. Yet several require far more than nebulous agreements. Service realization, for example, often means that the marketing and sales department have some way of notifying customer care of any new activities that might impact customer contact volumes. Yet it is not unusual for this process to be compromised by tenuous links between marketing and customer care. Several companies insist on service agreements between customer care and other departments in order to ensure that any failure to act on critical information can be tracked to a responsible party.

Also worthy of particular consideration is the fact that it is not always apparent from disparate process maps exactly what the scope of potential contact transfers, escalations, commitments, and after-call work (including manual workarounds such as remote faxing, etc.) really involves. By eliciting information on those calls not likely to be resolved at the first point of agent contact, the call center manager can evolve a "real world" picture of those contingencies that are likely to adversely impact service levels. For example, if detailed investigation of the troubleshooting process reveals that of the fifty problem types defined, twenty two are likely to result in call-back commitments, the customer care manager must construct the workforce model to reflect this contingency. At the same time, a task force should examine each potential callback type and determine whether the agent's inability to resolve this contact immediately will be due to empowerment constraints, training shortfalls, or technological inadequacies. By conducting this type of root cause analysis up front, management can then take whatever steps are necessary to avert repeat customer calls and outbound callback commitments. If it is determined that certain contacts are being escalated because their content is so cryptic that the agent was never trained in that area, then it is mandatory for management to ensure that the online knowledge base contains this information in a format that is easily followed. If other contacts are being escalated because these involve some degree of decision-making ability, then management must conduct a cost/benefit analysis to ensure that the inability of a frontline agent to credit a few extra dollars to a customer's account is not seriously affecting service levels. Clearly defined processes will also allow customer care management to determine exactly how long each transaction should take, thereby performing a "sanity check" on the workforce management model.

This book follows a model of customer care that establishes reciprocity between the needs of the business and systems development solutions. Business process improvement is the only conduit for the successful deployment and maintenance of any online customer care system. By defining the processes that facilitate multimedia access to customer care facilities, as well as those that define requirements for systems design, user interaction, content provisioning, and data gathering, a company can ensure that a transition to the rapidly evolving world of online customer care is conducted in a way that benefits both management and customers alike.

Take the example of a service that regularly adds new features in order to maintain a competitive edge. The first critical link is between product management and/or marketing with customer care. A common scenario occurs when product management or marketing simply decide to interact directly with the local development group rather than the remote customer care facility, resulting in changes to the customer care system that even call center management cannot explain. Involving customer care strategists from the outset means that the scope of the new feature and its likely effect on the customer care environment can be defined. The business process improvement team can then define the support responsibilities for the new offering, ensuring that both the content provisioners and process owners are fully cognizant of the necessary level of support. By ensuring that the process drives any system changes, there is a far better chance that the end users will get the type of system enhancements that make sense.

Customer-focused system design, development, and maintenance are critical to the realization of world-class customer interaction. As companies adapt to increasingly demanding customers, so too must the traditional model of customer care evolve to include new channels of communication and seamlessly integrated systems. Typical examples include integrated system functions based on user workflow patterns, robust data-gathering facilities, intuitive user interfaces, ability to track escalated trouble tickets, easy-to-use billing system interfaces, commitment tickler systems, presence of alternative (e-mail, fax, etc.) handling and routing facilities, and relevant, accurate, and complete content.

Technology Considerations

The use of technology in a customer care environment may be viewed as a *value-added* strategy that attempts to achieve competitive advantage by augmenting the customer's decision to invest in a company product or service. In an era of rapid technological change and increasing customer demand for premium service, therefore, a lengthy development cycle followed by a negligible maintenance budget is an unacceptable outcome.

There are hundreds of software companies vying for niches in the evolving world of interactive communications, so the goal for many systems development managers has become one of *adapting off-the-shelf* products rather than funding expensive in-house development of new systems. Companies are now seeking to take advantage of technologies that will drive superior customer care without becoming bogged down by internal development cycles. Rapid integration and robust maintenance are key factors in facilitating this scenario. Those companies who attempt to produce a total customer care solution by maintaining adaptive links to these latest software technologies are striving for an immediate upswing in customer satisfaction.

Failure to *actively* and *continuously* involve the user population in systems development rarely results in the exponential rise in productivity that management anticipated when funding the project. Systems developed through incremental refinements and high-profile user involvement are the least likely to meet with resistance, whereas those developed externally and representing radical change are sometimes rejected by the user population. The problem for most companies is that incrementally developed, user-friendly systems are likely to take so long to evolve that what might have been perceived as state-of-the-art three years ago has now become a technological dinosaur. The key to resolving this enigma lies in a combination of senior management commitment to innovation tempered with the identification of user needs through techniques like rapid prototyping, as well as the ability of internal system development groups to integrate outstanding off-the-shelf software with existing systems in order to consistently ensure that the customer care environment maintains a competitive edge.

Companies who have spent years nurturing legacy systems may struggle to remain competitive in an era in which customer demands for total service continue to grow. Those managers who have remained shielded from the demands of the marketplace, focusing instead on protecting their interests in a system that handles a diminishing part of the business environment, may seem prone to a myopia that obscures the vulnerability of their position. Massive companies whose bureaucracy ensures that a consolidated approach to technological innovation is virtually impossible will find it very difficult to offer bundled solutions to deter the low-cost, high-quality endeavors of upstart competitors.

Ironically, customer care appears to be suffering from an outbreak in technology. There are many "off-the-shelf" products that can provide piecemeal solutions, such as integrated troubleshooting and contact tracking systems. Yet even after years of enhancements, it seems that the majority of customer care environments still have dozens of processes that beg for automated solutions. Many companies have just begun to explore the nuances of alternative media, such as e-mail and the World Wide Web. It is this total integration, driven explicitly by user needs, that can save high-volume environments countless dollars.

Regardless of the system toolset, there are certain shared traits of successful customer care applications, as follows:

- *The system facilitates interaction with the customer.*
  Anyone who has observed inbound call center agents using online systems has probably witnessed the scrolling of interminable lists while the agent deciphers to which call category a particular customer contact belongs, or spending several minutes of after-call time writing voluminous notes (which most often are used only for contact history purposes, rather than as a viable source of market intelligence), or retyping the same information several times because the application the agent is using was poorly designed, or waiting interminably for a response to

a routine database inquiry, or trying to perform troubleshooting with paper manuals or an online file by rapidly scanning several hundred lines of text. Certainly, the agents can learn how to work with the system, but how much time is being wasted on unnecessary tasks, and what effect is that having on customer satisfaction? What will happen when a company tries to take these poorly designed systems and put them on the Web, so that customers can solve their own problems? The most obvious answer is not to even think about deploying a system until there is certainty that it will fulfill the customer's—as well as the business—need.

Perhaps the most complex challenge facing online customer care today is designing systems that facilitate human interaction. For the call center agent, that my mean integrating the contact tracking system with the online documentation, trouble ticketing, billing, customer callback, and troubleshooting applications. To the customer (who can be defined as the purchaser of a product or service), perhaps that means automatically receiving a callback after he or she has conducted a fruitless search of the website for an answer to a problem.

Successful human–computer interaction is an art that is not always well understood by those who design and develop online customer care systems. While the programmer admires the successful implementation of a function, and the artist admires the beauty of a picture, the good user interface designer or human factors engineer will consider both elements from the user's or customer's perspective by asking the simple question: "What does the user want to do?" The answer resides in continual user testing and feedback loops to ensure that the system works intuitively in the real world.

- *It is easy to find the right information.*

Superbly designed customer care systems often do nothing more than create elaborate placeholders for content. Users who cannot find the information that they are looking for quickly are entitled to dismiss even the most sophisticated systems as useless. It is pointless spending millions of dollars to implement integrated systems if users have to perform unnecessary or cryptic tasks in order to resolve their needs. For example, it is not unusual to see an agent vainly try to locate information relevant to a particular customer query by using a systematic search facility. After a few "no matches found" messages, the agent concludes that there is no useful information available online and makes a decision to either escalate the call, arrange a callback, or give the customer an often inaccurate recollection from some long-forgotten training session. It may be something as simple as a missed hyphen, but its potential cost to the company is enormous.

Those responsible for acquiring information, composing it, and ultimately presenting it online should always position themselves as close to the user as possible. Just as the human factors engineer is responsible for ensuring that the system is easy to use, the content engineer is responsible for ensuring that information is easy to find. Call center agents may tend by nature to be more tolerant than customers in general. While an agent may give the content engineer the benefit of the doubt, the customer will not hesitate to pick up the telephone and go back to the traditional form of customer care, quickly rendering an online customer care system obsolete.

- *The information is understandable.*

Perhaps a company boasts about its carefully designed online customer care system. Perhaps it is remarkably easy to find the right information. Perhaps the only question that remains for the call center agent is "Can you comprehend the information as it is presented?" This contingency highlights the critical content issues of style, vocabulary, legibility, presentation, and interpretation. For the agent who is "dual processing" (i.e., listening to the customer while trying to understand the information on the screen), this task is key to increasing productivity. The faster the agent can assimilate and even convey the information as presented, the sooner the call will end. For the customers who "surf the net," the same scenario applies, although they will have the option of calling the agent for clarification.

- *The information is accurate.*

This contingency not only illustrates the necessity for continual feedback loops within an organization; it also highlights the importance of rapid content maintenance. Just as the call center agent does not want to trip over price plans that were relevant last June, the customer does not want to access your website to read about a promotion that ended yesterday. The processes for gathering information (a.k.a. knowledge acquisition) and developing robust and timely information update channels across an organization are key factors in the successful implementation of online customer care.

Systems Design

One of the most effective traits of Baldrige Award winners is the fact that these successful companies have not only a long-term commitment to process improvement, but also an effective focus on technologies designed to enhance, rather than unwillingly hinder, customer interaction. For example, a particular problem that plagues human–computer interaction today is that of information access. Every day, massive corporate databases, news services, electronic mail, and text-retrieval facilities can provide agents with countless facts and figures. Information alone, of course, is not knowledge. The problem is how to find specific information with minimal difficulty. Presentation, speed of access, and ease of use are all important. Special care is needed in constructing computer applications so that the agent can easily find the required information. World-class customer care environments constantly involve frontline agents in designing systems that enable the rapid resolution of customer inquiries and problems by conducting task analysis, rapid prototyping, and usability testing throughout the development cycle.

As computer technology has become available to more and more people in a greater variety of devices and contexts, the need for accessibility and ease of use has grown more and more pronounced. People with a greater variety of skills and points of view have become involved. Those who study thought, language, entertainment, and communication—as well as those who study algorithms, hardware, and data structure—all have a role to play in interface design.

When the concept of interface design first began to emerge, it was commonly understood as the hardware and software through which a human and a computer could communicate. As it has evolved, it has come to include the cognitive and emotional aspects of the user's experience as well. While developers and users often have differing views on how we should interact with computers, no one doubts that the best way to unleash the power of a specific application is to make the process of human–computer interaction as natural as possible.

A few years ago, the graphical approach represented a radical departure from the way people traditionally interacted with computers, which was via character-based user interfaces. Character-based applications are easy to program and cheap to produce, and are still widely in use today. Users are often confronted by cluttered screens of text and blank spaces—or worse still, blank screens with a solitary blinking cursor—which offer little, if any, indication of what to do next. Such applications compel the user to learn a complex and somewhat arbitrary syntax.

Ease of use is of primary importance in any user interface design. It reduces training and support costs with a well-designed interface. It allows users to perform tasks more easily and reduces complaints and customer support problems. It is a more intuitive, direct means of interaction with software. However, users may not understand menu labels, may not easily identify icons, and may not remember mouse functions. Therefore, an interesting graphical user interface may promote ease of use, but is not a sufficient condition for it. After all, the graphical prowess of today's computers has encouraged the production of a plethora of unreadable graphics. There is one other step that may be taken in the attempt to ensure user satisfaction—the addition of "intelligence" to the user interface.

Systems Integration

Another crucial aspect of system development for customer care is that of integration. No matter how well designed a particular application may be, lack of integration with existent system functions may mean that the agent has no way of associating a particular customer, inquiry, or problem with a previous transaction. This can give a strong impression that the company is either disorganized or unconcerned with the welfare of its paying customers.

Some typical scenarios that require systems integration would be as follows:

• A customer is contacted by an outbound telemarketer and advised that he or she is eligible to receive the company's newest service at a significant discount. The customer at first declines, but then decides to accept the offer. The customer no longer has the telemarketing response number, but when he or she calls customer care, the agent is able to retrieve a record of the time and date of the original offer, thereby confirming the customer's eligibility.

• A customer calls the toll-free number to inquire about her account balance. The interactive voice response unit script prompts the customer for account information (or uses automatic number identification or computer-telephony integration links to search the database), initiates the billing database search, retrieves the information, and presents it verbally to the customer. The customer's record is automatically updated.

• A busy customer calls the toll-free number to acquire instructions on how to configure new software to recognize his high-resolution monitor settings. Rather than transcribe directions over the telephone, the customer asks the agent to fax or e-mail a written explanation. The agent finds the relevant instructions and then initiates the appropriate response template, which is automatically populated with the customer's name, e-mail address, and other information. The agent systematically attaches the instruction to the template, and sends it directly to the customer.

• An agent is confronted by an irate customer who demands that the company adjust what she claims is an erroneous service establishment fee. According to the customer, that fee was waived as part of a special promotion that her village store advertised at the time. The agent searches the policies and procedures using the term "disputed service establishment fee." The online documentation system not only describes how to deal with disputed charges, but also provides linkages pertinent to recent promotional activity. The agent uses a locator to contact the store directly and resolve the issue. The fee is waived and the customer's account adjusted. The agent quickly ensures via the system that the promotional code is charged accordingly.

• A customer accesses the World Wide Web site and initiates the online troubleshooting system. Based on an interactive question and answer session with the customer, the system suggests a probable solution. The customer accesses procedural details associated with this solution by retrieving an associated user instruction from the online documentation system.

• As a result of a training shortfall, many agents are unfamiliar with the several new fields and functions added to the customer care system as a result of a new release. By initiating the online help system, these agents are able to access a self-explanatory description of each new feature.

• A relatively new agent is unable to remember the steps necessary to complete a particular transaction with a customer. By initiating the online scripts, the agent is given a step-by-step description of the normal procedures.

• An agent is given fifteen minutes each day to become familiar with the various aspects of the customer care operation, including tips on how to deal with customers, system functions, internal operations, telephony, and the like via computer-based training modules.

• The system automatically gathers information relevant to the context of a particular call by storing any troubleshooting scenario or user instruction titles accessed by the agent during the course of a contact. Based on this information, the system suggests the call categorization that is most closely linked with the contact activity. The agent may choose to confirm this selection, or manually choose a different category. This information, together with any manual or auto-notations, is then used to drive management reports. A similar categorization, this time without agent intervention, is used to gather data on World Wide Web and interactive voice response contacts.

Systems integration requirements for information retrieval systems are without doubt one of the most important—yet most neglected—areas of customer care today. More often than not, a sophisticated off-the-shelf system can fall far short of its potential, not only because its content is poorly maintained, but also because it exists as a stand-alone application, without any links to other customer care functions.

The key point is that, in terms of agent productivity, nothing is more time-consuming than the combination of individualized contact categorization, notations, information searches, and verbal procedural explanations. Failure to provide systems integration means that the agent may have to perform one or all of the following unnecessary tasks, often adding several minutes to contact lengths:

- Manually choose the contact categorization from a list that may contain several hundred selections without any automated assistance (based on system interaction during the course of the contact). While some systems attempt to facilitate the agent by cascading the lists into subcategories, this time-intensive task often results in inappropriate categorizations, with the consequence of misleading market intelligence reports.

- Manually create notations that might otherwise have been gathered by the system, such as billing adjustments, troubleshooting remedies, and user instructions. Not only does this result in inconsistent descriptions of similar interactions (resulting in reports that might be interesting to the customer care manager, but which are virtually unintelligible from a trending or even a root cause analysis standpoint), it can also cause unnecessarily lengthy after call work for the agent, especially those who have never been trained to compose consistent shorthand notations.

- From an integration perspective, the most obvious marriage of all should be that of the troubleshooting system with the online documentation system. Given that most troubleshooting systems are engineered purely to ascertain probable cause and remedy for a particular problem, it is reasonable to assume that the user may then link directly from that system to a detailed procedure or explanation relative to implementing the proffered solution via the information retrieval system. Failure to integrate these two systems means that the user must conduct redundant searches and risk potential failure to find the correct information.

- Agents often spend inordinate amounts of time verbally explaining procedures that they read directly from user manuals or online documentation systems. It is a painstaking process, especially in the case of more complex procedures, as the customer attempts to transcribe the agent's instructions. The proliferation of fax and e-mail facilities, and most obviously the World Wide Web, involves system requirements that link response templates to online procedures—meaning that the agent can select a template and attach a procedure for e-mail or fax purposes within seconds.

There may be several reasons why support systems rarely realize their full potential in a customer care environment. Customer care managers who have only recently been exposed to the plethora of contact tracking, troubleshooting, information access, and trouble ticketing applications available today may not necessarily be aware of the potential for integrating these applications in a manner that replicates the real-world tasks of the agent while gathering key data for management reports. Other managers may give little or no credibility to customer care systems, relying instead on training and agent initiative. Developers, on the other hand, may not be aware of certain agent activities that could be streamlined by integration. After all, if the system is thought of only as an occasional support mechanism for the user, then it is certainly unlikely to be considered a prime candidate for any type of integration.

The evolution of media like the World Wide Web, and the drive to exploit online customer care, should change the emphasis toward applications such as online documentation and troubleshooting. Now that customers are being given the opportunity to resolve their own problems and inquiries online, without the benefit of training, it is clearly imperative that these systems be as intuitive and useful as possible. Also, there is no way for a company to track customer activity on the Web unless these systems are fully integrated. This should pave the way for more sophisticated forms of auto-notations and interpretive reporting, thus giving customer care applications the prominence they deserve in terms of systems integration.

Content Considerations

The task of gathering, compiling, and maintaining online information for customer care environments is widely recognized as so challenging and time-intensive that many customer care managers are willing to allow remotely located systems development groups and supporting teams of knowledge and documentation engineers to collaborate independently in order to provide content mechanisms such as online documentation systems, troubleshooting systems, online help, scripts, computer-based training, and so on. In so doing, customer care managers often isolate themselves from the processes and technologies that most need their support and involvement in order to succeed. Properly implemented information retrieval systems can result in not only higher levels of customer satisfaction, but also reduced costs through increased agent productivity and enhanced market intelligence through automated data-gathering functions. This reveals the inherent complexities and rewards of online content provisioning for customer care.

Content can be narrowly defined as the information required in order to enable a user, whether an agent or a customer, to resolve a particular inquiry or problem. Therefore it should be distinguished from other customer care endeavors, such as contact tracking (i.e., customer profiling, contact history reviews, contact categorization, notations, and follow-ups) and routine management information system database access (billing, order, and repair status, store locations, etc.). Based on this definition, content may include troubleshooting information, user instructions, policies and procedures, and any other information that might be useful in the context of a customer contact, such as organization charts, vendor contact numbers, marketing promotions, press releases, and the like. Essentially, content provisioning is an endeavor that attempts to provide knowledge to users in a timely, usable, relevant, clear, complete, accurate, and integrated manner.

On a broader level, content for customer care environments can involve any or all of the following:

- User instructions
- Policies and procedures
- Troubleshooting scenarios

- Scripts
- Response templates
- Computer-based training
- Online help
- System messages
- Contact categorization

Collectively, these components may be referred to as *information retrieval systems.* The migration of these systems to the World Wide Web has already had a profound effect on traditional models of customer care, as customers are provided direct access to database information. Although interactive voice response mechanisms involve a limited degree of direct access, the graphical environment of the Web provides unprecedented levels of online customer interactivity. Nevertheless, with the majority of customer contacts continuing to be made via voice, at least for the foreseeable future, the development and maintenance of scripts will remain an integral part of content provisioning. Embedded applications, such as online help and system messages, also need to be provided as part of an overall effort to assist users wherever there is a need. Some customer care organizations even invest in stand-alone computer-based training applications to augment classroom training, an endeavor that also constitutes a part of the content provisioning effort.

Agents may achieve the majority of content knowledge through training, offline resources (such as paper documentation or subject matter experts), or information retrieval systems, or a combination of all three. In operations that are sufficiently large to support a centralized call center, adequately designed and maintained content applications are the most consistent and efficient means of reducing costs, increasing customer satisfaction, and gathering product or service feedback in customer care environments. Used in concert with classroom training, these systems not only facilitate resolution of customer inquiries and complaints on first contact, but also help to minimize contact time (thus maximizing accessibility) and optimize management reporting. Management support for carefully planned implementation and maintenance of information retrieval systems can have a positive effect on employee satisfaction in highly pressured call center environments, and therefore can contribute to a decrease in agent turnover. Finally, information retrieval systems can be migrated to media such as the World Wide Web, thus enabling direct customer access to information that might otherwise have necessitated a telephone call to a call center.

In many cases, information retrieval systems can augment and sometimes replace more traditional forms of information sharing, such as classroom training and offline resources. For example, training for contemporary customer care environments, particularly call centers, is an unenviable task. Trainers must not only tutor new agents on how to deal with customers, they must also teach them how to log calls and gather customer data and feedback, as well as familiarizing them with company policies and procedures. The majority of training time, however, may be spent on mastering cryptic computer system functions as well as learning the intricate details of a particular product or service. This type of training, particularly in high-technology environments, can be extremely involved and time-consuming. Most trainers don't have the luxury of keeping new agents in the classroom for what might be considered an adequate period of time. Instead, they have to contend with an industry trend of diminishing budgets, resulting in lower-paid agents and higher turnover rates. Increasing competitiveness and more demanding customers may also mean that trainers have to deal with rapid changes and innovations in a product or service. Retraining agents becomes an issue, as hard-pressed customer care managers are judged more on accessibility than the arguably more nebulous benefits of enabling their staff to attend training on the latest product upgrade or service enhancement. The result is that agents often have to rely on rather sketchy details from perhaps a one- or two-hour training session.

Typically, customer care environments provide a certain amount of "on-the-job" training for new agents. In call centers, this normally involves working alongside an experienced agent or subject matter expert who is capable of coaching the new agent as they handle customer contacts. This practice is useful in helping to reinforce any classroom training the new agent might have received, in addition to familiarizing the agent with what are considered the standard practices of the call center. During this period, the new agent is given strong indicators as to how the best performers handle customer inquiries and complaints. In customer care environments (and there are many) that do not require agents to ensure consistency and accuracy of content information by first validating their responses through reference materials, the experienced agents may rely solely on their own knowledge and respond to the customer accordingly. Even in environments where management requests that agents validate their responses, reference materials (whether on paper or online) are often so poorly maintained that, even if the agent does find a reference, it may be completely outdated, cryptic, or incomplete.

Subjectivity of response becomes most evident in troubleshooting scenarios where experienced agents may be able to pinpoint a problem within seconds, while newer agents struggle with their outdated and poorly designed materials, or sift anxiously through the "cheat sheets" they or their peers composed during on-the-job training. If the option is available to them, new agents in this predicament will put the customer on hold and attempt to retrieve the answer by asking any available peer. As a last—but not uncommon—resort, the agent will advise the customer that the problem needs to be handled by a specialist or technician. At this point, the agent will attempt to escalate the call. If no "internal help desk" agents are available, a callback time frame is arranged with the customer. In the meantime, several minutes have elapsed, leaving only a dissatisfied customer, a perplexed or embarrassed agent, potentially several more minutes of after call work (scheduling the follow-up, creating a trouble ticket, and composing a note about the customer's problem), more work for an already overburdened internal help desk group, and an immediate drop in the call center's service level.

Some call centers encourage agents to listen to internal help desk agents resolving customer problems, particularly in the case of online transfers. While this practice appears to make sense, it is a reactive process that clearly does not involve information sharing across the agent population. In other words, the only one to really benefit is the agent who happened to receive the call that resulted in the contact escalation. This sort of selective information sharing is endemic in customer care environments in which knowledge retrieval has not been made a priority.

The task of ensuring that reference materials are updated and distributed in a timely manner is both daunting and time-consuming, especially in large or distributed customer care environments. Even in organizations that have employed a team of technical writers to ensure that paper documentation is kept up to date, a secondary problem emerges: The documentation is so abundant that finding the right information at the right time is highly improbable.

In summary, implementing and maintaining an online content application not only requires a significant amount of analysis and design, but depends upon substantial management commitment in order to succeed. Too many information retrieval systems become the brunt of users' criticism as a result of poorly planned implementation and virtually nonexistent maintenance practices. The success of any information retrieval system is contingent on meeting business requirements, some of which may have been derived from the overall goals of the customer care environment. For example, a customer care manager with the goal of increasing calls *resolved on first contact* from 78 percent to 90 percent, while *reducing contact times* by 40 percent, may use a combination of these metrics in addition to savings on materials and reductions in training costs to determine the return on investment from an information retrieval system. The original business requirements might have included the following:

The information retrieval system will:

- Respond to user search requests within x seconds
- Present a structure and interface that is intuitive to any user
- Automatically capture specific user interactions for root cause analysis purposes
- Automatically capture data for contact tracking purposes
- Retrieve information that is relevant to the customer inquiry or problem
- Retrieve information that is easily understood
- Retrieve information that is complete
- Retrieve information that is accurate

Every process and technological implementation is consequently driven by one or more of these properties—a concerted effort involving users, managers, analysts, designers, developers, trainers, human factors engineers, knowledge engineers, and documentation engineers.

For many customer care environments, the decision to implement information retrieval systems represents a tremendous paradigm shift from the days in which a clerical worker would drop a few sheets of company policy directives on the desk of each agent, or a technical writer would spend six months preparing or updating a user manual. Yet, in an age of commodities and demanding customers, few can afford to be complacent. Rapid, satisfactory answers to customers' inquiries and complaints not only can improve customer care operations, but can also encourage customer loyalty even while gathering market intelligence and establishing intraorganizational feedback channels.

Ideally, information retrieval systems will encompass the following essential properties:

- *Accessibility*

Accessibility is a measure of the *speed of response* and *ease of use* engendered by an information retrieval system. Speed of response may include the time taken to initiate the system and the time taken to respond to user input, such as a database search. If either of these mechanisms is unreasonably slow, leading to user frustration or stress, the system is likely to be rejected as unusable. Customer care management must ensure that in-process metrics driven by best in class scenarios constitute the minimal acceptance criteria for speed of response.

Ease of use is a term usually applied to the human factors issue of making system usage intuitive to a user. For the purposes of an information retrieval system, this would involve elements such as searching, information structure and presentation, and automatic data capture. A cumbersome user interface can cost precious seconds at the agent level, and is especially detrimental at the direct customer interaction level (e.g., the World Wide Web), where it can result in calls to customer care that should have been resolved by the customers themselves.

• *Integration*
The most effective information retrieval systems are capable not only of resolving customer inquiries and complaints, but also of automatically gathering data that can later result in useful management reports, assisting in root cause analysis, helping agents by automatically updating customer records, and even generating electronic information to be faxed or e-mailed to the customer. Deploying information retrieval systems as "stand alone" entities is counterproductive and one of the most detrimental, yet common, system deployment decisions found in customer care environments today.

• *Relevance*
If a user has to spent time sifting through the results of a search in order to determine which, if any, information retrieved is relevant to a particular inquiry or complaint, this may be indicative of a poorly designed database or inadequate user interface. Information retrieval systems may employ a variety of search mechanisms or "engines" in an effort to facilitate a relevant response.

• *Clarity*
Once relevant information has been retrieved, it is critical that the user can quickly assimilate the contents (and, in the case of a call center agent, convey the information in real time to the customer). This requires not only outstanding communications skills, but also a tremendous amount of planning and maintenance on the part of the documentation and knowledge engineers.

• *Integrity*
Completeness and *accuracy* are the two components of integrity. It is reasonable to assume that when an information retrieval system is first deployed, it will not contain the answer to every customer inquiry or problem, and those that it does address may not always be accurate. Rapid turnaround on incomplete, erroneous, or previously nonexistent information is therefore the goal of every documentation or knowledge engineer assigned to *maintain* the integrity of information retrieval systems.

In concert, therefore, a strong management focus on collaborative process, technology, and content provisioning can pave the way for outstanding customer interaction. Continuous process improvement, integrated system design, and vigorously maintained content results in "village store" customer loyalty and retention. For senior management, however, it must also result in the opportunity to gather meaningful market intelligence, in order that the company can continue to make customer-focused product and service decisions.

Modeling the Optimal Customer Care Environment

While it is understood that no two customer care environments are exactly similar, there are certainly processes that involve the same operations, such as answering a call, looking up an existing customer's record, changing account information, conducting a troubleshooting session, responding to an e-mail, and the like. Building on the premise that an outstanding customer care system will provide a satisfactory response on the first contact, as well as gathering sufficient data about the call to improve market intelligence and elicit feedback to help prevent any such calls in the future, it is apparent that such a system must automate all feasible processes. However, in an era in which most systems development groups are focused on automating processes in order to minimize human involvement, it is important to recognize that automation that leaves residual tasks for the human can become a significant and recurring training problem. With an automated system, operator compensation for system deficiencies is often more difficult and might even be prevented by the automated component. If humans are to remain an essential ingredient in organizational effectiveness (which, of course, they must), design and training for automated systems must converge to ensure that operators can perform their assigned roles adequately.

Consider the customer care system that does not track contacts. Very often, a small percentage of the customer base can constitute the majority of all calls. Typically, these repeat callers are low-usage, low-revenue-creating customers. Many are complainers who call several times in a row, hoping to get the agent who will step beyond normal company policy and give them, for example, a brand new replacement product for the one they purchased six months ago. A worthwhile contact tracking system can help alert agents to repeat callers and provide a rapid overview of previous transactions. Once recognition of the frequent caller is established by the system, it is up to customer care management to determine the appropriate policy.

There are two business endeavors that directly affect technology from a customer care perspective. The first is a company-announced plan to release a new product or service, and the second a company decision to reengineer all or part of its customer care environment. The first of these challenges is normally far less drastic in terms of system iteration than the latter. It is also more time-intensive and prone to sudden changes in direction that may adversely effect the design and development cycle. The second, depending upon budgetary constraints, may be thought of as a rare opportunity to implement a state-of-the-art customer care system. From the process perspective, it affords the opportunity to rectify all of the workarounds encompassed by the previous new product or service offerings. It also demands a more user-focused atmosphere, as any changes made at this level can have far more significant ramifications or the effectiveness of customer care in general.

New Product or Service Support

The first step in modeling the optimal customer care system is to understand the process of supporting new products or services. A concerted effort must be made from the outset to ensure that responsibilities, handoffs, and outputs are well understood. Strategists, in concert with product management, marketing, and senior customer care management, must outline the scope (boundaries), budget, release dates, and forecasted contact volumes to the business process improvement team, who in turn will distribute pertinent information to process owners. Policy, partnerships, competitive analysis, prospective customer profiles, and initial direct measures of quality should also be ascertained and shared. It is important that senior management should recognize the ramifications of any policy changes made after this point. New product or service offerings often involve extremely short development cycles, and even seemingly insignificant changes can cause a ripple effect that may jeopardize the readiness of customer care support.

Similarly, the development organization should interact directly with customer care process owners rather than product management on matters pertaining to the functional support of a new offering. It is often too easy for process owners to be excluded from this dynamic and frantic environment, resulting in system iterations that do not correlate to the accepted practice. Once deployed, new system releases are far harder to change than process, so the end result is that the process owners have to adjust to the limitations of the system, often resulting in suboptimal performance.

The customer care business process improvement team should also act as the conduit for the creation of content support for any new product or service. The team itself, a combination of major process owners such as billing inquiry and technical support, together with representatives from training, knowledge engineering, and operations, will act upon the scope of support as defined by the strategists. By defining these boundaries of customer care from the outset, those involved in gathering and distributing content can define their suppliers as part of the acquisition process, as well as coordinating with technical support to determine the necessary service agreements for handoffs to other organizations. Major process owners can redefine existing processes or create new ones based on the forthcoming offering, which in turn will provide documentation engineers with the policies and procedures necessary to support this endeavor. The outputs of both the knowledge engineers and the documentation engineers should then be channeled through the product management and legal departments in order to verify accuracy.

As indicated, from a technology perspective, any changes to the agreed upon functional support can often result in a direct line of communication between the development organization and product management. Because these changes tend to occur with increasing regularity as the release date approaches, the customer care process owners are simply not aware of them until the iterated system is released. Not only does this potentially impact the authenticity of existing processes, it can also cause significant problems for knowledge and documentation engineers, as their carefully crafted online content is quickly rendered inaccurate. Sometimes, these inconsistencies are recognized only after several customer contacts, leaving the agents questioning the credibility of the online customer care support system and the process owners with a sense of helplessness at being the poor relations in the business life cycle. The relative involvement of the process owner is going to be driven by the company's core strategy—whether to differentiate itself from the competition on the basis of price, product quality, or customer support. If it is clearly not the last item, then no amount of "lip service" to customer care will enable the process owner to adequately prepare for the first contact.

From the functional perspective, tight time frames engendered by new product or service offerings often mean that the development organization will be unable to adequately test iterations to the system with the user population. The training department is often left to conduct a crash course in using the new functions a few days prior to release. In many cases, trainers are the first to point out inconsistencies between the new release and the existing process or content material. The worst-case scenario occurs when trainers have to conduct their classes before the last set of functional iterations to the system is complete, resulting in later confusion about the intended purpose of a particular user interface component. Often, the trainers are so busy trying to develop curricula and conduct classes that they have no time to coordinate their findings with other process owners. Clearly, while content, training, technology, and process are all being developed in parallel, it is only through adherence to a universally recognized business process improvement model that customer care will be ready to provide outstanding support for a new product or service.

Customer Care System Reengineering

The second scenario pertinent to the development organization for customer care is that of reengineering all or part of the support system. Large-scale endeavors of this nature can sometimes take years to complete, and require substantial upper management support to succeed. Others are driven by short-term goals pertinent to automation and workforce reduction. Whatever the motivation, there is no question that relative success or failure is driven by user needs. It is fair to say that users, from call center agents to Web-surfing customers, respond well to being included in the system design process, and *extremely* well to seeing that their input was valued.

The business case for developing new customer care systems usually focuses on a reduction in contact time. Computer-telephony integration (CTI), for example, is getting a lot of attention because of its promise to reduce talk-times in addition to providing end-to-end contact tracking capabilities. For a company receiving 10,000 calls a day, that could mean significant workforce reductions. Similarly, interactive voice response (IVR) units attempt to force customers to classify their calls before speaking to a human, and they also present an opportunity to offload calls by providing online billing and account information, troubleshooting scenarios, and general information.

The other focus of the business case is invariably the promise of increased customer satisfaction. After all, it seems reasonable that the natural outcome of decreased contact time is a more satisfied customer. This means not only routing the customer efficiently, but also having someone available to deal with the inquiry or complaint. Thus forecasting, staffing, and scheduling software exists to ensure that each contact is answered in a reasonable period of time.

Of course, simply answering a contact in a reasonable period of time is not necessarily going to realize customer satisfaction. The accuracy, clarity, and completeness of the response is also critical. If the agent is poorly trained or unempowered, or relies upon an inadequately populated and poorly designed online system to provide responses to the customer, then satisfaction levels will plummet and talk times will naturally increase.

While call handling and routing technologies are generally established as cost savers, and forecasting, staffing, and scheduling software applications are clearly preferential to manual processes, the area that continues to demand the most improvement is at the agent–computer interaction level. It is apparent that countless minutes are being lost as a result of poorly integrated and maintained systems in the area in which it is most evident to the customer—the actual interface with a company representative. Not all such problems can be attributed to poor system design, of course; low quality or insufficient online content can sometimes render even the most proficient agent helpless to immediately resolve a customer inquiry.

In summary, every customer care environment must seek to emulate the performance of the successful village store owner in terms of personalized service, thus facilitating the goals of customer loyalty and retention, while also embracing the acquisition of new customers through cross-organizational cooperation. In centralized call centers, these targets can be achieved only through continuous process improvement, user-focused systems design, and rigorous content maintenance, coupled with the distribution of useful market intelligence to decision makers throughout the organization.

3
Media

Overview

While the vast majority of contacts with customer care environments continue to be made via telephone, the rapid evolution of "alternative" media has allowed companies to offload these expensive voice-to-voice calls using technologies that have become commonplace in the consumer arena—such as e-mail, fax, interactive voice response, and the World Wide Web.

Using contemporary technology, it is feasible that any type of customer inquiry or problem that, by customer preference or company policy, is routed to an agent can be presented in a unified format on the desktop. In other words, these disparate forms of communication can be chronologically received and logged in much the same way as calls are handled today. This type of universal contact handling will become increasingly important as the use of alternative media for customer care proliferates.

Today, receiving and responding to a customer e-mail, fax, or even a letter can be a time-consuming chore for those customer care environments that are neither procedurally nor technologically equipped to handle anything but voice-to-voice communications. In many cases, e-mail messages can be misrouted or even ignored because of these limitations, postal correspondences are not associated with previous or ongoing customer contacts, and even routing and handling faxes may involve significant amounts of agent "not ready" time. These inefficiencies are more apparent in those customer care environments that fail to accurately assess the evolving capabilities of the customer base in terms of using these alternative media.

The move toward so-called multiple application platforms, which allow the integration of several data and voice applications, means that systems development groups will ultimately contend with far less complexity in the development and maintenance of customer care systems. The shared resource environment permits access to a variety of information media, including voice, fax, video, graphics, and data to be accessed through a single, integrated platform.

For call center management, integrating the media resources that may be available to the customer in order to compile a complete contact history log, in addition to gathering useful market intelligence, is a task that demands careful business planning and systems implementation. Achievement of this goal can have a resoundingly positive effect on customer relations, particularly as alternative media become more commonplace and acceptable to both consumer and business customers alike. It is not unreasonable to assume, for example, that World Wide Web sites and call centers will continue to become closely integrated through technologies like computer-telephony integration (CTI).

Until recently, however, even what many CTI proponents would describe as a relatively facile endeavor, such as synchronizing inbound telephone numbers with existent customer accounts, remained an expensive and often time-consuming chore. Automatically linking World Wide Web activities with voice-to-voice communications, together with any other customer activity via e-mail, fax, and the like, is an integration issue that presents particular problems for most customer care–related systems development efforts. It is certainly feasible, however, that a customer who has been exploring a company's website and who has requested "live" assistance can be identified and, based on known preferences and even current interaction with the Web (e.g., searching for a solution to a particular problem type), be routed to an appropriate agent. Yet even from a nontechnical aspect, significant business process reengineering acumen is required in order to understand all of the ramifications of provisioning multichannel customer care facilities.

The following sections examine the various types of "alternative" media available to handle customer inquiries, particularly the rapidly evolving areas of electronic mail, the World Wide Web and interactive voice response.

Electronic Mail

For years, electronic mail (e-mail) has enjoyed prominence as a proven and cost-effective internal communication vehicle. Until recently, however (with the notable exception of technologically advanced business-to-business environments), external customers had to rely mainly on telephone services in order to resolve their inquiries and problems. The emergence of networks like the Internet, and the growing commercial success of the World Wide Web, together with the phenomenal growth of personal computing both at home and work, have converted e-mail into a viable and cost-effective business communications tool. The Internet, for example, provides a convenient way for customers to report a problem electronically at any time of day. Recognizing the potential of this medium for low-cost customer care, in addition to its power as a marketing device, companies are creating "websites" with e-mail facilities at an unprecedented rate.

It is, after all, a straightforward process. After accessing a company's Web page, a customer can send an Internet e-mail message with minimal difficulty. At the touch of a key or click of a mouse button, users are provided with a preformatted template upon which to type their request. A simple action sends the message, and often the customer will receive immediate confirmation that it was successfully received. There are no long waits in queue, no time-consuming transfers, and no telephone tag; it is up to the company to find the right person to handle a message, and to respond within what is considered to be a reasonable period of time. Today, it is the ideal medium for those who are not in a *critical* hurry to resolve an inquiry or complaint. Tomorrow, perhaps e-mail will have evolved to the point at which certain customers find it a more efficient communications medium than voice.

When an online information system doesn't meet the customer's needs, many companies strive to avoid a lengthy call by giving the customer an e-mail facility. This can enable the receiving agent to capture the customer's profile as well as a written record of the problem, *in the customer's own words,* for further analysis. This is a relatively novel way of interacting with the customer. Before the Internet became available on a widespread basis, e-mail communications were limited to internal business and were not even considered as a viable means of customer care. That has all changed, but relatively few companies have given much thought as to how to utilize this powerful medium in a customer care environment.

The evolution of e-mail has particular ramifications for customer care. The agent of tomorrow will require excellent writing as well as verbal communication skills. Supervisory text editors, highly trained on company policy, will be required to peruse outbound e-mail (particularly if the agent is forced to deviate from a set of templates, approved by the legal department, which are designed to handle the most common types of customer contact). Customers who take the time to compose e-mail messages are likely to be more specific and detailed about the nature of their inquiry or complaint than they would normally be via the telephone.

The commercial success of the Internet ensures that e-mail will continue to flourish by augmenting and in some cases replacing both voice communications and postal service. Some companies may even consider eliminating their toll-free telephone numbers in favor of e-mail because it costs virtually nothing and, most importantly, they discover that their customer base has a strong presence on the Internet. Coming at a time when companies are outsourcing their customer care functions to low cost-per-call service agencies and telemarketing bureaus, the advent of global e-mail facilitates a resurgence of personalized care, as well as providing an opportunity to more easily track and integrate inbound contacts.

From the customer's perspective, the relative time and effort involved in composing and sending an e-mail message is considerably less than that involved in writing a letter. After all, it does not involve the use of paper, envelopes, stamps, addresses, or copy machines. The customer can easily attach any electronically stored file, such as a spreadsheet, graphic, or text composition, to the message. The e-mail is retained on the computer and the sender can know within seconds whether or not the correspondence was received. The customer composes and sends the message when it is most convenient, and retrieves the response in similar fashion. It is also considerably less costly than sending a fax, which also can be a troublesome effort in terms of composing cover sheets, encountering busy lines, and uncertainty that it was ever received by the addressee.

In terms of *cost per contact,* properly handled e-mail communication defeats the telephone with consummate ease. For example, researching and ultimately explaining a technical procedure to a customer over the telephone can take an immense amount of time as the customer painstakingly transcribes the verbal instructions, whereas accomplishing the same goal via e-mail can take just seconds. All research is done "offline," and any procedural information is simply attached to a response template. In addition, the customer "screening" process facilitated by e-mail can ensure that nonroutine issues such as customer complaints can be channeled appropriately, rather than thrust upon some unsuspecting agent, as is the case with voice-to-voice customer care (one reason for high agent turnover!). In other words, an expert "receiving agent" can review cryptic, inappropriate, or misdirected e-mails before routing to a frontline agent, rather than the converse.

The unprecedented shift to online customer care, however, while embraced by many companies, places new demands on systems and employees alike. Today, many companies have little or no way of methodically storing, sorting, routing, interpreting, integrating, reporting, and responding to e-mail messages. Many messages vanish into "black holes" as a result of untracked escalations and poorly executed processes. When e-mail volume climbs to a significant level, then routing becomes of prime importance, and many companies are simply not prepared to deal with the nuances of e-mail tracking and distribution.

An electronic mail facility is an ideal medium for the customer who doesn't have the time or patience to endure lengthy hold times, who may have looked around a company's website and not found an answer, or whose inquiry or complaint is not so critical that it has to be resolved immediately. In many cases, as with toll-free telephone service, the need for e-mail customer care could be viewed as a testament to what's wrong with a particular product or service, or (more recently) the usability and content of a company's website. From a management perspective, the ultimate goal would be to eliminate the majority of customers' e-mail communications by making each incoming message a learning experience to be channeled back to marketing, product management, and Web content providers. However, because traditional customer care management is used to focusing on voice-to-voice communications, it is not unusual today to see many call centers treating e-mails as an inconvenience, and rather than advocating the use of this medium, it is being neglected, resulting in slow response times, inadequate resolutions, and consequently customer dissatisfaction. Those companies who have recognized the full potential of e-mail and have implemented robust processes and technology solutions are reaping the rewards of inexpensive and efficient online customer care.

The World Wide Web

As we have discussed, little more than a quarter of a century ago the telecommunications industry persuaded businesses that they needed toll-free telephone numbers in order to provide outstanding customer care. As the turn of the century approaches, protagonists are attempting to convince companies that the optimal supplement (or in some cases, replacement) to that form of support is to allow customers direct access to information via the World Wide Web. The "Web," as the graphical offspring of the Internet, has demonstrated a global reach far beyond expectations, and in so doing has opened up a new vista of possibilities in customer care. To many, it is the greatest communications medium since the advent of the telephone, and thus the facilitator of a new realm of customer interaction.

As the World Wide Web becomes more sophisticated, it is likely that companies will put more emphasis on online customer care, diverting as many calls as possible from toll-free telephone lines and consequently looking to downsize or even eliminate costly call centers. For many, the Web may become the focal point of all customer care, with an auxiliary force of telecommuting agents dealing with e-mails, faxes, and exceptional telephone calls. In the longer term, customers may even be charged a premium for *not* using the Web or some other similar medium, akin to the situation today with automatic teller machines. For that to happen, of course, the Web has to become as ubiquitous and accessible as the public telephone. In the interim, progressive companies will put as much information as possible online, giving the customer the ability to search knowledge bases, update their personal account information, review bills, place orders, and so forth. Optimally, the "Webcentric" customer will have the same access to personally relevant information as the average call center agent.

Before examining the potential benefits of the Web, it is worth investigating exactly what today's customer might be losing by going online to seek the answers to inquiries and problems. The most obvious answer is human contact—engendering courtesy, intelligence, and sympathy. It is reasonable to assume that even the best answers on the Web will not placate an angry customer. Nor will the continuing difficulties with natural language reasoning (i.e., the ability of software applications to interpret freeform textual or verbal input) be sufficient to provide relevant responses to complex searches. Customer recognition and acknowledgment of privilege and contact history also remain far-sighted endeavors for most websites. Speed of response is clearly a principal issue that is unlikely to be resolved prior to the turn of the century, yet, with the long waits in queue that are the hallmark of many voice-to-voice customer care environments, this is not always going to be a deterrent—even to the most impatient customer. Impersonality and technological limitations, therefore, are currently the primary drawbacks of Web usage.

On the positive side, the World Wide Web promises the customer access to large amounts of information at any time of day or night. The graphical presentation of this information makes it easy for most customers to explore a website and discover interesting facts that may enhance their enjoyment of a product or service. For routine inquiries and problems, the Web is ideal. The existence of direct telephone links to agents from a website gives customers an immediate "out" when they have apparently exhausted their search options. For customers who are not in a hurry, the ability to send an e-mail directly to customer care is also beneficial. A key to the success of the Web will be a company's ability to convince repeat callers that whatever is represented online is also advocated consistently by every customer care agent and supervisor. The Web then becomes the recognized medium for company policies and procedures, with a database reflecting perhaps 80 percent or more of the contacts normally received by the customer care environment. Customers on the Web can also interact directly with a company's interactive voice response system in order to conduct transactions and/or order an item from a fax-on-demand facility. If voice-to-voice interaction with an agent becomes necessary, the customer can link to the call center via Internet telephony, or at least receive a confirmation message advising approximately when an agent is going to call.

From the technology perspective, many believe that the World Wide Web will put the Internet in a death spiral, unable to support demands for data from millions of concurrent users. There are predictions of rival networks capable of channeling millions of bits of data to home computers each second—not surprising, considering the phenomenal data-carrying capacities of fiber optic cable. Regardless of the outcome, the enormous popularity of interactive multimedia ensures that networks like the Internet will continue to flourish and evolve. In the near future, increased bandwidth, shared applications, and increased processing power will see the Web migrate into a world that comes far closer to emulating today's video game environment—an interactive, visually stimulating medium that enables customers to visit company sites and conduct business, solve problems, and learn about the latest product or service offerings.

Just as concerns about the safety of the railway encouraged the development of telegraphy, and the subsequent emigration of large numbers of individuals led to the proliferation of the telephone, the spread of Web-based technologies has already changed the way some companies communicate. Similarly, many inbound call centers would not exist today if companies did not see a viable reason to placate customers after a product has been purchased. Yet diminishing budgets, long hold times, and inadequate answers from poorly trained agents who rely on equally poorly written documentation can do more to alienate the customer than encourage loyalty.

A robust customer care environment on the Web, handled properly and with an amenable audience, will potentially save a company thousands of dollars each day. The Web already facilitates around-the-clock (7×24) access, coupled with automatic data gathering and reporting on customers contacts, and minimal network costs. Of course, many people still prefer human contact, but if a large company can divert even a small percentage of callers to its website, the savings will be potentially enormous.

Interactive Voice Response

Interactive voice response (IVR) is a relatively new technology that has its origins in call centers, where it was first used to offload inbound customer calls by using scripts to answer frequently asked questions. Today, the IVR platform (sometimes referred to as voice response unit or VRU) is used in other areas, such as employee benefits, human resources, and internal help desks. Because they can be linked directly to company databases via computer-telephony integration, many IVRs are used to actually resolve a customer inquiry or problem, such as performing a small billing adjustment, retrieving account balances, citing recent customer transactions, validating credit card information, buying and selling stocks, resolving a common product problem, or making a reservation. IVRs can be available even if the call center itself is closed, thereby providing value-added seven days a week, twenty four hours each day.

Voice products vary greatly in cost and capabilities. The most simple example of this type of technology is the telephone answering machine, which announces a prerecorded message to the caller and records the response. The automated attendant delivers a prerecorded message, but also asks the caller to select his or her destination from a list of choices. Voice mail provides large message storage capabilities together with sophisticated features to ensure appropriate routing and manipulation of incoming and outgoing messages. Audiotex enables call centers to provide prerecorded information to customer on a wide variety of subject areas, which are normally accessed through Touch-Tone selections. Most IVR manufacturers can cater to both small and large customers by offering systems that allow call center managers to add features, lines, and upgrades as the need demands.

Despite a burgeoning presence on toll-free service lines, prohibitive integration costs mean that many IVR units exist as stand-alone screening devices (akin to automated attendants) whose only function is to force customers to make selections from a multitude of menu options. As a result, customers and ostensibly threatened call center agents often perceive IVR as an excuse for poor service—as an admission by the company that it does not care enough about them to have a human available to answer the telephone. The fact that IVR can often handle calls at 10 percent to 20 percent of agent cost, however, makes it a popular choice for companies who are focused on operational enhancements, if not always on customer satisfaction.

Original IVR units were relatively difficult to program and did not always integrate with existent call routing facilities. Vendors attempted to convince call center managers that interactive voice response not only cut costs and facilitated call management, but also was being enthusiastically embraced by customers as a quick means of resolving routine inquiries. As a result, the technology flourished to the point at which today it is considered an easy-to-maintain (via graphical user interfaces) and essential part of the call center infrastructure.

Voice recognition is also an important component of evolving IVR functionality. Rather than asking the customer to endure seemingly interminable keypad entry requests, the system facilitates the use of voice to provide instructions and respond to questions. Although voice recognition has not progressed as quickly as expected, research facilities have made strides toward the ultimate goal of "universal" voice interpretation (i.e., the ability to recognize utterances from any human voice without "training" the application). Given that the voice recognition vocabulary will continue to expand, some vendors are attempting to link similar advances in natural language interpretation to provide "intelligent" customer interactions with the IVR unit. It is reasonable to assume, therefore, that vendors may ultimately provide a more user-friendly alternative to voice-to-voice interaction, thus promising significant return on investment for any busy call center environment.

Other Media

Postal Service

A much maligned, low-technology, and often obscure medium in many contemporary call center environments, customer correspondence delivered via the postal service is nevertheless a stumbling block that can cause significant problems in terms of repeat contacts, time-consuming responses, and, most importantly, customer dissatisfaction. Consider, for example, (1) the company whose auditors discovered that over six months of incorrectly addressed customer care mail was heaped beneath a part-time administrative assistant's desk, or (2) the call center whose outbound correspondence processes were so convoluted that even mailing one piece of correspondence took an agent offline for over ten minutes, or (3) the customer care division of a major service provider that had completely disparate systems for recording inbound customer calls and mailings.

Companies who rely heavily on customer care correspondence for areas like billing payments and inquiries, of course, are benchmarks for all others. Online templates for outbound correspondence, imaging systems for inbound correspondence, administrative support, and stringent adherence to well-defined processes can ensure that no customer mailing is neglected. Instead, "hard copy" documents are treated as an integral part of the customer care operation. Inbound letters are scanned and distributed to appropriate online resources, and ultimately handled much the same way as an inbound call. After call work is appropriated to call center agents as necessary to ensure that such mailings are handled and resolved in a timely manner. Outbound correspondence processes are fully automated from an agent's perspective, with predefined templates automatically populated with customer information, leaving minimal "tweaking" prior to being routed online to a mailing facility. Any attachments are defined by the agent and fulfilled by administrative support.

Those customer care environments that overlook the inherent value of highly defined correspondence processes—even when such correspondence constitutes a small percentage of all inbound customer contacts—would do well to conduct a cost/benefit analysis as necessary to determine the viability of automating these processes. It is fair to say that, despite the intense focus on voice-to-voice calls inherent in many of today's operations, neglect of even small-volume correspondence support can cause a ripple effect that can be debilitating to service levels.

Fax

As more consumers and small businesses invest in fax capabilities, the greater the reward for providing customers with "just-in-time" faxing capabilities, such as fax-on-demand, fax mailboxes, e-mail to fax transmission, and other functions. For call center managers, there are two discrete processes that must be addressed in order to ensure that fax correspondence is addressed in a timely and satisfactory manner. The first of these, inbound fax processing, considers the issues surrounding the receipt, routing, and handling of incoming faxes. The second process involves the routing of faxes from the agents desktop or fax server to the customer.

Fax has been a useful customer contact medium for over twenty years. Used primarily as a support mechanism for voice-to-voice customer contacts, it can facilitate the rapid distribution of complex procedural instructions, proof of contractual obligations, bill copies, and other material that is ideally conveyed in a "hard copy" format. Many customer care environments enable agents to send and receive faxes directly from their desktop, thus eliminating the time-consuming chore of sharing limited facsimile resources with others. Also, by allowing customers to access fax-on-demand facilities, seven days a week, twenty-four hours a day, companies can alleviate voice-to-voice calls for routine information.

Fax is most viable in business-to-business environments, although the proliferation of personal computers that are preloaded with fax software ostensibly means that more and more consumers may take advantage of this technology. For the majority of call centers, however, fax will remain a useful, if not pervasive, medium for interaction with customers.

Video Services

The emergence of broad bandwidth facilitators such as fiber optics, coupled with burgeoning computer processing capabilities, will continue to encourage consideration of customer care video services. As technology evolves, video-enabled customers can expect companies to provide face-to-face communications with agents. Just as video kiosks heralded a novel form of customer-agent interaction, continuing strides in the telecommunications industry promise to make these facilities available on a more widespread basis.

Companies who rely on high-powered contact with their most lucrative customers, or those who cater to high-technology clients, are already adding video services to their arsenal of customer care tools. Although such concepts are nothing new, the latest videoconferencing devices are economically within reach of most consumers. The question becomes one of determining how far a company will go in order to provide "personalized service." Some would argue that the need to actually see an agent (particularly when the majority of customers are never likely to see that agent again) is questionable. Preferred customers who are designated to a specific agent may indeed benefit from the experience, but it is more likely that downloading a video clip from the Web or other facility will have greater rewards for the quality of the customer experience, at least in the short-term.

Summary

The return on investment for implementing alternative media in an effective manner is potentially substantial. Given a customer base that is willing to use electronic mail, the World Wide Web, or interactive voice response to resolve routine inquiries and problems, many companies have found that voice-to-voice communications can be at least somewhat reserved for more complex issues. This situation can result in a base of highly trained and skilled agents handling customer problems. Given the erstwhile lack of "instantaneous gratification" inherent in communications via fax and postal services, however, it is apparent that such media are generally not suitable for resolving immediate customer needs. With the widespread availability of broadband networks, video services will continue to evolve and will be most useful in establishing personal rapport with highly valued customers. Ongoing procedural and technological development in the automated handling of electronic mail will continue to enhance the viability of this medium for customer care. Interactive voice response and fax-on-demand are already being used by many companies as a means of resolving routine customer calls, and the World Wide Web is clearly paving the way for a new age of customer interaction. These paradigms will evolve rapidly as consumers gain cost effective access to all forms of digital communication.

4

Business Drivers

Overview

If company executives were asked to document their strategic view of customer care as succinctly as possible, the result would probably be something akin to *satisfying the customer at the lowest possible cost while gathering usable market intelligence data*. From this simple statement, the framework of a multibillion dollar industry unfolds. Hundreds of processes, vast telecommunications networks, countless lines of code, and massive databases exist to help humans fulfill the goal of world-class customer interaction.

By treating each element of this strategy as an individual business driver, a more defined model of customer care begins to emerge:

Satisfying the customer. . .

Customer satisfaction could be narrowly defined as "giving customers what they want as proficiently and quickly as possible." At the marketing level, it means fulfilling a perceived customer need with a product or service, while at the customer care level this would hinge upon accurate contact forecasting, empowered staff, and rapid access to relevant information (possibly through several media), thus resulting in a high rate of resolution on first contact.

. . . at the lowest possible cost. . .

Providing a product or service so flawless that the only reason a customer contacts the company is to place an order would be the optimal scenario. Given that this does not occur too often, it is fair to state that lowering customer care costs is intertwined with the relative level of customer satisfaction with postsale care. In other words, everything that applies to increased customer satisfaction from the customer care perspective also translates into a more cost-effective environment for the company. Additionally, one of the most obvious ways to lower costs in a customer care environment is to reduce the amount of time an agent spends with each customer, thereby reducing telecommunications costs as well as creating possible opportunities for downsizing.

. . . while gathering usable market intelligence data.

Initial customer registration is an opportune time to gather market intelligence. A satisfied customer will certainly be more likely to respond to a few survey questions than one who has been in queue for twenty minutes and still failed to have a problem resolved. The irritated customer will be more apt to criticize the customer care operation than to impart useful suggestions about how a company could improve its product or service.

Gathering product or service feedback is a prime function of any customer care environment. Every troubleshooting contact and every customer complaint, suggestion, or comment presents an opportunity to gather valuable and inexpensive information. The question becomes one of whether the agent or system is gathering usable data, and secondly, whether the recipients of that information are actively using it to improve the product or service. In many cases, neither contingency is being met.

Customer satisfaction, cost reduction, and market intelligence, therefore, constitute the three major business drivers behind every successful customer care environment. The question, of course, is how these seemingly incongruous elements can be realized in a world of diminishing budgets and rising customer demands.

These elements also constitute the first part of a model for outstanding customer care consisting of *business drivers, requirements,* and *solutions* that rely on *process-driven* design and the development, deployment, and maintenance of technology and content. These processes can be applied to customer contacts via *media* such as voice-to-voice, electronic mail, the Internet, fax, interactive voice response, video, and the postal service. Each of these media provides a route for customers to directly contact a company for the purposes of presales advice or postsale support. In order to provide this support, the online customer care environment relies on *components* such as systems design, user interaction, content provisioning, and data gathering. These components, in turn, are contingent on the existence of many processes and subprocesses that are designed to ensure that every customer contact successfully achieves the minimal criteria imposed by the business drivers. Systems development, for example, incorporates the selection, integration, release, and maintenance of every customer care application. In concert with user interaction and as a conduit for content provisioning and data gathering, systems development is the gateway to enabling fewer agents to cope with increasing customer demands.

By maintaining the affiliation between business drivers, requirements, and solutions derived via these media and components, a customer care environment can continually focus on the customer, rather than viewing each business endeavor as some sort of isolated initiative to provide better customer support. Process-driven customer care, therefore, can ensure that business strategy and tactical endeavors remain synchronized, thus avoiding "boondoggle" enterprises, which can ultimately be more harmful than beneficial to a company's relationship with its customers.

As indicated, there are three principal business drivers for customer care. These are customer satisfaction, cost reduction, and market intelligence. By striving to satisfy each of these drivers, a company can ensure that the process of providing customer care is perceived as a profitable venture that can result in greater customer loyalty and continual product or service enhancements based on direct customer feedback. The following sections provide a high-level description of each of these drivers.

Customer Satisfaction

Two key requirements for the realization of customer satisfaction with regard to a call center transaction are the ability to *resolve calls on the first contact* while also *maximizing customer access* to the center. These requirements may be explained as follows:

- *Resolve on First Contact*

The requirement, "resolve on first contact," generally means that after the *initial* call the customer has no need for any further contact with the call center. In some cases, however, operations managers may consider a resolution on first contact one in which the customer describes the reason for contacting the center and subsequently receives a scheduled callback from an agent with an appropriate resolution. This is an important distinction, as the latter path is clearly more apt to produce favorable metrics, but less likely to satisfy the customer.

- *Maximize Access*

The second requirement associated with customer satisfaction—"maximize access"—refers to customer care's ability to respond to a contact in a timely manner. For an inbound call, this means answering the call in the shortest time possible. Most call centers use some form of auto attendant or IVR facilities to immediately pick up incoming calls, placing the onus on the customer to select the correct prompt for routing to an agent. In the case of IVR, it is hoped that the customer will take the initiative to explore online information resources rather than always attempting to reach an agent. Given that this is not usually the path that most customers would choose to take, maximizing access to a call center also means reaching an agent as quickly as possible. In terms of customer satisfaction, this means that the call center manager must understand the customer's tolerance for delays versus the number of agents available to answer the call. This balancing act has been a challenge since inbound call centers first opened, but in an era of staff reductions it becomes an even more difficult requirement.

Consistently Meeting Customer Expectations

Any interaction with a customer should be measured against *inferred* or *known* customer expectations. Customer care managers don't need a technical study to tell them that the sooner a contact is answered and the faster the customer's inquiry or complaint is resolved, the more satisfied the customer will be. This logical ideal is clearly *inferred* from normal human behavior. However, it is implausible to always meet the most demanding customer expectations. So customer care environments generally measure themselves against, and attempt to surpass, what is normally called best in class for a particular industry. A good starting point is the traditional inbound voice-to-voice call center environment. The goal of the call center is to provide the best possible care to its customers at the lowest possible cost. For example, in the event that company management discerns that one of its competitors is resolving 85 percent of all customer calls on the first contact, with an average speed of answer of under fifteen seconds and a talk-time of three minutes, then it will naturally strive to do even better. If a company has no immediate competition, or finds that its competitors have such an abysmal level of service that they are forced to align themselves with best in class from an associated industry, then that call center's metrics are initially somewhat arbitrary, driven purely by cost constraints and management's best guess at what might constitute "world-class" customer interaction.

On the other hand, *known* customer expectations are derived from surveys, interviews, and unsolicited customer feedback. In many cases, known customer expectations reveal far more complex issues than the comparative effectiveness of the competition. They may reveal critical flaws in the company marketing strategy, in the product or service itself, or even in something as seemingly mundane as the bill format. These are all scenarios that may affect the call center in terms of volume, but are not the direct responsibility of the center itself. Instead, they must be effectively channeled to other parts of the organization for resolution. This gives the call center an opportunity to prove its true value to the company as a direct (and often the principal) conduit for customer feedback.

Other known customer expectations, however, have direct implications for the effectiveness of the call center itself. Notwithstanding the *one ring, right first time* ideal, if a significant proportion of customers indicate that they are dissatisfied with the amount of time they are spending on hold, or the quality of the answers they are receiving from agents, then it could be indicative of several major problems at the center. While this kind of feedback may not specify precise expectations, it is up to company management to establish measures in order to ensure that the number of dissatisfied customers is reduced to at least manageable proportions.

Measures in a customer care environment are generally a mixture of inferred and known customer expectations. Based on the outcome of customer feedback and competitive analysis, a company might decide that a six-minute talk time is a reasonable goal for its first-level technical support. It might also add that a 90 percent resolved on first contact rate is desirable, and that all calls should be answered within ten seconds. Decisions such as these clearly have significant effects on the workforce model, but the call center's ability to realize these goals depends upon a plethora of other mechanisms and processes, which could be termed *contingencies*.

Contingencies are defined as *events that may occur but are not likely or intended*. Customer care contingencies are avoided by carefully designed *processes*. Some contingencies are more problematic than others. The ability of a call center to answer customer inquiries, for instance, may depend upon the existence of a building that houses sufficient lines and agents to address inbound calls. This contingency is a "given," whereas others, such as those dictating the ability to convey a response that satisfies a customer, are far more subjective.

Take the example of a call center that determines that all calls should be answered within ten seconds and concluded within 220 seconds, with a 1 percent abandon rate, no blocked calls, and a resolved on first contact rate of 90 percent. Regardless of whether these metrics were driven by budgetary constraints or inferred/known customer expectations (or a combination of both), suffice it to say that the call center has allocated its resources and configured its schedules accordingly.

In order to meet these service-level goals, the call center may rely on a significant number of everyday contingencies. First, there are those contingencies that facilitate interaction with the customer, but which do not actually provide the customer with a solution to a problem or resolve an inquiry. These can be referred to as *supportive* contingencies. Examples of supportive contingencies for an inbound call center may include:

- The toll-free network is available.
- The switch can handle all incoming calls.
- The interactive voice response (IVR) unit is functioning.
- The automatic call distributor (ACD) is configured correctly.
- The computer-telephony integration (CTI) functions are available.
- The call management system is being appropriately managed.
- Workforce management is facilitating all incoming calls.
- The agent's desktop system is functional.

The second set of contingencies is based on effective business processes. This is where the customer actually receives a response to a query or complaint. Given that, in the majority of cases, operational contingencies (with perhaps the exception of workforce management) augment rather than adversely effect a call center's level of service, it is fair to assume that it is at this secondary level where most jeopardies can occur. These may be referred to as *customer-facing* contingencies. Unlike operational contingencies, these represent areas where the success or failure of a particular contact with a customer does not depend upon the existence of powerful technologies that are normally hidden from view. Instead, they depend upon the agent's ability to conceptualize and comprehend, to design and to implement, to review and to improve. These are the areas where, for managers and decision makers, there exists an opportunity not just to deploy the latest call monitoring software, but to really ensure that customers are being handled appropriately and in a productive manner. Notwithstanding the agent's ability to interpret the customer's needs and provide a consistent and acceptable response, examples of customer-facing contingencies for an inbound call center would include the ability of the system to facilitate interaction with the customer, and the agent's ability to locate, understand and convey accurate and complete information quickly.

Each customer-facing contingency describes a critical conduit for a company's ability to distinguish itself from the competition. Coupled with *organizational* contingencies (i.e., the ability of the organization to provide a superior product or service and adapt to the needs of the customer based on market intelligence), these points represent the foundation of customer care today. Behind every customer-facing contingency are the three essential realms of *process, technology* and *content,* each of which, working in concert, can help a company to realize world-class levels of customer interaction.

Cost Reduction

The second business driver involves a concerted, company-wide productivity initiative that clearly requires vigorous executive support and a formalized company policy or position as the basis for addressing productivity as a strategic issue. There are two key requirements for reducing cost in a call center environment—minimizing contact time with the customer and minimizing agent turnover.

- *Minimize Contact Time*
Given that many customer care environments are now contending with staff reductions in addition to handling ever more demanding customers, the requirement to maximize access has become synonymous with reducing contact time. Many senior managers appear to believe that the answer to this enigma is to implement the newest customer care technologies as a one-time major cost offset by the workforce reduction savings. The problem is that the association among technology deployment, process improvement, and content development is often obscured by the seemingly disparate organizations involved. While the contracted development group remotely designs and develops the ultimate system, process owners hold meetings in corporate headquarters with marketing and product management to determine the best way to support new service offerings and gather customer data, and the knowledge engineering group discuss the optimal presentation of content with agents at the call center. Essentially, the absence of a universally understood process relegates the system's effectiveness before it is even implemented.

- *Minimize Turnover*
The requirement to reduce cost is contingent not only on staff and contact time reductions, but also on the ability of the customer care environment to reduce existent staff turnover. Clearly, the longer a call center can retain its best staff, the more likely it is that the customers will be satisfied and contact time will be minimized. Also, depending upon the technicality of the product or service, the potentially substantial costs of training replacement agents are avoided. Many companies also perceive outsourcing as an effective cost reduction by enabling them to take advantage of existent facilities and staff, as well as a low cost-per-call rate. High turnover, however, can be an even bigger problem in the highly competitive and streamlined world of outsourced customer care.

Implementing Cost Reduction

Productivity measurement is a key element of most customer care environments. For the call center manager, productivity usually means assessing how many calls are being taken by each agent. In centers with high rates of escalation or customer callback, it should also mean tracking how many calls were resolved on the first contact. For senior management, however, productivity may typically be measured under the general heading of, for example, "sales per employee." In labor-intensive environments such as call centers, that usually means reducing staff while overtly maintaining service levels—in other words, getting the most support for the least amount of money.

Cost reduction in customer care, therefore, normally focuses on increasing human productivity while implementing new technology solutions. On the human side, management might examine the effective cost of an employee, per unit of time, for the tasks covered by that employee's job description. In the case of a call center, nonproductive time might engender improvement of convoluted processes for outbound correspondence (e.g., addressing envelopes, copying forms, composing customized responses), bill reconciliation (e.g., manual calculation of discrepant information), and the like.

Productivity in contemporary customer care environments can be adversely affected by many elements, including such things as the absence of usability testing in the design of online systems, the absence of empowerment, limited agent capabilities, inappropriate rewards and recognition, inadequate data gathering, and the absence of feedback loops. Conversely, productivity at the expense of customer satisfaction (e.g., hurrying the customer or subjecting the customer to interminable and confusing menus) is extremely detrimental to the concept of "best in class" customer care. Using technology appropriately can help customer care managers realize the optimal blend of customer satisfaction and productivity.

Technology implementation is the usual direction taken in an effort to lower costs, increase productivity, and increase customer satisfaction in the customer care arena. The business case for deploying technology in toll-free telephone number environments is invariably compelling, for example:

- Computer-telephony integration (CTI) promises to reduce talk time by as much as 30 seconds per call.
- Decision support tools can provide even newly hired agents with rapid solutions to customer problems.
- Interactive voice response (IVR) facilities can offload a significant percentage of inbound telephone calls.

Measures of productivity can help a customer care environment to heighten company awareness of specific needs by providing the basis for tracking rates of improvement, serving as a planning tool, and permitting the call center to measure itself against the competition. The best ideas for improving productivity often emanate from the front lines, that is, the agents and customers themselves. The ability of a customer care environment to raise the productivity of its agents through the use of technology can enhance the quality of every interaction with a customer, thus engendering both loyalty and cost-cutting proficiency.

Decisions within the marketing environment can have a significant logistical effect on customer care. It is important, therefore, that the ramifications of certain promotional decisions be fully understood prior to implementation. The offering of a new service feature at a low price to a large sector of the marketplace can have a devastating effect on customer care productivity. It is not uncommon for customer care to have no prior knowledge of the latest marketing campaign. In fact, many agents discover the existence of a campaign from the customers themselves. This situation is compounded in a call center environment where information is passed by word of mouth. The result, of course, is that productivity and morale plunges as agents scramble not only to handle an influx of calls, but also to learn as much about the promotion as possible so that they can give at least the impression of competence.

Whereas traditional customer contact–driven environments will continue to focus on talk-time and after-call work as a principal measure of productivity, those companies who wish to be perceived as value-added product or service providers will ensure that customer care is perceived as a critical function of the overall marketing strategy rather than as an obligatory cost center. While such a strategy may drive certain types of contact time upward, the correct blend of technology and human intervention will ensure that both customer satisfaction and market intelligence benefit significantly. A process-focused approach is the only way to ensure that each of these marketing "influencers" does not disrupt the customer care environment.

Market Intelligence

Customer care facilities present a unique opportunity to gather useful market intelligence. Rather than receiving an intrusive telephone call, or even a polite request for written feedback, it is the customer who is contacting the company with a question or a comment. It is at this juncture, which some companies term as a "moment of truth," that the customer, consciously or otherwise, imparts some form of market intelligence to the business. Perhaps it is simply a request for directions to the nearest store which, based on frequency of occurrence by location, may ultimately indicate a need for a new facility in a certain part of the country. Or perhaps it is the first indication that there is something wrong with a recent batch shipment. Or maybe it is the third request that day for a new service feature, and so on. Whatever the reason for the customer contact, the ability of the customer care environment to gather and analyze contact information in a timely and efficient manner will dictate its relative value to the company, as follows:

- *Gather Customer Data*
  The requirement to gather customer data is one that is facilitated to some degree by most customer care systems, at least in call center environments, but it is also one that is rarely effective in helping a company understand its customers. The pertinent question is "why gather customer data at all?" From the customer care perspective, it is clearly important that any contacts with the customer are logged, in the event that further discourse on the same subject is required. By capturing the date and time of the contact, the reason why customer interaction was necessary, and any pertinent follow-up work, the customer care environment can maintain an historical database of all contacts with customers. The second reason why customer data is gathered is to provide product or service feedback, complaints, and suggestions to marketing, product management, legal, and other departments within a company. The proliferation of online support for cus-

tomers, particularly through nonmediated forums such as the World Wide Web, presents a new type of challenge for gathering this type of information.

- *Conduct Root Cause Analysis*

The basic premise of many customer care environments is, first, to answer the customer problem or inquiry, but secondly to reduce postsale customer contacts by gathering data that may be used to enhance the overall product or service. This process, known as *root cause* or *preventive* analysis, can help a company identify opportunities for improvement, such as

- ♦ Identifying reasons for missed sales opportunities or account cancellations
- ♦ Recognizing potential product or service improvements
- ♦ Realizing potential customer contact improvements
- ♦ Identifying potential cost-cutting opportunities

While it is generally agreed that a toll-free number or e-mail address is an excellent conduit for complaints and suggestions, in most cases the information collected is not easily analyzed and disseminated throughout the company to effect necessary change to a product or service. Instead, notations and categorizations relevant to customer contacts become an unintelligible library of random facts and opinions attached to customer profiles. Root cause analysis becomes increasingly difficult for larger customer care environments. A call center with 10,000 contacts per day but without an automated data gathering facility, for example, needs to practice extremely focused notations and categorizations in order to enable analysts to identify why customers are calling and how the company can act to improve customer satisfaction.

Quite often, the only really useful data that are generated from a customer care environment are those reports that enable call center management to monitor talk time, abandonment rates, average speed of answer, and after call work. This situation is perpetuated by the fact that, in many instances, these are the only metrics that really interest the call center manager, because they are the measurements upon which the relative success of the operation is determined. Demands from other company departments for more data gathering are often viewed as impositions that are likely to compound service-level problems and result in suboptimal evaluations for call center management.

Creating useful reports requires collaboration between the end users, information technologists, operations, and senior management. Not only do business requirements have to be defined, but a trade-off has to be negotiated in terms of additional talk time and after call work time (hence workforce management requirements) verses the relative business need for a particular element of information. Most importantly, report formats must reflect management needs for easy-to-assimilate customer information. Ideally, the end product will be data gathering and reporting mechanisms that do not irritate the customer, require minimal end-user time and effort, and which provide management with mission critical information.

By defining management reporting needs from the outset, a company can ensure that the customer care operation is a profitable endeavor and an extremely viable extension of the marketing process, rather than a cost center that has to struggle for budgetary recognition each year. Determining how the frontline associate should input this information with minimal time wastage is a critical step (i.e., negotiation of after call work as necessary, coupled with an intuitive user interface design), as is database design and definition of the functional requirements that may be necessary to generate certain types of reports. Actual report content and layout are often a much neglected step that can make or break the usefulness of the entire reporting environment. Giving management mind-boggling amounts of information is unlikely to score any points for the business acumen of customer care.

One of the principal management complaints from frontline agents is that nobody seems to do anything about their feedback. By providing a robust reporting mechanism, a company can significantly reduce this type of employee dissatisfaction, thereby encouraging agents to contribute as much as possible to the flow of direct customer contact information to all levels of the company.

CHAPTER

5

A Case Study

Setting the Stage

While recognizing that every customer care environment has unique business issues, it is nevertheless worthwhile exploring how the principles of world-class customer interaction can be put into practice in a hypothetical situation. Take the example of an international company that not only produced equipment, but also provided installation advice over the telephone or dispatched field technicians as necessary to meet the customers' needs. This company, who had several hundred field sites, wanted to centralize its product and service support by opening a call center. The business case for this endeavor was based upon increasing the level of customer satisfaction and market intelligence gathering, while also reducing costs. As such, the call center manager, who had been promoted from an operations role at a major field site, determined that resolving calls on first contact, maximizing customer access to front line agents, minimizing contact time, reducing agent turnover, gathering customer feedback, and conducting root cause analysis would facilitate the accomplishment of these goals.

In order to support this endeavor, the company considered outsourcing the entire operation, as well as entertaining the idea of routing after-hours calls to a European country that promised an educated workforce and low corporate tax rates. Ultimately, the experimental nature of the project prompted management to keep customer care in house, at least for the first year of operation.

Studies from the field had indicated that inbound call volumes could be as high as four million per year, and as a result the call center manager decided to advocate the purchase of an automatic call distributor, rather than using a private branch exchange or even the local telephone company's switching system. In order to assist with forecasting and scheduling, the manager also decided to purchase a workforce management application.

57

In anticipation of fairly involved technical and procedural calls, the manager had recruited a mixture of experienced field staff, local college graduates, and even agents from other call centers, in addition to some part-timers, such as retired corporate employees. The manager had also hired several supervisors with a view to establishing a ratio of ten frontline agents to every supervisor. These supervisors were expected to coach each agent with telephony skills, as well as establish adherence and other performance measurements.

In anticipation of the systems development group's decision to purchase an off-the-shelf contact tracking system, the manager had contracted with a group of training consultants, in addition to using process engineers and a part-time telephony consultant to prepare new agents for frontline interaction with customers. A five-week training curriculum had been designed, with agents spending one week learning about business processes, one week at an offsite location, two weeks using computer systems (including the new contact tracking application and corporate legacy systems), and a final week taking mock telephone calls. After going "online" new agents were receiving a further week of on-the-job training from supervisors and peers.

The team of process engineers worked with subject matter experts from the field to ensure that every potential customer contact inquiry was adequately described. This team suggested significant improvements in many existing business processes, and it was anticipated that ongoing systems development and integration would facilitate the realization of these goals. The process engineering effort also identified those areas in which frontline agents would need additional empowerment or immediate access to decision makers within the company in order to resolve the customer call on the first point of contact. By exhaustively flowcharting these contingencies, the team was able to establish measurements relative to the execution of each process. Test scenarios were established, and approximations of average talk time and after call work for each type of customer contact were used to establish the workforce management model.

Several weeks prior to the opening of the call center, the systems development group recommended the purchase of a highly regarded contact tracking system, which would enable the customer care environment to capture customer demographics, call categorizations, escalations, and follow-up commitments, as well as specific customer comments and complaints. Using the business requirements that had been developed by both the field representatives and management, the development group was able to describe functional requirements for integrating the customer care application with existent corporate systems. This would involve ensuring that pricing, ordering, billing, and other customer data were being shared across the entire network.

By the time the call center opened, the manager was relatively satisfied that all possible steps had been taken to meet the business criteria for a successful customer care operation. Workforce management projections indicated that there were more than enough agents to answer the majority of customer calls within the accepted target of twenty seconds, even at peak calling times. This projection was based upon what process engineers had described as a "reasonable" average talk time of 210 seconds, coupled with an average after call work time of 90 seconds, and given that agents would be occupied at their workstations at least 85 percent of the time.

Early Warnings

Within a few weeks of operation, however, it became clear that all was not going well at the call center. Customer contact reports indicated that not only were call volumes rising beyond even worst-case scenarios, but it was taking agents almost twice as long as predicted to handle calls. As a result, queue times had risen to an average of over two minutes on every call, and abandonment had jumped to almost 7 percent. To make matters worse, supervisors estimated that agents were requesting assistance or escalating calls over 30 percent of the time. Random call monitoring also suggested that up to 20 percent of all nonmisdirected customer contacts were resulting in call-back commitments from agents. While resolution on first contact plummeted, agent turnover was climbing alarmingly. Within the first six weeks, over 10 percent of full-time staff had been fired or had resigned for reasons ranging from incompetence to incompatibility.

Attempting to resolve these operational issues was clearly the major priority, but the call center manager was also disconcerted to find that reports being generated by the contact tracking system were virtually useless from a market intelligence perspective. Not only were the majority of calls being classified as "Other," but the agent notations accompanying each call were cryptic and inconsistent.

The first inclination of the call center manager was to focus on hiring and training inadequacies as a root cause for the seemingly excessive contact times, as well as the high rate of escalated calls and follow-up commitments. It also seemed rational to surmise that better-trained agents would be more productive, as well as enjoying greater job satisfaction and less stress, thereby increasing customer satisfaction and reducing turnover.

The manager decided to appoint a task force in order to identify opportunities for improvement throughout the operation. After five days of call monitoring, interviews, questionnaire responses, and documentation reviews involving process, technology, and content considerations, the manager was presented with several findings, which could be summarized as follows:

• The relative complexity of the product and service offerings meant that agents were constantly searching for a plethora of business policy guidelines, instructional procedures, troubleshooting advice, and general information such as directions to the nearest store or branch location, hours of operation, current marketing and sales promotions, planned upgrades to existing products, comparisons to competitors services, and so on. Clearly, much of this information could not be conveyed to agents during training, so a number of references were being used, including technical manuals, loose-leaf binders, job aids, reference sheets, and a variety of handwritten notes posted around the agent's workstation. It was found that in the majority of cases, agents were either unwilling or unable to execute a timely and acceptable solution to a particular customer inquiry by using these materials. Instead, the agent who could not immediately respond to the inquiry would either place the caller on hold and verbally request assistant from a peer or supervisor (which was happening as many as five times per call), ineffectively look through the available references for a suitable response (in which case nearly all calls were escalated or resulted in a callback commitment), or would immediately suggest that the customer should receive a callback within twenty-four hours.

• Another area of focus for the task force was that of systems support. Agent feedback indicated that not only was the new contact tracking system difficult to use, but information "feeds" from corporate legacy systems were notoriously inaccurate, and it was difficult for the agent to identify existing customers. It was found that the development group, ostensibly as a result of an overly aggressive management schedule, had been forced to deploy the new system without evaluating its suitability to the tasks that were being performed by agents. Instead, the development team had decided to release the system in an "as is" state, with a view to identifying a prioritized list of usability problems through process engineering focus groups. Also, systems integration was proving to be a more time-consuming and costly task than had ever been imagined, and in the meantime agents often had to enter the same information in disparate systems.

• Not surprisingly, it was found that queue times were increasing as a result of excessive amounts of talk time (as agents struggled to resolve calls on the first point of contact) and after call work (as agents struggled to explain via the contact tracking system why the majority of calls were not being resolved). Another major contributor to this problem was the fact that only 10 percent of all callback commitments were being met in a timely fashion, resulting in excessive numbers of repeat calls from customers, which in turn was steadily driving call volumes far beyond reasonable estimates. Supervisors were then instructing agents to stop any after call work and continue receiving inbound calls until such times as queues became manageable. Like a vicious cycle, increased contact times, inability to resolve the contact, and missed commitments due to excessive queue times were causing a steady decline in customer satisfaction.

• The goal of cost reduction was also being thwarted by excessive agent turnover at the call center. Here it was found that training did have to bear some responsibility for the fact that new agents were relatively unprepared for the rigors of online customer care, particularly when it involved a base of increasingly frustrated customers. Despite the fact that 20 percent of the training curriculum was devoted to "mock" customer calls, inexperienced agents, including those who had been recruited from the field, had been less than prepared for the constant pressure and (depending upon call segmentation and routing) the monotony of answering one customer call after another. There were other contributors to agent turnover, including complaints of inadequate salaries, lack of supervisory support, the fact that rewards were being linked to group—rather than personal—performance, and, not least, the fact that frontline agents were being given little or no authority to resolve customer demands for product or service retribution, such as demands for replacement products and credit adjustments.

• There was a great deal of information being gathered by frontline agents via the contact tracking system, including attempts to categorize the reason for the call, customer comments and complaints, and notations on customer-agent interaction. From a market intelligence perspective, however, the information was virtually useless. Not only were agents struggling with a lengthy list of call categories, but notations were being made in an individualistic style which, given the number of inbound calls, precluded any possibility of root cause analysis. The fact that management had not allocated any resources to address preventive analysis from the outset was also seen as a cause for criticism. There appeared to have been an erroneous presumption that meaningful management reports would automatically be generated from the contact tracking system, ready for distribution to marketing and product management, without any need for human intervention.

• While it was acknowledged that the process engineers had done an exceptional job of documenting the processes relevant to particular types of customer contact, such as billing inquiries, pricing, credit and collections, general inquiries, and troubleshooting, it was also found that these processes, rather than being automated wherever possible, had been rendered virtually obsolete by ongoing system development efforts. Weeks, even months, of effort were being undone by technological limitations caused by a combination of tight time frames, limited budget, and lack of in-house programming expertise. It was also found that call center processes for handling escalations, internal referrals, customer callbacks, marketing initiatives, new product development, postal correspondence, fax, and electronic mail had been overlooked by the supervising process engineer. This had resulted in many inconsistencies, including missed customer commitments, lack of response to written customer inquiries, and outdated reference materials.

The call center manager recognized that, despite what had been considered fairly elaborate preparations, the current operation had no hope of achieving hoped for gains in customer satisfaction, cost reduction and market intelligence. While the basic requirements for achieving those goals remained valid, such as resolving calls on the first contact, maximizing access, reducing contact time, minimizing turnover, and gathering customer data, it was apparent that a far more stringent solution set would need to be considered. Based on the recommendations of the task force, the call center manager decided that the majority of these problems could be most efficiently resolved through increased systems support. For example, the manager decided to provide frontline agents with the ability to conduct a consolidated search for information *online*, rather than by using an assortment of desktop reference materials. The manager rationalized that outstanding cross-organizational processes and technological implementation in this area would reduce talk times and increase resolution on first contact, creating a ripple effect in terms of reduced repeat calls, lowered queue times, decreased after call work, and consequently reduced agent turnover and increased customer satisfaction. The manager was also optimistic that, by even marginally freeing up staff, some resources could be devoted to root cause analysis for market intelligence purposes.

Proposed Solutions

Aware that any technological enhancement was likely to be expensive, the call center manager decided to augment the business case by conducting a cost/benefit analysis on every major system adjustment. At a high level, the manager proposed to:

• Improve resolution on first contact by ensuring that processes are described for every possible call center contingency, including cross-organizational service agreements, root cause analysis, customer contact criteria, customer satisfaction, content provisioning and improvement, marketing initiatives, and system change requests.

• Reduce escalations and callback commitments by empowering frontline agents with an online information retrieval system that enables agents to provide accurate, clear, consistent, and complete responses to customer inquiries and problems. This would include information on policies, procedures, troubleshooting, and general inquiries.

• Reduce call volumes and increase accessibility by providing customers with multichannel access to the customer care environment, specifically through the establishment of a sophisticated electronic mail facility, a customer care–oriented World Wide Web site, and a systems-enabled interactive voice response unit.

• Further reduce talk times and after call work by implementing a user-focused systems design process, including task analysis, rapid prototyping, and usability testing. This approach would involve standardization of user interface design principles and execution of key systems integration requirements.

• Generate useful market intelligence by improving contact categorizations, automating notations, and standardizing manual data gathering, in addition to assigning human resources as necessary to conduct root cause analysis and ensure integrity of management reports.

In terms of cost/benefit, the manager summarized technological investment recommendations as follows:

• Customer surveys indicated that as many as 30 percent of all callers were willing to use an *interactive voice response* unit to resolve routine inquiries and problems, provided that the system

♦ Used scripts that were easy to follow
♦ Enabled rapid access to relevant information
♦ Allowed users to "opt out" and speak to an agent at any time

In order to fulfill these requirements, the manager planned to subject every script to a human factors evaluation, in addition to discovering those functions that could easily be integrated into the IVR unit, such as routine problem solving, account balances, order status, credit adjustments, and so on. The manager also decided to provide every customer with a graphical depiction of the IVR structure, in order that the user would know in advance exactly which numbers to select in order to quickly resolve an inquiry. Based on current call volumes, the manager estimated that the successful implementation of such a system would potentially reduce call center headcount by 5 to 8 percent within one year, while also contributing to improved service levels.

• Implementation of a fully integrated information retrieval system (i.e., both online documentation and intelligent troubleshooting system) was the most expensive proposition, but also the one that promised the highest return on investment. In this case, the manager estimated that a fully functional system, which could be purchased "off-the-shelf" and fully integrated within six months, would potentially save the call center in excess of one hundred hours of contact time per day, purely by virtue of increasing resolution on first contact by at least 10 percent. (A detailed cost/benefit analysis on the implementation of an information retrieval system is depicted later in this book.)

• By enabling the system to capture automatic notations relevant to each customer call, the manager estimated that 15 to 50 seconds of after call work could be saved on each contact (thus enabling higher service levels and potential headcount reductions), in addition to providing more consistent management reports and root cause analysis opportunities. This systems integration endeavor was expected to involve not only corporate billing and ordering systems, but also the call center's information retrieval systems. Again, working on these estimates and a projected three-person systems development involvement for a total of four months, the manager estimated a return on investment of less than one year.

• Customer surveys also indicated that up to 30 percent of the customer base had access to electronic mail and World Wide Web facilities. By providing a robust interpretation, routing, and response process that could be facilitated by emerging technological solutions, the manager estimated that as many as 10 percent of all calls could be ultimately handled via these media. The existence of the Internet meant that implementation would be restricted only by the deployment of the necessary hardware and software at the call center and the preferred Internet service provider (ISP) location. Although the initial cost would be relatively high, the return on investment was potentially immense in terms of reduced call volumes, particularly when nonproprietary information retrieval system access was enabled from the website.

• The manager also decided to implement a fax-on-demand service that would enable customers to call in for routine document access at any time. As the majority of the customer base used home telephones to call the center (i.e., increasing the possibility of a database match), a decision was also made to implement standard "screen pop" computer-telephony functionality, based on time savings from automatic retrieval of customer data (synchronous with agent acceptance of the inbound call).

• Given the continued evolution of unified messaging and computer-telephony integration applications, a decision was also made to conduct an in-depth examination of integrated customer care functions, such as automatically tracking customer contacts made via the Web, interactive voice response, electronic mail, voice mail, fax, and postal services, as well as voice-to-voice, on a unified contact tracking platform. This vision, however, was tempered by the fact that integration efforts using evolving technologies could lead to an extremely lengthy, as well as costly, development cycle that could be preempted by the emergence of increasingly sophisticated "off-the-shelf" software solutions. As such, the manager decided to focus on more mature technologies and integration endeavors, while also monitoring these innovative developments.

While these solutions clearly suggested a strong focus on systems support, the call center manager also recognized several other opportunities for improvement, including flaws in the organizational structure of the call center, such that supervisors were expected not only to coach frontline agents as well as handle escalated calls, but also to deal with scheduling, performance reviews, special projects, and other ongoing administrative duties. As such, the manager proposed the creation of an internal "escalation desk," staffed by high-performing agents, in addition to assigning clerical staff to handle routine agent and supervisor chores, such as copying bills, retrieving contracts, and faxing and mailing correspondence. The manager also considered the formation of an "offline" agent group to deal exclusively with those customer contacts that required additional research above and beyond normal contact times.

Rather than deal with unexpected peaks in call volume by relying on part-time agents to be at the call center on short notice, the manager decided to advocate the use of internal resources, such that management staff would be prepared to devote a proportion of their time to answering customer calls. By involving other areas of the company in the customer contact process, the call center manager gained support for the concept that an awareness of customer problems would infiltrate the entire organization. Additionally, it was suggested that a business case should be created to allow certain part-time resources to receive customer calls remotely, using residential ISDN and computer-telephony integration.

In an effort to address the agent turnover issue, the manager decided to adopt a more in-depth screening process, which would include the scripting of a telephone interview via the interactive voice response unit, including questions regarding previous call center experience, salary requirements, current employment status, and so on. Suitable applicants would then be contacted to set up a fifteen-minute voice-to-voice telephone interview with a telephony skills consultant, who would grade the applicant based on items such as articulation, listening skills, cadence, vocabulary, grammar, courtesy, and empathy. The applicant would then be invited to participate in a short training scenario that would involve using the computer to input data, in addition to answering a "customer" call, the goal of this exercise being to assess the applicant's ability not only to work under pressure without becoming defensive, but also to enter error-free typewritten information in a timely manner. Given the strategic geographical location of the call center, the manager believed that even with such a rigorous screening process there would be no shortage of suitable applicants.

From the training perspective, the call center manager decided to expose new agents to the "real world" of customer interaction far earlier in the process, ostensibly by staggering the training curriculum to include at least two weeks of on-the-job training after a high-level classroom introduction to business policies and procedures, systems support, and telephony skills. The manager believed that this type of exposure would potentially cut costs by enabling new agents to quickly determine whether or not voice-to-voice customer care was still considered a desirable occupation. The manager also determined that a combination of individualistic and team-oriented reward and recognition approaches would be used, in addition to financial incentives for assuming internal help desk responsibilities.

In order to effect these changes, the manager created a number of new roles within the call center environment, most of which were filled internally. For example, by deciding to increase the supervisor-to-agent ratio marginally, the manager was able to secure the services of an appropriate individual to lead a root cause and quality analysis effort. The technical writers who maintained various reference materials at the call center were assigned to lead online content development, while a human factors engineer was chosen to be the call center liaison with the systems development group. A high-performing agent with a background in design was initially appointed to work on the customer care website, while another worked with the process engineering team to optimize the interactive voice response and electronic mail initiatives. A process improvement team addressed the internal call center processes that had been originally overlooked, as well as instigating involvement in a cross-organizational team involving marketing, product management, sales, and systems development.

At this stage, the manager might also have examined those considerations that could be directly impacted by the collaboration of process, technology, and content, such as empowering agents, providing multichannel access, reducing contact time, providing rapid system response, providing intuitive system design, providing outstanding content, facilitating data gathering, and providing contact tracking tools (see Table 5.1, Building a model for online customer care). While the remaining considerations (such as improving training, improving scheduling, increasing staffing, providing incentives, conducting customer surveys, and providing analysis tools) are clearly important, these involve processes that are not directly impacted by the implementation of information retrieval systems and alternative forms of customer interaction, which constitute the essential elements of online customer care.

Empowering Agents

Many call centers rely on an initial period of classroom training to provide agents with the in-depth knowledge required to resolve a customer problem on the first point of contact. In technical environments, or those that handle a wide spectrum of customer interests, this has resulted in a segmented workforce and, arguably, an increase in the number of escalated contacts due to misdirects (e.g., the customer selected the wrong prompt and was routed to an agent who was not empowered to resolve his or her

⬚ TABLE 5.1.   Building a model for online customer care.

Business Drivers	Goals	Requirements
Customer Satisfaction	Resolve on first contact	**Empower agents** Improve training
	Maximize access	**Provide multichannel access** Improve scheduling Increase staffing **Reduce contact time**
Cost Reduction	Reduce contact time	**Provide rapid system response** **Provide intuitive system design** **Provide outstanding content** **Facilitate data gathering**
	Minimize turnover	Improve screening Provide incentives
Market Intelligence	Gather customer data	Conduct customer surveys **Provide contact tracking facilities**
	Conduct root cause analysis	Provide analysis tools

inquiry). This approach also encourages tremendous inconsistency as agents interpret training recollections into a customer response. Despite the proliferation of written reference materials around the agent's desktop, many find it virtually impossible to find the right information at the right time. Apart from random monitoring, the absence of systematic information sharing can mean that busy agents have little or no way of assessing whether or not they are giving the customer the optimal response. Such a goal can be most consistently and cost effectively achieved by providing a constantly updated and easily accessed online information retrieval system that provides not only answers to technical problems and billing/general inquiries, but also management approved guidance on issues such as product returns and complaints.

Providing Multichannel Access

Clearly, workforce management techniques such as forecasting and scheduling will continue to be a key factor in facilitating rapid customer access to agents. Recognizing that even the most accurate forecasts and intuitive schedules will not appease cost-cutting executives, however, many call center managers monitor the rapid growth of alternative media for customer care—a situation that will continue to present opportunities to offload customer contacts from call center agents to facilities such as interactive voice response and the World Wide Web. Although it is not envisioned that such media will preempt voice-to-voice communications, the proliferation of personal computers, modems, and fax machines, coupled with the growth of "self-service" on contemporary toll-free service lines, certainly creates the prospect that more customers will find answers to their problems and inquiries via these alternatives.

Reducing Contact Time

It seems reasonable to assume that customer access to a call center can be maximized by reducing the amount of time each agent takes to resolve a particular customer problem or inquiry. Not only is reducing contact time a potential customer satisfier, therefore, but it can also contribute directly to cost reduction by enabling agents to become more productive in terms of the number of customer contacts handled. Of course, a great deal depends upon the approach to minimizing contact time. Abruptly escalating calls after five minutes' talk time or terminating conversations after giving customers incomplete answers may indeed contribute to a decline in contact time, but will also result in a far higher number of callbacks (and a subsequent decline in customer satisfaction). The ideal situation, therefore, is to not only reduce contact time, but also to ensure that the customer is satisfied with the response.

Providing Rapid System Response

The provisioning of rapid system response is a critical technical issue that can "make or break" an online customer care system. Several seconds' delay is far more than a minor irritation to an agent who is attempting to placate an impatient customer. The simple fact is that unless the system responds to an agent command within what is considered a *reasonable* period of time, the system will be regarded as more of a hindrance than a help, and the agent will devise personal workarounds that may or may not be optimal. Even if system content is outstanding, poor response time will render it useless to time-pressured employees. Interestingly, a time lapse is probably more acceptable to the customer who is interacting with a website or interactive voice response unit, than with another human being. Customers clearly expect immediate and articulate advice from agents—not an uneasy silence.

Providing Intuitive System Design

Rapid system response must of course be accompanied by an intuitive system design. Users should be able to quickly navigate through an *integrated* customer care system that provides all of the functions required to answer routine problems and inquiries, in addition to gathering data relevant to the customer contact. Process improvement, workflow or task analysis, rapid prototyping, and usability testing are all critical elements of good system design, yet these are often neglected by those development groups whose only goal is to produce a system that more or less meets high-level business requirements within the constraints of time and budget. In such cases the absence of strong cooperation between management, users, and systems development results in a functional system that does little to improve agent productivity and can even diminish customer satisfaction.

Providing Outstanding Content

Content maintenance is the bane of many customer care environments. No matter how fast and how intuitive the system may be, the absence of accurate, relevant, and complete content information will ensure its downfall. Troubleshooting systems that cover only a small percentage of known customer problems, user instructions that are poorly written and presented, scripts and online help applications that serve only to confuse the user, and policies that no longer reflect management initiatives are all indicative of a system that was deployed under the misguided assumption that technology alone would provide some sort of "magic bullet," rather than to interactively assist users by adhering to continuous improvement processes. Reducing cost and increasing customer satisfaction mean that users can immediately retrieve the information they need in a way that makes sense to them. If the information isn't available, then a management-driven quality improvement process will ensure that it is there in the future.

Facilitating Data Gathering

There are two reasons to collect data on customer contacts. The first is to keep an historic record of the transaction so that it may be recalled should the customer be engaged in future contacts with the company. The second is to gather market intelligence that may be used to identify opportunities for improvement with regard to the company's product or service. Properly documented customer inquiries, problems, complaints, and suggestions can clearly help marketing and product management teams understand ways in which they can gain new customers while retaining the existing base. More often than not, however, customer comments are obscured by inconsistent and unclear data-gathering techniques, and further impeded by systems that fail to facilitate analysis of that data, leading to an obscure mass of information that does little more than fill storage facilities. Unstructured manual note

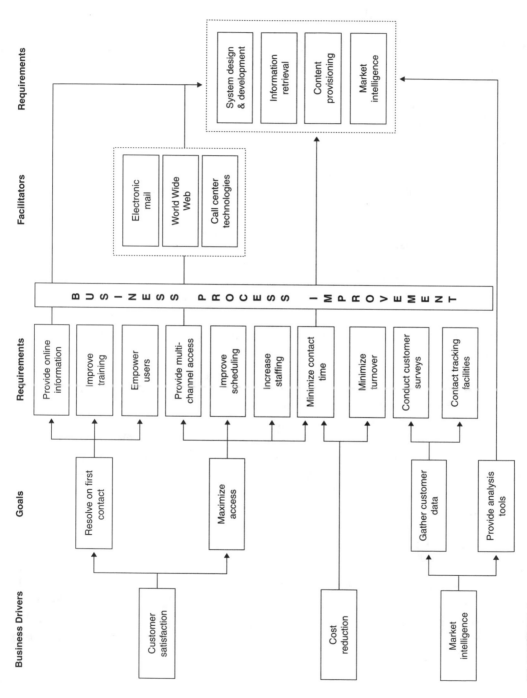

■ **FIGURE 5.1** Online customer care

taking by agents, for example, is often a counterproductive exercise that contributes to significant after call work and has a detrimental effect on customer access. A customer care system must facilitate automated and interpretable data gathering wherever possible.

The emergence of direct customer access information channels such as the World Wide Web means that companies must either automate the gathering of market intelligence data or forgo any knowledge of customer activities through that medium. Given that direct access will continue to flourish, it is reasonable to assume that most companies will want to monitor and interpret customer activities wherever possible. As computer-telephony integration is applied to this scenario, companies are not only able to monitor activities at a website, but also to associate that activity with a particular customer. If the customer chooses to speak to an agent, therefore, the agent will be aware of the customer's prior activities, such as the use of search strings. The point is that regardless of whether it is an agent or a customer interacting directly with the system, consistent, interpretable, and useful data can be gathered without human intervention.

Summary

The case study discussed in this chapter describes a situation that is familiar to many call center managers. Such situations negate any type of competitive advantage engendered by the provisioning of centralized customer care, and can often be more damaging than beneficial to a company's reputation. Instead of the call center generating useful customer information, the operation becomes reactive, constantly negotiating a tightrope of inbound calls verses agent availability, with the management team struggling to maintain any semblance of value-added service.

In this case study, the call center manager has been given the latitude to implement what appear to be plausible solutions to a difficult situation (see Figure 5.1, Online customer care). By using process-driven system design and development, information retrieval, and content provisioning as critical customer care *enablers*, coupled with investigation of both emerging media (electronic mail and the World Wide Web) and evolving call center technology, the manager has opened the door to outstanding customer interaction. The following chapters explore each of these considerations individually, with a view to examining how each might be justifiably applied to contemporary customer care environments. When perusing these chapters, it is recommended that the reader keep this study in mind as a benchmark for examining how a company might move from a potentially damaging cost center situation into the realm of world-class customer interaction.

CHAPTER

6

Process Considerations

Overview

World-class customer care providers empower their agents and realize greater productivity by developing processes that ensure that every agent knows what is going on throughout the company in terms of marketing initiatives, product or service enhancements, innovations, and changes to company policy (see Figure 6.1, Product and service realization). By using technology as a conduit for sharing this information and rewarding frontline agents for augmenting the system by providing new information, these companies ensure high levels of productivity in addition to providing a value-added service.

The basic premise of business process improvement is that it crosses organizational boundaries and provides the best possible form of customer care. A fundamental question for every customer care process engineering team is whether the objective is to impress management with voluminous output or to ensure that the process flows have a direct correlation to the "real world." It is certainly easier to achieve the former, the accuracy and completeness of which may never be tested, then archive the flows with a combined sigh of relief for a job well done, so that team members can go back to the assignments for which they were originally hired. The process flows may even be used to derive an initial set of policies and procedures, and may constitute a part of the training curriculum for new hires, but accountability for their accuracy is often lost with the disbanded team. Ensuring that the flows reflect reality is a far more tedious process, yet one that builds the foundation for continuous process improvement.

One of the first steps toward business process improvement is the appointment of process owners. These individuals are chosen to lead and direct, keep a group on schedule, support and encourage team members in their improvement efforts, and

72

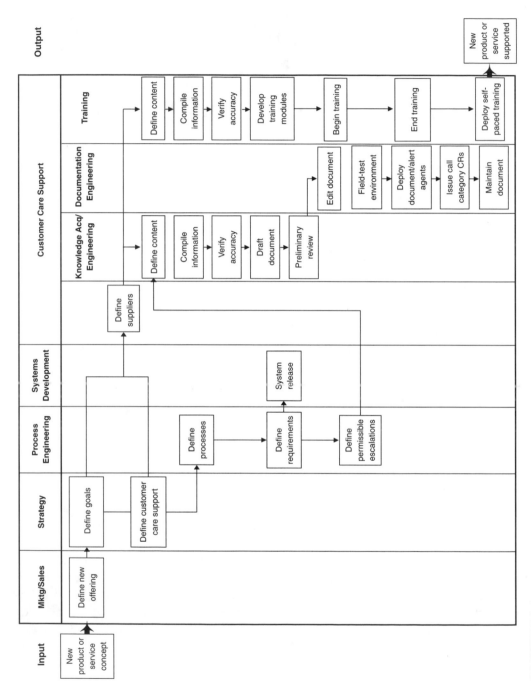

Input

Mktg/Sales

Strategy

Process Engineering

Systems Development

Customer Care Support

Output

Input

New product or service concept

Mktg/Sales

Define new offering

Strategy

Define goals

Define customer care support

Process Engineering

Define processes

Define requirements

Define permissible escalations

Systems Development

System release

Define suppliers

Customer Care Support

Knowledge Acq/ Engineering

Define content

Compile information

Verify accuracy

Draft document

Preliminary review

Documentation Engineering

Edit document

Field-test environment

Deploy document/alert agents

Issue call category CRs

Maintain document

Training

Define content

Compile information

Verify accuracy

Develop training modules

Begin training

End training

Deploy self-paced training

Output

New product or service supported

▨ **FIGURE 6.1** Product and service realization

meet commitments on schedule. It is a position that requires the vigorous support of senior management to fulfill. While business process improvement as a concept may be less formal than a rigorous evaluation like ISO 9000, it can ensure that these initial efforts to baseline customer care processes are not doomed to obscurity. Process owners, through the medium of the business process improvement hierarchy, will not only flowchart the process but also gather several other key pieces of information, including

- Compiling cost information (identify departments involved and their activities, and estimate time spent on the process and any subprocess costs involved)
- Establishing measurement points and feedback loops
- Reporting effectiveness (such as the percentage of contacts completed within three minutes)
- Gauging efficiency (such as the percentage of time spent on follow-up contacts) and change status

Process owners may also conduct value-added assessments of the process (just how much value is the process really adding?), as well as relating customer expectations to the process itself. This latter task is critical to the establishment of measures of quality, which benchmark a customer care environment against perceived "world-class" standards (see Figure 6.2, Multichannel measures of quality).

The Measures of Quality—Process Relationship (see Figure 6.3) illustrates how direct measures of quality are applied to a typical customer contact. In this example, the customer has initiated a toll-free telephone call to a call center. Based on a mixture of market research, competitive analysis, and subjective decision making, in this case management has determined that the following measures of quality should apply to these types of contact:

First contact resolutions:	95%
Average speed of answer:	25 seconds
Talk time:	<= 8 minutes
Escalations:	<= 15%
Customer rating:	=> 85% (very good/excellent)

The ability to meet these expectations for the sum of all voice contacts to the call center depends upon many variables, or *contingencies*, which can include

- The ability of the call center to
  - Hire adequate numbers of agents to answer incoming calls
  - Select and hire high-quality, customer-focused agents
  - Adequately train and empower agents
  - Motivate poorer performing agents
  - Accurately forecast call volumes
  - Appropriately schedule agents to meet incoming call demands
  - Provide an efficient call-handling infrastructure
  - Provide clearly defined and well-understood call-handling processes
  - Provide integrated contact tracking applications
  - Provide well-maintained information retrieval systems

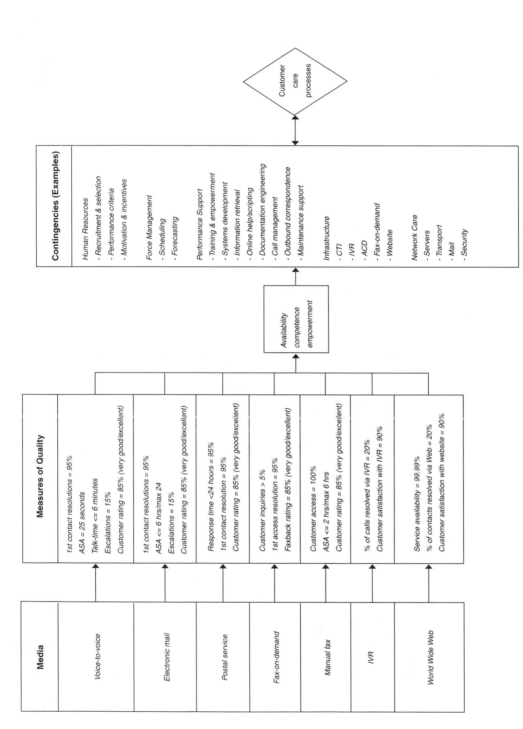

FIGURE 6.2 Multichannel measures of quality

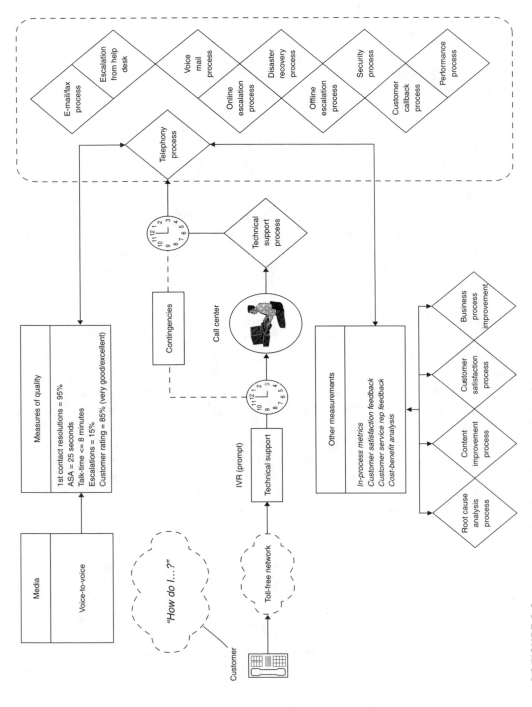

☒ **FIGURE 6.3** Measures of quality—Process relationship

75

By meeting these contingencies as necessary, thus attempting to ensure the *availability, competence* and *empowerment* of all agents, call center management can viably formalize strategies to fulfill any reasonable direct measures of quality. A breakdown in any one of these contingencies, however, can obviously result in detrimental performance and subsequently inadequate levels of service and decreased customer satisfaction.

For example, the agent may be primarily concerned with measures of talk time. Based upon a predefined frontline telephony process, the agent may follow a routine of greeting and identifying the caller (a scenario that may be enhanced by computer-telephony integration), perusing the customer's profile and contact history (if any), determining the customer's specific need, invoking the information retrieval system, attempting to resolve the customer's inquiry or complaint (and escalating the call or scheduling a callback if necessary), gathering any customer feedback, and closing the contact.

If the process works correctly and systems respond adequately, the agent will fulfill the constraints of talk-time. If the call is escalated, it adversely affects both the *resolved on first contact* and *escalations* measurements, and probably also has a detrimental effect on the *customer rating*. Normally, escalations indicate either inadequate training, disempowerment of the agent, or inaccuracies/omissions in the information retrieval system, most of which can be rectified by a robust quality improvement process.

In a process-driven customer care environment, analysis of the outcome of any given customer contact could reveal flaws that would ultimately result in changes to either the process, the supporting technology, the content, or even the product or service itself. Much depends upon the ability of the agent and/or the system to gather data that can contribute to viable root cause analysis, overall product or service quality, and process improvement. Of course, allowing the system and/or the agent to capture information in an ad hoc manner is not conducive to effective root cause analysis, so it is clearly important that management reporting requirements and parameters be established as early as possible in the development cycle. For example, encouraging agents to capture customer comments or contact transactions using free-form text fields is not going to assist the root cause analysis process in a high-volume call center. These type of notations make interesting reading for the next agent who happens to peruse that customer record, but from a management perspective they are virtually useless.

While full-scale business process improvement enterprises will use histograms, cause and effect, pareto diagrams, scatter diagrams, force-field analysis, mind maps, and statistical process controls in order to achieve their goals, that is often a resource- and time-intensive task rarely afforded to the low-budget, reactive world of customer care. Often all that process owners can do is to keep up with the ramifications of a marketing decision to tout a half-finished product, or the release of an "integrated" customer care system that isn't integrated enough. Customer care process owners who do not enjoy supportive and understanding management often find themselves facing new crises and change-control situations on such a regular basis that considerations of statistical process control become as rare as delighted customers. It is up to senior management to shield the process owner by ensuring that cross-organizational handoffs and notifications occur in a timely manner, so that the customer care environment has sufficient time to prepare for an onslaught of contacts.

By including customer care in the strategic decision-making process, senior management can exemplify the much-vaunted "competitive differentiation" that drives the concept of outstanding customer care. One example of this might be reengineering of the end-to-end billing process, which usually involves every department in the company. By horizontally crossing the organization, the senior management team driving business process improvement can quickly discover how, for instance, the inability of billing operations to process adjustments made by customer care agents before the next bill cycle was causing hundreds of unnecessary callbacks from irate customers, or how the inability of the system to process credit card rejection notifications had resulted in a hopeless backlog of work for the customer care billing inquiry manager. Identifying these critical business issues with organization-wide ramifications can help to demonstrate the difficulty of providing "world class" customer care and thus ensure that process ownership does not become the least desirable position in the organization.

Defining Customer Care Processes

As discussed previously, there are several contingencies relevant to meeting customer expectations through business processes. These contingencies drive processes that may be *organizational, supportive,* or *customer-facing.* At this point, one may assume that management has developed a product or service that satisfies what is believed to be a customer need. Marketing has subsequently compounded that need in the targeted market. As a result of these endeavors, the company expects to receive many contacts from customers. Based on contact volume forecasts, the company has budgeted a customer care offering to answer customer inquiries and problems, gather market intelligence, and perhaps cross-sell other products and services. In order to achieve this goal, customer care will have established a baseline for existent processes. This baseline may require a best in class comparison with other customer care operations, identification of the features, functions, and technologies of the ideal customer care environment, and observation and tracking of contact types, lengths, follow-ups, and other postcontact activities.

The following list represents a potential high-level grouping of some typical customer care processes:

Organizational Processes

    Management
- New product/service support/marketing activity notification
- Disaster recovery (loss of telephone or computer network)
- Customer contact root cause data gathering and analysis
- Customer satisfaction data gathering and analysis
- Facilities management
- Screening and hiring
- Partnership and service agreements

- Customer care quality analysis and improvement
- Agent appeals
- Agent rewards and recognition

Scheduling
- Agent shift preference
- Agent vacation scheduling—Initial choice process
- Agent vacation scheduling—Change processes
- Agent time-off scheduling
- Agent closed time scheduling

Supportive Processes

Information Support
- Interactive voice response (IVR) customer script maintenance
- Initial and continuation training
- Methods and procedures information for customer contact handling
- Agent help system support (for customer care systems)
- Agent script development and maintenance
- Content development for new product/service ("how to" instructions)
- Content maintenance for existing product/service ("how to" instructions)
- Problem-solving support for new and existing product/service (knowledge acquisition/engineering)

Systems Development and Maintenance
- Interactive voice response (IVR) functional improvements
- Systems change request—Prioritization and implementation
- New systems definition, prioritization, and implementation
- Database administration
- Systems administration

Customer-Facing Processes
- Routing inbound customer calls to appropriate agents
- Classifying, routing, and responding to
  ♦ E-mail messages
  ♦ Fax messages
  ♦ Postal correspondence
  ♦ Voice mail requests
  ♦ Website communications
- Opening a customer contact—Agent tasks
- Handling customer account maintenance, such as
  ♦ Change customer address
  ♦ Change pricing plan
  ♦ Responding to returned mail
  ♦ Renew or cancel contracts
  ♦ Modify credit limit

- ◆ Change billing responsibility
- ◆ Record customer comments
- Resolving presales requests, such as
  - ◆ Pricing inquiries (noncustomer)
  - ◆ Feature availability
  - ◆ Nearest branch/store location
- Handling customer orders and reservations, such as
  - ◆ Inventory location
  - ◆ Credit approval
  - ◆ Price negotiation
- Resolving general inquiries and problems
- Resolving billing inquiries, including
  - ◆ Pricing inquiries (customer)
  - ◆ Request for invoice copy
  - ◆ Change billing cycles
  - ◆ Explain first bill
  - ◆ Explain feature charges
  - ◆ Create revised bill
  - ◆ Explain taxes
  - ◆ Produce on-demand bill
- Handling collections, including
  - ◆ Response to late notice
  - ◆ Response to treatment report
  - ◆ Response to nonpay deactivation
- Handling customer complaints
- Handling misdirected calls
- Online escalation of customer calls
- Customer agent callback commitment handling
- Handling customer-initiated callbacks
- Closing a customer contact—Agent tasks

Regardless of whether or not customer care management decides to document processes, there obviously has to be some sort of process understanding in order for the operation to exist at all. This common knowledge may have been conveyed verbally during training, or informally by peers and managers. It is not unusual for a manager in a small call center to verbally convey a change in process or policy for all those who were within earshot on a particular day. Often, there appears to be presumption that any agents who were absent for that announcement will adhere to the change by some sort of osmosis. Given that inconsistency in dealing with the customer is one of the primary reasons why call centers experience repeat calls, it is remarkable how many managers exacerbate the problem through failure to ensure rigorous communication and adherence practices. In some cases, the agent may come across a method and procedure that explains what to do in a certain situation. How consistently the process is applied and how effectively it works can be determined only by formal measurements. The critical question applied to these customer care environments becomes "how many of our processes will break when we start getting a lot of customer contacts?" If that question is not addressed, even hiring two hundred new agents to handle increased volume will not have the desired effect.

Identifying Process Flaws

One way of identifying process flaws is to document, analyze, and quantify costs in those areas that are viewed as particularly damaging to customer relations. These areas may be defined independently, or derived from agent and customer feedback. For example, the process of answering customer questions relating to billing, product problems, and account maintenance are most likely to be dependent upon the existence of robust systems support. In the event that such support is unavailable, the result is a huge backlog of customer callback commitments, with extremely detrimental ramifications for the customer care environment. Quantifying the cost of working around this issue should include consideration of not only additional resource requirements, but also the impact on customer satisfaction resulting from an inability to resolve calls in a timely manner. An example of identifying flaws in the process of resolving customer contacts may be depicted as in Table 6.1.

Implementing Overall Process Improvement

In order to meet customer demands for outstanding customer care, a concerted organization-wide process improvement effort is required. From the customer care perspective, "outstanding service" could be defined as the ability to immediately contact customer care by telephone, fax, e-mail, or directly from a website. It would also require a satisfactory result, including the acquisition of a clear, accurate, and complete response on the first contact. Finally, it would demand that, in the event a follow-up contact with the customer was required, it would be carried out in a timely and mutually agreed manner, avoiding the situation in which a customer calls back, citing a missed deadline.

Direction for creating customer care processes generally emanates from strategic quality-planning teams comprised of senior managers. Management strategies, cou-

TABLE 6.1.   Identifying detriments to world-class customer interaction.

Issue	Examples	Results/Implications	Cost to the Company
System downtime during normal business hours, which prevents agents from resolving calls on the first point of contact	Client-server failures resulting from an excess of user logons, agents cannot change a customer bill cycle while the account is being billed, etc.	Additional closed time required as a result of customer commitments is now exceeding fifteen minutes per agent per day. Service levels during system downtime are 20% below normal Repeat calls as a result of customer impatience and missed commitments have increased 30%	Agents × closed time minutes × cost per minute Additional ASA minutes × cost per minute Excess repeat calls × talk time × cost per minute

pled with a strong customer focus (measuring customer expectations, defining customer satisfiers, invoking direct customer feedback, and employing rigorous process performance management based on these data), will guide organizational improvement efforts through process improvement teams at the customer care level.

Customer care is the dynamic functioning of a set of interrelated processes. The first step in any business process improvement endeavor is to baseline the current processes, which can most easily be accomplished in the form of flowcharts. In order to ensure accuracy, the responsible process owners must first be identified. The process boundaries should be clearly defined, and any technical, procedural, or organizational issues documented. Interfaces and feedback loops with external processes and organizations should also be demonstrated. Finally, measurements such as in-process metrics relevant to each process should be established as they relate to customer satisfaction and cost, with regular reports on efficiency, effectiveness, adaptability, and cycle time as part of continuous process improvement.

In addition to ensuring the quality of information being channeled to and from the customer, teams need to be formed in order to identify processes in need of improvement based on the following criteria:

- External customer problems and/or complaints
- Internal customer problems and/or complaints
- High-cost processes
- Long cycle-time processes
- New technology solutions or system change requests
- Benchmark studies

Processes selected for improvement should be prioritized based on key considerations, such as whether or not the customer is really impacted by the output of the process, whether it is financially feasible to fix the process, an assessment of how damaged the process actually is, how important the process is to the business, and whether or not there are resources available to support any changes to the process.

A typical customer care business process improvement team structure to handle these matters would consist of an executive leadership team together with representatives from marketing, product management, vendor management, customer care infrastructure, service strategy, customer care operations, and customer contact. The customer contact team leader would represent areas such as technical support, billing inquiry, request for service, training, knowledge engineering, documentation engineering, the development organization, and process performance measurement. Major processes like technical support and billing inquiry would involve subteams with representatives from frontline and internal help desk support, billing operations, and network operations. Operations would include input from human resources, force management, and scheduling, while infrastructure would encompass telephony, systems interfaces, and communications.

The objective of this structured approach is to ensure that any changes to existing processes take place at the appropriate level, and that no changes are made without the knowledge of affected entities. For example, it should not be possible for an executive decision maker to make sweeping changes in established technical support processes without channeling a change request through the business process improvement hierarchy, thus ensuring that everyone who needs to know and adjust to the change is fully aware of its ramifications. Conversely, this approach also ensures that existing processes are fully explored from front-line customer care operations to the executive level.

In established hierarchies, a horizontally based business process improvement initiative such as the one described above is often viewed with skepticism and concern. A typical response to such an initiative would be "We're not quite ready for that yet!" Personalities and turf wars can derail the best efforts to ensure that a business provides a customer with outstanding service. Most organizations find it easier to exist in relative acrimony, where marketing can blame product management for unfulfilled promises, and product management can cite ill-prepared customer care for delaying the launch of a new offering. In turn, customer care can accuse the development organization of failing to provide an adequate contact tracking and troubleshooting system, and the development organization can blame management for imposing unreasonable deadlines and inadequate budgets. Management, in the absence of a global process improvement structure, will issue decrees based on perceived flaws in each of these departments. The overall effect is one of fire fighting, rather than proactive improvement. The customers will blame the company regardless.

One of the most critical outputs of any process development and improvement process is the discovery of the necessary policies and procedures that will guide the agent through any interaction with the customer. Quite often, a new call center manager will discover that many policies have never even been thought of in the context of call center operations. For example, in a distributed customer contact environment, such as a regional network of branches, each branch may have dealt with the customer on a first-name basis, bending the known rules wherever necessary to appease the customer's needs. Such inconsistencies cannot be replicated at a centralized call center, therefore the company must establish a plausible "middle ground" for the majority of customer contacts. Quite often, it is extremely difficult to gain upper management approval for every policy and procedure that emanates from a customer care process, therefore at some point the customer care manager must "drive a stake" into the ground and advise agents (preferably via an online documentation system) that one consistent policy must be adhered to for a particular customer contact situation. Unless this step is taken proactively, the likelihood is that agents (especially more experienced representatives) will convey their best guess as to the correct course of action in a specific instance. It is only through process evaluation that such contingencies can be appropriately described—a factor that can significantly affect the integrity of the entire customer care operation.

At the highest level, the ideal online customer care environment, whether for customer usage on the Web or agent assistance at a call center, would provide rapid response time, an intuitive user interface, a single, integrated system, instant account updates, 24-hour access (no down time), electronic communications (such as e-mail, fax, broadcast and online chat forums) and virtually eliminate manual processes such as account reconciliation, pricing plan analysis, requests for bill copies, paper filing and envelope stuffing. From the content perspective, the system would facilitate online troubleshooting and document retrieval, contact tracking, trouble ticketing, online help, scripting, and outbound correspondence. At the feedback level, the system would provide meaningful and accurate data, and timely reports in an understandable format. The only viable way to ensure that all of these ideals are met is through rigorous process adherence and continuous improvement techniques designed to ensure that customers and agents alike appreciate the value of a company that views customer care as a critical facet of the marketing endeavor. At this point, it is worth examining some of the processes that might be applied to a world-class customer care environment.

Quality Improvement Process

The key to the successful maintenance of online information and channeling of market intelligence is encompassed by the quality improvement process (see Figure 6.4). This process spans several tasks, including training, knowledge engineering, documentation, the development organization, customer satisfaction, root cause analysis, and customer contact categorization. A quality improvement team should be formed to review daily customer contact reports and pending trouble tickets, in addition to gathering and analyzing feedback from agents and customer care managers. The core team should include part-time representatives from training, knowledge engineering, documentation, and the development organization, in addition to an expert agent and a front-line agent representative. The goals of the team, which may also include special projects, could be stated as follows:

Overall Goals

- Increase the number of problems and inquiries *resolved at the first point of contact* by empowering both customers and agents with accessible, accurate, understandable, and complete online information
- Reduce *contact time* by improving both the speed of response and ease of use through continuous process improvement, efficient database access, and intuitive user interface design
- Establish robust *market intelligence* and *product or service feedback* loops throughout the organization

Specific Goals

- Determine missing or inaccurate online policies and procedures, user instructions, troubleshooting scenarios, contact categories, and other information that may be relevant to customer contacts
- Assist process owners in identifying inefficient online system processes and suggest improvements by means of system change requests and cost/benefit analysis
- Facilitate root cause analysis of customer contacts for management reporting purposes
- Assist in the analysis and integration of customer satisfaction survey results

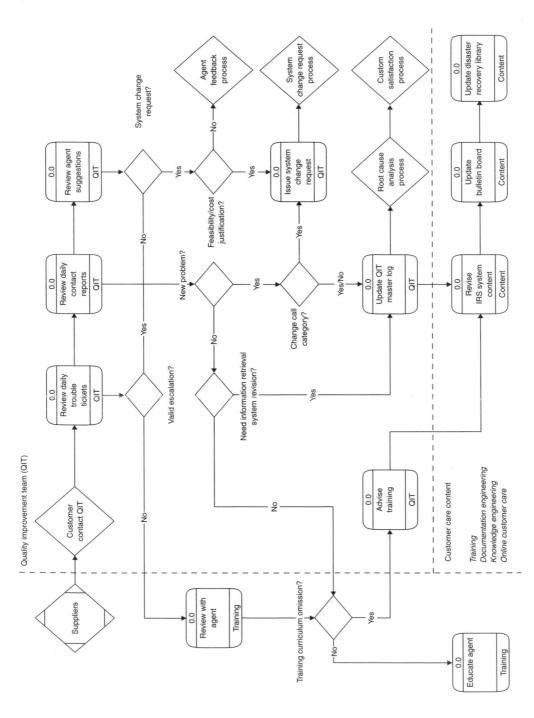

■ **FIGURE 6.4** Quality improvement process

As with any successful endeavor, the quality improvement team must adhere to a mutually agreed process in order to ensure that these goals are achieved. Given the fact that the team is usually composed of individuals who are also key players in other areas, this necessarily streamlined process would normally include designating certain tasks to team members prior to each team meeting, such as reviewing the previous day's customer contact and trouble ticket reports for content, collecting and interpreting any agent suggestions, and gathering customer survey results. Special projects might include assessing the cost/benefit of a mutually agreed system change, conducting root cause analysis of customer contacts and channeling the results to management, and assessing the relevance of current contact categories. The team meetings themselves should be held on a regular basis, usually thirty minutes every day, with each participant recommending action based on the results of his or her designated tasks (see Table 6.2, Quality improvement tasks). The goal of each meeting should be to gain consensus on each recommendation, thus allowing the relevant "process owner" to take action as appropriate.

A typical daily scenario for the quality improvement team would be as follows:

Premeeting Activities: Review Escalation Reports

- Given that every customer inquiry or complaint not resolved on the first point of contact is a potentially costly customer dissatisfier, the designated "expert" agent(s) review the previous day's escalation reports from the website to the front-line agent, and from the agent to the internal help desk support in order to determine the authenticity of the escalation.

- If the customer accessed the customer care website before contacting the agent, then the contact is marked for the Web content owners (usually knowledge or documentation engineers).

- If the expert(s) decide that a particular contact should not have been escalated from the front line to the internal help desk, then that contact is marked appropriately for channeling to the training representative.

- If a contact was escalated due to *missing* online information at the front line, then the report is channeled to the knowledge engineers.

- If a contact was escalated due to *erroneous* online information at the front line, then the report is channeled to the knowledge and documentation engineers.

TABLE 6.2.   Quality improvement tasks.

Task	Output
Training	Curriculum improvement and individual agent retraining
Knowledge engineering	Revised troubleshooting scenarios and links to documentation
Documentation	Revised policies and procedures, user instructions, and other information
Systems development	System change request and cost/benefit analysis results
Customer satisfaction	Analysis and integration of survey results
Root cause analysis	Management feedback on contact reasons and customer suggestions
Contact categorization	Updated contact categories based on frequency of occurrence

---

The information retrieval system 48-hour maintenance cycle flowchart (see Figure 6.5) is intended to demonstrate a potential process for maintaining the integrity of troubleshooting and online documentation information. Once the quality improvement team has determined that additional information or changes need to be made to the information retrieval system, the first determination is whether or not knowledge engineering is required in order to format the information in a way that is meaningful to the documentation engineers. If knowledge engineering is required for a *known* issue (i.e., the result of *inaccurate* information), then the *only way to meet the 48-hour deadline for information turnaround is for the knowledge engineer to use the solution proposed to the customer by the agent.* If this solution is found to be incorrect, the presumption of the knowledge engineer must be that the correct solution will emerge on the next iteration. Although this is a somewhat controversial point, the only other way to ensure that the solution is correct is for the knowledge engineer to conduct independent research on each problem. This is clearly going to jeopardize the chances of turning around information within a short period of time, and is also likely to entrench the knowledge engineer in time-consuming research—to the ultimate detriment of the overall information retrieval system.

Gathering Contact Data

A primary function of the call center is obviously not just to answer customer questions, but also to record each call in order that multiple contacts from one customer can be tracked and handled according to company policy, as well as to provide feedback to management on the reasons why customers are calling. Contact history is important because it should allow agents to understand exactly what has transpired in the past with a particular customer. This is usually derived from a combination of system-generated notations (based on transactions that have occurred in the past, such as billing adjustments), in addition to any comments that previous agents may have entered in free-form text.

From a management perspective, notations are one of the most revealing, yet also the most time-consuming and inconsistently executed areas of customer care today. Depending upon the environment, the time taken to create a note can often exceed the actual length of the customer contact itself. Poorly trained agents dealing with highly technical problems can take several minutes to compose a laborious note, which can clearly have a devastating effect on service levels. Coupled with the fact that most agents are not hired for their writing skills, note-taking can become a painstaking chore for those who may be outstanding in verbally dealing with the customer. In the following example, the agent has carefully constructed a paragraph within the confines of a 273-character notes field:

> The customer called to advise us that his e-mail was not able to transmit messages. He had changed the configuration and internal settings, but it still didn't work. I told him we would call back after we had done some additional research on this matter.

After a few adjustments for length, this note took the agent just over three minutes to complete, yet its value is extremely limited to the customer care environment. The note is revealing for a number of reasons, including the fact that any time-saving

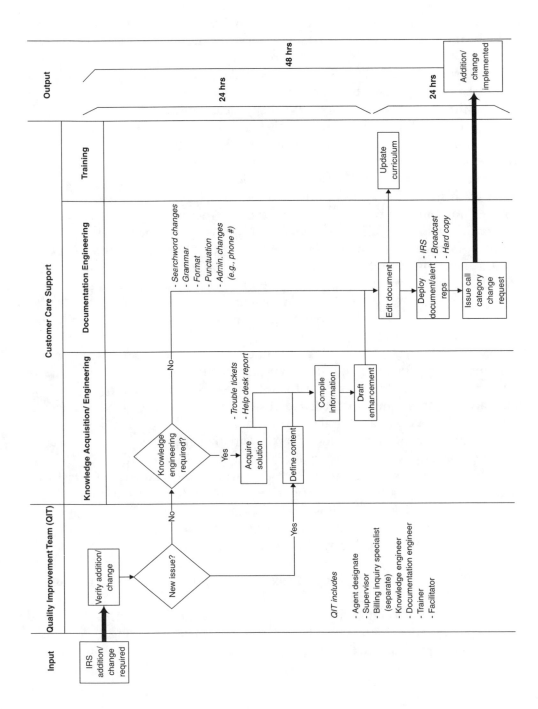

■ **FIGURE 6.5** Information retrieval system (IRS)—48-hour maintenance cycle

87

advantage gained by installing contact handling and routing technology is clearly negated, and there is an obvious failure by the company to recognize the importance of training agents to construct concise, consistent, meaningful, and useful notes. The entire context of this note could have been capably handled by a carefully structured call categorization function on the contact entry screen, such as "e-mail transmission," coupled with a simple choice of "Unresolved" (which in turn would have initiated the follow-up or tickler application), and linking the contact to any effort the agent may have made to resolve the problem using an online troubleshooting system. From a reporting perspective, the note is virtually meaningless and provides customer care management with virtually no substantive data for root cause analysis.

Other agents, especially those in high-volume/low technology call centers, may take as little as ten seconds to write a consonant note, for example "cst cld nt gt grn lcs" (customer could not get green laces), but which makes perfect sense to peers and managers. In this case, the agent has clearly tried to write a concise, consistent, and innately meaningful note. Yet even in these instances, the question becomes whether or not the note will be useful. It seems that in most instances, agents make notes on every contact because that is what they were told to do. Most of the information is cryptic and never used, and should have been systematically captured in the first place. In effect, the company must go one step further and define instances in which the agent *should* take a note, such as when the customer makes a suggestion. Other notes, such as the exact amount of a billing adjustment, should be automatically generated by the system.

Customers who access customer care facilities at a website will not be interested in taking notes and sending them to the company for analysis, but instead may leave a system-generated audit trail of their activities. It is this latter scenario that perhaps best illustrates the trend into nonmediated customer care and which exemplifies the question as to why agents have to take notes at all.

Many agents have only a vague idea why they are making notes on *every* customer contact. The presumption is that someone, somewhere, sometime, is going to read the note and take some kind of action. Perhaps it will be the next agent to deal with this customer, or maybe it will be a manager who is trying to understand why people are contacting the company. The most valuable aspect of the notes that agents generate is in identifying the types of calls that have not been covered by the call categorization function, and as such may never have been used in the root cause analysis process.

Perhaps the best way to eliminate unnecessary notes is to implement tracking of all agent (or customer in the case of website activity) actions during the course of a contact. A significant amount of time can be saved by capturing the titles of accessed nodes of documentation or functional attributes and then presenting these to the agent or customer in a compiled list format.

Escalations

In many cases, what initially appears to be a fairly incongruous customer contact may escalate into a saga of repeat calls, missed commitments, and an increasingly hostile customer relationship. Such an episode most often results from an agent's inability to convey credible and/or consistent information, or a financial empowerment issue, or a complete lack of focus on resolving every possible call on the first point of contact. The examples of typical process flow charts (see Figures 6.6–6.9) for both online and offline escalations, as well as customer initiated callbacks, demonstrate the importance of systematically tracking and fulfilling any unresolved customer contacts. Ironically, these are the processes that are most often overlooked in new call center environments. It is as if there is some presumption that the frontline agent will rarely need to escalate a call, when in fact the converse is all too common in many contemporary operations, particularly those that deal with decentralized branch offices, or those who handle highly technical problems.

The task of tracking and resolving escalations or commitments is clearly critical to the achievement of world-class levels of service. Technology that supports management and agents in achieving this goal must be considered an outstanding selling point for any contact tracking system.

Follow-up Work

By traditional definition, customer follow-up work is instigated in response to calls that cannot be resolved on first contact—that work which has been *deferred* to a specific period of time (uninterrupted by inbound calls) and which has either been scheduled by management or is allowable as extended time provided after concluding a call with a customer. Also known as *closed key* time, follow-up work involves

 Case in Point: Disparate Trouble Ticketing Systems

One call center used an off-the-shelf trouble ticketing system to log escalated customer contacts. Several of these escalations could not be resolved by the internal help desk group at the center, so they were escalated to a technical group operating from company headquarters. The problem was that the technical group had chosen a noncompatible trouble ticketing system with which to track their own tasks, so although they had the capacity to receive and interpret the customer care trouble tickets, they could not update them based on work in progress. As a result, there was no way for customer care to discover the status of an escalated trouble ticket unless they called the technical group. Usually, such a call was prompted by a customer requesting status on his or her problem. In many cases, the call center was unable to reach a representative of the technical group, so the customer was advised that the problem was "still being worked on." To make matters worse, the "word of mouth" process meant that nobody bothered to update the original trouble ticket, causing even more confusion at a later date. Again, the lack of systems planning and integration caused significant problems for customer care, in terms of both time wastage and customer dissatisfaction.

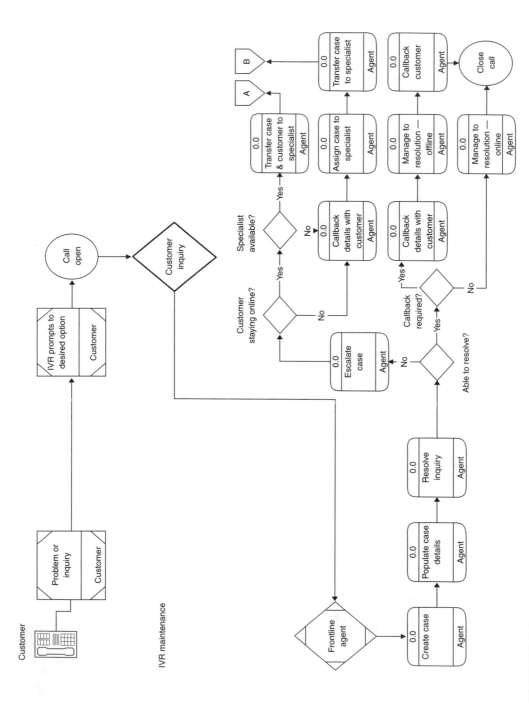

FIGURE 6.6 Customer contact—Example

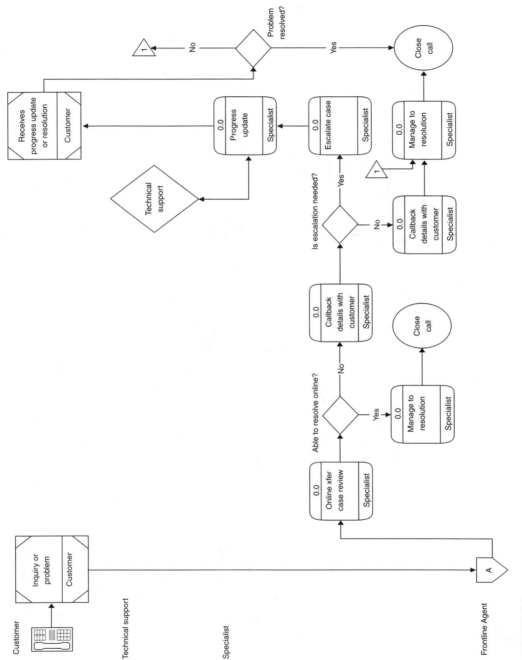

◩ **FIGURE 6.7** Online escalations/transfers—Example

91

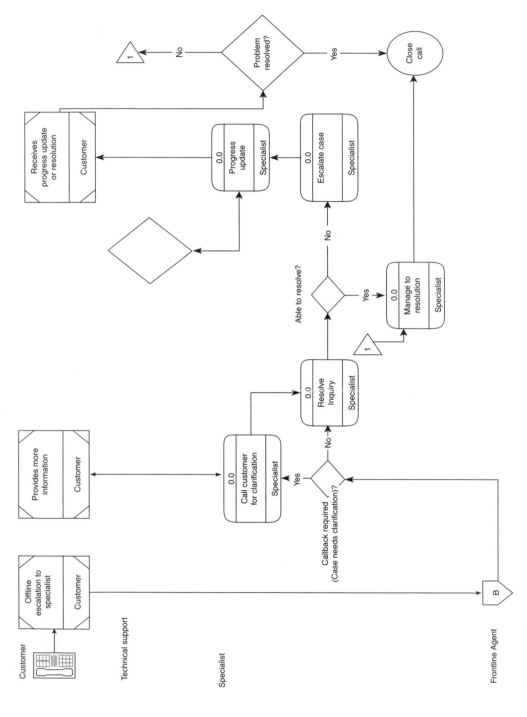

FIGURE 6.8 Offline escalation to specialist—Example

92

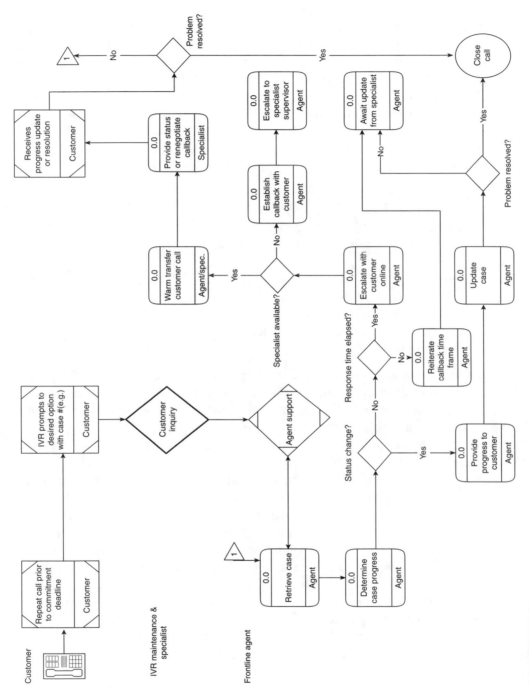

FIGURE 6.9 Customer-initiated callback—Example

93

actions that the agent and/or the customer decided were not feasible during the call itself (or within the normal jurisdiction of *after call work*). Asynchronous communications, such as outbound e-mail, fax or letter responses (or even outbound calls in response to a customer communication via these media), may also be classified as follow-up work as they do not necessitate direct communication with the customer.

In general, follow-ups to customer contacts are the most poorly executed tasks in the entire customer care environment. Customers who have been told to expect a callback "within x hours," for example, may wait several days (if they receive a callback at all). More often than not, the customer is forced to contact the company again to discover the status of the problem or inquiry. This is also a common occurrence with nonvoice communications, where the customer sends a fax, e-mail, or letter to the company only to have it disappear into what may appear to be a technological "black hole." There may be several generalized reasons for these situations, including

- Absence of well-defined follow-up processes
- Insufficient closed key time for agents
- Poorly designed contact tracking systems (particularly for nonvoice media, such as e-mail)
- Insufficient upper tier or support staff to deal with escalated problems
- Incompatible trouble ticketing systems between tiers
- Nonexistent or inadequate follow-up "tickler" systems
- Absence of personal accountability for follow-ups
- Absence of monitoring for follow-up content quality or timeliness

Typical examples of follow-ups include troubleshooting difficult or unusual product and service problems, copying and mailing customer bills, instigating pricing plan changes, and reconciling misapplied payments. While customer care environments seek to avoid follow-ups wherever possible, this often requires the provisioning of new technologies to alleviate the time-consuming manual work that prompted the agent to offload the work in the first place.

In companies that support more technical products and services, the most common follow-ups are escalated troubleshooting problems. These types of follow-ups can be the most time-consuming of all, particularly when agents are bereft of powerful troubleshooting tools. Usually there is a significant loss of context and continuity when agents are disposed to schedule follow-ups for technical problems. No matter how well written the accompanying notations for the original call may be, the return call to the customer (unless initiated by the original agent, which is uncommon in larger customer care environments) almost always requires reiteration of the original problem—a factor that can alienate and frustrate customers even further.

As a rule, the tardier the follow-up contact, the costlier it becomes to the company, in terms of both customer loyalty and the time taken to resolve the original issue. Missing a follow-up sends an overt message to the customer that he or she is not important to the company, an impression that even the most apologetic agents cannot assuage. Of course, the ultimate goal of any customer care environment is to eliminate voice-to-voice follow-ups completely by providing agents with the training and tools needed to successfully resolve a call on the first point of contact. Follow-ups to alternative media communications such as e-mail and fax, on the other hand, require management to embrace a paradigm shift in both process and technology that many companies are only now beginning to explore. The following case study is intended to explore the ramifications of a poorly defined and implemented follow-up process, as well as examining the ways in which management hoped to rectify the situation.

 Case in Point: Fulfilling Follow-up Commitments

A major service provider had a particular way of resolving escalated contacts that occurred due to product problems. In such cases, the agent would advise the service center that a customer was having difficulty using a product. Instead of the service center contacting the customer directly, a representative would convey the resolution to an originating agent, who in turn would call the customer back and attempt to explain the remedy. The technical nature of these remedies was not always well understood by the agent, and it was common for a series of follow-up calls to take place, often with substantial delays, until the matter was resolved to the satisfaction of the customer. The general absence of troubleshooting expertise among agents, in addition to the fact that there was no systematic troubleshooting information available, contributed to a costly and ultimately unsatisfactory process.

Secondly, newer agents protested that they had neither been trained nor provided adequate tools to reconcile a customer's account. A mistake in one month's bill may have resulted in a promise that the error would be rectified, yet the agent, who was measured on volume of calls answered, may never have followed up on this promise, resulting in a secondary error the following month, and so on for months until it took even an experienced agent more than thirty minutes of closed key time to rectify the errors.

As with many call centers, agents measured on volume of calls answered were not necessarily focused on resolving the customer's problem on the first contact. Escalations to the service desk (i.e., senior agents and supervisors) were considered a quick passport to poor evaluations, so the agents preferred to contend with irate customers than draw attention to themselves in this manner. Furthermore, management had no systematic way of identifying follow-up jeopardies, and it was only through random call monitoring that untimely customer follow-ups were occasionally discovered.

Results of this study indicated that follow-ups were usually caused by

- Absence of accurate and complete online documentation
- Inadequate training and high staff turnover
- A strong reliance on voice mail communications, which often resulted in information loss. It was not unusual for an agent returning from lunch to have up to twenty messages in the mailbox. These messages were a

Continued

mixture of customer referrals, administrative announcements, policy changes, and personal contacts.
- System downtime
- Absence of a follow-up "tickler" system, resulting in missed commitments and inadequate management reports
- New contracts being manually generated as a result of price plan changes
- Absence of an online troubleshooting system
- Absence of system checks for misapplied codes
- Inaccuracies in customer names and addresses
- Time-consuming processes for sending outbound correspondence (such as e-mail, fax, and postal) to customers
- Inaccurate information from point-of-sale representatives
- Insufficient support staff
- Inadequate tracking of inbound correspondence (e-mail, fax, and postal)
- Manual calculation of billing adjustments
- Manual searches for bill microfiche and paper contracts
- Filling out paper forms.

Improvements

During this study, management described a number of proposed enhancements that were expected to minimize the amount of follow-up work required to satisfy a customer request. These enhancements included

- Installation of an optical scanning system for contracts and correspondence
- Enhancement of interactive voice response functionality to include customer account maintenance
- 24-hour inbound correspondence response process
- Billing support group to offload time-consuming adjustments
- Expert agent profiling for call routing based on customer need
- Internal help desk personnel for complex troubleshooting calls
- Implementation of bill rerate and price plan analysis software
- Greater financial empowerment for frontline agents
- Online help facility for quick reference to codes and functions
- Predefined point-and-click notations
- On-demand bills for customers.

In addition to the general enhancements planned for each center, the systems development group also planned the following systematic improvements:

- The online customer care system will track and manage customer follow-up commitments.
- Transaction history (automatic notations) will be captured by the system.
- Outbound correspondence templates with systematic field generation features will be available.
- Agents will be automatically notified of pending follow-up commitments.

- Reporting capabilities for follow-up commitments will include status, past-due items, and percentage of follow-ups resolved/unresolved customer contacts.

The proposed enhancements promised a significant decrease in the amount of follow-up work. However, it was noted that, with the exception of the planned follow-up "tickler" system and also the analysis software for bill rerates and price plan options, the content deficiencies that were leading to multiple follow-ups (i.e., the absence of a troubleshooting system and online documentation) were not immediately addressed. The existence of these systems could have also facilitated a more robust notation facility that would not have been limited to a few key phrases (instead, being driven by the actual topics that the agent explored during the course of a call). Management's insistence that agents, rather than billing support personnel, continue to correct erroneous customer bills was one of the most controversial topics in a call center where agents were rewarded based on volume of calls answered.

While some customer care environments frown upon any type of follow-up commitment, others acknowledge that follow-ups are an inevitable outcome of their business, and attempt only to limit the number of scheduled follow-ups on an individual basis. One large call center (over 1,000 agents), handling nontechnical contacts, used forecasting to ascertain the levels of follow-up support vis-a-vis incoming calls. Based on the product offering at that time, management decided that no more than 0.8 percent of all customer contacts should result in follow-ups. Agents who consistently exceeded that average were monitored and coached as necessary.

Agent productivity relative to follow-ups at the same center was measured based on the quantity of follow-ups completed in 30-minute intervals. For example, the system would "batch" follow-ups based on time and motion studies. It was determined that a particular type of order processing follow-up should take ten minutes, and another type should take five minutes. The system therefore might batch (10 minutes × 1) + (5 minutes × 4) = 30 minutes. Most follow-up tasks are not as easy to measure, however, and opinions on the standard number of completions within a given time frame can be purely subjective.

The same call center preferred to use outbound correspondence as an alternative to customer callbacks. Instead of making expensive and time-consuming outbound calls, agents are provided with online templates designed to cover every type of standard customer interaction.

Timing and Prioritization

Timing guidelines for follow-up contacts are usually motivated by the following factors:

- Customer insistence on callback within a certain time frame
- Investigation—The agent calculates the amount of time needed to accomplish a task

- Adjustments—Scheduled for completion ten days prior to the issuance of the next customer bill
- Priorities for follow-up contacts are often established by category based on management predetermination, for example, Orders (Priority 1), Presales (Priority 2), Billing (Priority 3), Troubleshooting (Priority 4), and so forth.

Customer care follow-ups can do much to augment the sales and marketing process by following up in a timely and definitive manner with customers. Computer-generated order confirmations, presales incentives such as e-mailed or faxed maps showing the route to the nearest store, or coupons that can be printed out from a website or faxed to the customer as a result of an inquiry all help in promoting sales and affirming a positive impression of customer care.

7

Systems Design and Development

Overview

The emergence of call centers as a viable medium for customer care, coupled with the evolution of computer systems, created a unique opportunity for companies to gather and leverage customer information. The first logical step was to create an online database of customer contacts, which could be augmented by notations and special handling instructions. Capturing a succinct reason for the customer call was another useful addition, as was giving call center agents the opportunity to view customer ordering and billing records. As products and services became more complex, and customers became more demanding, the need for a more efficient information retrieval methodology became apparent, encompassing a mixture of online documentation and intelligent troubleshooting systems. More recently, the emergence of the World Wide Web, together with the growing utilization of electronic mail and fax, has highlighted the need for a systems facilitated "end-to-end" view of customer interaction. Overall, the majority of centralized customer care environments now rely on the computer to an extent that could scarcely have been envisioned thirty years ago.

The proliferation of computer systems at once led to the emergence of scientifically oriented individuals whose goal was to master complex machine languages and present responses to standard queries from users. The initial focus, therefore, was to execute a function that presented data more efficiently than any manual procedure. This led to tremendous variance in the way information was presented. Essentially, it was up to the human to interpret the response appropriately. It was not until high-level programming languages and more sophisticated user interface design tools emerged that computer science opened its doors to those who were concerned with making computers more accessible to "ordinary" humans.

Contemporary corporate environments rely on computer systems not only to process, store, and retrieve information rapidly, but also to present it in a way that is immediately understandable. This latter requirement has encouraged the emergence of individuals whose task is to ensure that no unnecessary time is wasted either inputting relevant information or interpreting the output from the computer. This endeavor, known as the study of human–computer interaction, can encompass many disciplines, including software development, artificial intelligence, cognitive psychology, sociology, linguistics, and ergonomics.

Effective human–computer interaction is especially crucial in the time-intensive world of call centers. Average talk time and after call work time are key metrics that can obviously be adversely affected by poorly designed computer systems. In an era of increasing customer demands for outstanding care, coupled with high agent turnover, it is clearly desirable that supporting systems are responsive, intuitive, and relevant to the user's needs. For example, waiting twenty seconds for a response to a billing inquiry, or scrolling a two-hundred-item list to find a logical categorization for a particular customer call, or attempting to interpret a company policy that is written in legal jargon—these can all be extremely stressful situations for the call center agent who is being measured on, for example, the number of calls answered each day.

Those who study and optimize human–computer interaction are most often referred to as human factors engineers. In the deadline-driven realm of business systems development, these individuals rarely have the latitude to apply cognitive psychology or linguistic considerations to a particular application design, but instead work closely with both the systems developers and the user population to ensure that the user interface displays all of the necessary functions in an intuitive manner. The human factors engineer may also work with the quality improvement team to ensure that all information displayed on the screen is in a format that is easily interpreted.

In the best-case scenario, the human factors engineer and the system developer collaborate to ensure that all concepts presented to the user representatives are plausible in terms of both budgetary and time frame restrictions. There is mutual respect, for both the task understanding of the human factors engineer and the ability of the developer to provide adequate or even exceptional online solutions to expressed user needs. In the worst case (and this is not uncommon), user interface design becomes a contentious battle between the human factors engineer and the systems developer. The developer may perceive the human factors engineer as an unqualified pretender who knows nothing about the inherent difficulties of programming certain functional depictions.

Process Meets Technology

Typically, business process owners will be engaged for several weeks or even months prior to the opening of a new call center, designing "should be" processes. At the same time, systems designers and developers are starting to define what will and will not be included in the initial rollout of systems support. Much like the "chicken and egg" syndrome, when these two factions meet, one must give way to the other. Typically, the process owners are confronted with the stark realities of limited systems development resources and budget, and are forced to iterate their processes to conform with system limitations. Consequently, "should be" processes rapidly become "future generation" depictions, and the ideal is replaced by mediocrity.

In environments in which the process owners have achieved a high level of detail in their process mapping, the impediment of system limitations can be particularly disappointing. Essentially, this situation can also result in significant loss of time, as process engineers who should be evolving policies and procedures, training guidelines, and other outputs are consumed with discovering the latest round of system changes. Often, the end result of such a situation is that the call center operates with little more than a scaled-down systems support infrastructure and a plethora of flowcharts that are soon left to gather dust in some forgotten database.

The critical question, of course, is whether to use valuable process engineer support for an endeavor that is really dictated by the day-to-day discovery of functional or systems development limitations, or to wait for the systems environment to stabilize prior to revisiting the "should be" processes in order to create "as is" environments. This way, the original glimpse of the future is not compromised by technological limitations. In the meantime, process owners can spend constructive hours advising systems designers as necessary, in addition to documenting the business rules, policies, and procedures that will be an integral part of the agent's interaction with the customer. By having these elements of customer interaction available in an online documentation system prior to the opening of the call center, process owners can ensure that agents have adequate training and access to this information, thus ensuring overall consistency from the first customer contact.

The Importance of Systems Integration

The disparity of customer requests requires a multifaceted development environment that can involve several different groups working on discrete tasks. The failure of project management to view these tasks as part of an integrated design effort results in cryptic human–computer interaction as users attempt to memorize the user interface controls of each online customer care system deployed to resolve particular customer inquiries or complaints. Secondly, the absence of necessary functional integration between these disparate systems (i.e., viewing each system as an independent entity, rather than as an integral part of an overall task) contributes significantly to increased costs and decreased customer satisfaction. Resolving a customer inquiry or complaint becomes a situation that is analogous to a series of unsynchronized traffic signals on the same short stretch of road; as soon as one turns green the next turns red, and so on, frustrating those in a hurry to get home. It's just one more unnecessary set of obstacles that can be attributed to poor planning.

It is not unusual for agents to have to initiate several applications to resolve a call, such as contact tracking, troubleshooting, online documentation, trouble ticketing, follow-up, billing, and ordering. This would be acceptable if the lack of integration didn't force the agent to type or select basically the same information in order to populate the notes field, the incident report field, the documentation search field, the troubleshooting symptom field, the follow-up report, and the call category field.

In order to demonstrate the importance of a uniformly integrated development approach, it is first necessary to consider the many different online needs of a customer care environment.

Classes of Customer Care Systems

Overall, there are three basic categories of systems for customer care:

1. Contact tracking systems (also known as case management systems)
2. Information retrieval systems
3. Workforce management tools.

Contact tracking systems include customer information files, contact history, trouble ticket/repair databases, and follow-up tools. *Information retrieval systems* include online documentation, store or branch locators, pricing analysis, customer satisfaction matrices, and billing databases, as well as intelligent troubleshooting applications. *Workforce management tools* include forecasting and scheduling facilities. Some vendors continue to evolve what were originally problem resolution tools for the internal help desk market into more integrated solutions for the customer support environment by attempting to embrace all three categories. Certainly, it is far easier for those who have done the exponentially more difficult work of creating an intelligent troubleshooting system to move into the realm of contact tracking and inquiry management, rather than the other way around. The rapid evolution of alternative media for customer care, such as e-mail and the World Wide Web, however, means that even the most astute of these vendors are continually playing catch-up.

1. Contact Tracking Systems.
These systems support the following:

- Computer-telephony integration
- Logging of customer contacts
- Retrieval of contact history
- Contact categorizations
- Callback commitments
- Management reporting facilities

2. Information Retrieval Systems.
These systems can provide any or all of the following:

- Business policies and procedures
- Customer instructions
- Online system help
- Computer-based training
- Intelligent troubleshooting
- Facility locations and directions
- Outbound correspondence templates
- Interactive voice response

3. Workforce Management Systems.
These systems support the following:

- Customer contact forecasting
- Estimating workforce requirements
- Agent scheduling

System Functions

Most of these systems share three basic functions:

- *Retrieving* information (e.g., troubleshooting a customer's problem)
- *Processing* information (e.g., determining an optimal pricing plan)
- *Storing* information (e.g., gathering market intelligence data)

In general, the easier it is to rapidly retrieve and store *useful* information, then the lower the operating cost and the greater the level of customer satisfaction. Useful information may be defined as that information which *empowers* humans by fulfilling a specific need. The customer who needs to know an account balance after normal business hours, for example, may use an interactive voice response facility to obtain an immediate answer; the customer who wants to perform a particular procedure may access detailed instructions on the World Wide Web; the customer care agent troubleshooting a complex problem may use an expert system to reach an acceptable resolution; the marketing manager who needs to understand the perception of a particular market segment may review the latest customer retention reports; the product manager who is defining product improvements may analyze specific customer suggestions and complaints.

1. Retrieving Information.
Customer care environments typically retrieve multifaceted information from several sources in order to resolve a customer inquiry or complaint in a timely manner. This can include customer demographics, customer contact tracking, follow-up information, troubleshooting information, presales information, user instructions, policies and procedures, general inquiry, trouble ticket status, orders, billing inquiry, and store location information. These types of knowledge retrieval mechanisms, whether through agent mediation or direct database access (via the World Wide Web or Interactive Voice Response), could be classified as follows:

- *Status*
  - ⇒ Billing status inquiry   (What is my latest account balance?)
  - ⇒ Order status inquiry   (When will the product be delivered?)
  - ⇒ Trouble ticket status inquiry   (When will my service be fixed?)
- *General*
  - ⇒ Troubleshooting request   (Why won't my product work?)
  - ⇒ User instruction request   (How do I install this attachment?)
  - ⇒ General information request   (Do you have any current promotions? What are your latest prices? How do I contact an executive?)
  - ⇒ Location request   (Where is the nearest store that sells your product?)

- *Historical*
  - ⇒ Customer profile   (Has this customer contacted the company previously?)
  - ⇒ Contact history   (Why did this customer contact the company previously?)
  - ⇒ Contact tickler   (Which customers were advised to expect a callback?)

- *Help*
  - ⇒ Online help   (What is the purpose of this field?)
  - ⇒ Policies and procedures   (What is the procedure for returning a product?)
  - ⇒ System messages   (Error messages, etc.)
  - ⇒ Computer-based training   (Training modules)

- *Reporting*
  - ⇒ Ad hoc market intelligence reports   (How many contacts were concerned with . . . ? What are the most common customer complaints? What suggestions were made about this product? What is the regional breakdown of callers?)

2. Processing Information.

Customer care, unlike outbound telemarketing, does not typically involve agents in data processing. Tasks such as root cause analysis and billing reconciliations take place "behind the scenes" and have no impact on contact times. There are, however, several instances in which agents would benefit by having online assistance in order to resolve a customer inquiry or complaint. Typically, this would involve tasks such as creating a revised bill, or calculation of pricing plans. In a customer care environment that does handle such tasks, even on a relatively infrequent basis, it can be extremely

---

Case in Point: Analyzing Contact Types

A busy call center with a cumulative average talk-time and after-call time of 280 seconds received requests for creating revised bills at a ratio of only 1:525 calls. While it was generally understood that the newer agents tended to struggle with the complex process of manually revising customers bills, the real problem became evident only when it was discovered that the average time spent on *each* bill revision request was no less than 82 minutes—the equivalent of over seventeen average calls. By working with a core team of agents in order to create a program to assist in creating a revised bill, the development organization was able to reduce the average total time on these calls to just under ten minutes—an endeavor that reduced total talk time and after call work time for *all* calls by over eight seconds a call. At an average of 6,700 daily contacts, the customer care environment saved almost 15 hours of time each day as a result—realizing a full return on investment within three weeks of deployment.

important that agents are given adequate online tools to support the customer's request.

Billing systems that have been adapted for use by the call center are often inadequate for many of the tasks that agents have to perform. Many of these systems were designed for usage by financial planners and billing operations staff, and their task orientation has little compatibility with typical customer contact.

Typical examples of information processing tasks that are assigned to customer care agents:

- *Pricing and Billing*
  - ⇒ Credit adjustments   (I cancelled the service, but was still charged.)
  - ⇒ Creating revised bills   (I want my bill consolidated with my spouse's.)
  - ⇒ Pricing plan analysis   (How much would I be charged on plan B?)
  - ⇒ Rerates due to price plan changes   (I should have been on plan A since April 1st.)
- *Outbound Correspondence*
  - ⇒ Electronic mail, fax, or letter attachments   (Attaching a node of text or graphics to a message)
- *Order Processing*
  - ⇒ Calculating the cost of a new or revised order.

3. Storing Information.

Information storage in a customer care environment is always driven by two distinct needs—those of the customer and those of the company. It is certainly easier to gather and store information that the customer believes will facilitate the rapid resolution of a particular problem, as opposed to information that the company would like to use for market intelligence purposes. For example, an agent may request and readily receive demographic information, such as name, address, telephone number, and the like, in order that the customer can be rewarded by a follow-up contact regarding an outstanding product repair, whereas the customer may be loathe to answer survey questions that are not perceived to be of any value in helping to resolve the problem.

The emergence of the World Wide Web as a medium for customer care may be a significant opportunity for companies to lower operational costs, but it is also a potential deterrent to gathering certain types of market intelligence, such as impromptu customer comments and complaints. Regardless of the medium, however, every customer contact provides outstanding opportunities for storing information that will, in the correct format and with adequate root cause analysis, be inherently useful to the company. For example, storing a problem statement from a customer or tracking access to product-user instructions can not only help customer care management identify missing information, but can also assist company management in identifying inherent flaws in the product or service.

In summary, the needs of the user community must be fully understood before any database or system function is designed. It is not unusual, however, for a customer care environment to employ a conglomeration of systems and databases that, while fulfilling certain key functions, only partially satisfy the needs of the humans who utilize them. Typically, this does little to alleviate a preexisting condition of sub-optimal *resolutions on first contact* and high *contact times,* while also failing to realize useful market intelligence (thus augmenting the perception of the customer care environment as a costly, if necessary, endeavor). Indirectly, those retrieval, processing, and storage mechanisms that do not specifically address user needs will also fail to improve accessibility (i.e., rates of abandonment and average speed of answer). The return on investment for technological development and deployment in a customer care environment is therefore proportional to the amount of effort that was made by the development organization to understand and implement user needs.

Typical examples of information storage requirements for a customer care environment include

- Account maintenance (Creating new account/changing existing information)
- Contact tracking (Storing contact history, including
  - Contact history
  - Contact categorization
  - Auto-notations [transactions during contact]
  - Agent notations [special comments]
  - Customer suggestions)
- Contact tickler (Scheduling an outbound follow-up contact)
- Trouble ticket creation (Creating a new trouble ticket based on customer contact)
- Order submission (Creating a new or revising an existing order)
- Inbound correspondence (Storage of inbound e-mail and fax, imaging of inbound mail)

In summary, it is recognized that any system that may be utilized by customer care must pass information as necessary to the contact tracking system, which is usually the focal point of the entire enterprise. The number of systems involved usually means that there is a significant learning curve for users, due to disparities in human–computer interaction. Wherever possible, therefore, human–computer interaction for each of these systems should be as uniformly consistent as possible, using a combination of task and content analysis, rapid prototyping, usability testing, and industry standard graphical user interface conventions in order to ensure that the users have not only access to the functions they require, but also a user interface that behaves similarly for each system that is necessarily accessed.

There are also additional integration requirements that are sometimes overlooked by the development organization. It is necessary, therefore, to examine a consolidated view of all aspects of knowledge retrieval, processing, and storage in order to comprehend the technological design and development discrepancies that can result in a poorly integrated online customer care system (see Table 7.1).

Measures and Technology

It can be argued that systems development managers rely too heavily on internal measures of system performance, rather than focusing on how their endeavors fit in with

TABLE 7.1. High-level integration for online customer care systems.

Category	Task	System	Additional Integration
Retrieval	Billing status inquiry	Biller	—
	Order status inquiry	Ordering	—
	Trouble ticket status inquiry	Trouble ticketing	Technical trouble ticketing systems and notations
	Troubleshooting request	Troubleshooting	User instructions and trouble ticketing
	User instruction request	Online documentation	Outbound correspondence applications
	General information request	Online documentation	Outbound correspondence applications
	Location request	Locator	—
	Customer profile	Contact tracking	—
	Contact history	Contact tracking	—
	Contact tickler	Tickler	Contact tracking (retrieval)
	Online help	Online documentation	All
	Policies and procedures	Online documentation	—
	System messages	All	—
	Computer-based training	Online documentation	All
	Inbound correspondence	E-mail, fax, imaging	—
	Voice mail	Interactive voice response	—
Processing	Adjustments	Biller	—
	Pricing plan analysis	Biller	—
	Rerates	Biller	—
	Outbound correspondence	Contact tracking (E-mail, fax, postal)	User instructions and general information
	Code verification	Biller	—
	Order processing	Ordering	—
Storage	Account maintenance	Contact tracking	—
	Notations	Contact tracking	All
	Customer suggestions	Contact tracking	—
	Contact categorization	Contact tracking	All
	Trouble ticket creation	Trouble ticketing	Troubleshooting and Notations
	Order submission	Ordering	—
	Inbound correspondence	Contact tracking (e-mail, fax, postal)	—
	Online customer surveys	Contact tracking	—

the rest of the business. For example, measurements providing a customer's perspective of company performance could include the time it takes to fill an order, which is contingent on both the agents aptitude for the task and the system response time. Internal process measurements might focus on the processes for designing a system upgrade, while other measurements could apply to the development effort involved. In concert, these provide a strategic glimpse of corporate performance and future goals.

A customer care measurement for systems development that focuses on strategic and financial concerns is suggested, to balance internal measurements such as delivery time. Such an approach can act as a template for setting a value to computer systems. The approach would be first to list systems development goals for each of these perspectives and then to choose measurements to assist in achieving those goals.

Failure to collect data from all customer contacts results in not understanding why thousands of calls on unimportant or irrelevant issues are being received, as well as an inability to set priorities for prevention and customer education. Also, failure to conduct preventive analysis is considered a critical error: Few companies enhance their data utility by estimating the market cost of not acting to prevent or eliminate a problem. Other common issues include failure to incorporate satisfaction data into front-line evaluation systems (focus on productivity at the expense of the customer), and failure to evaluate the usability of systems during the pilot test (the "let's just get up and running and we'll figure out the flaws later" attitude), which can result in the loss of both agent productivity and customer satisfaction.

Often, the call center system development effort is being stymied by a combination of arbitrary management deadlines and budgetary constraints. For example, the development team may chose to focus on small-scale changes to an expensive "off-the-shelf" system. Such an approach should be tempered by adherence to the following requirements:

1. An intuitive call flow facilitated by a user interface that helps rather than hinders the agent. Ideally, supervisors and agents are the most appropriate resources to work with a human factors engineer and systems developer to overcome any difficulties with the system, which might include convoluted operations, cluttered screens, and navigational complexity.

   Risks:

   • Inappropriate use of the contact tracking system as agents have to "seek and find" functions that facilitate call handling and management reporting—a classic case of the system getting in the way of the normal flow of a customer call

   • Increased talk times and after call work due to a poorly designed and implemented graphical user interface (non-aligned with industry standards)

2. The ability to proceed immediately with content input to an information retrieval system that would be continually enhanced by robust feedback loops from the agent and supervisors to the quality improvement team.

   Risks:

   • Increased talk times as new agents attempt to locate information from hard copy documents

   • Inconsistent responses to the customer as agents share "word of mouth" interpretations of business policies and procedures

   • Increased after call work as agents research problems that should have been resolved online

   • A caveat relative to the success of the system is not only the ability of the content engineer to craft accessible, accurate, clear, and complete documentation, but also the commitment of management to its usage on a consistent, if not mandatory, basis

3. A notification or commitment process and system implementation that is understood and accepted by all parties. This major after-call work/closed time issue may require service agreements from cross-organizational resources such as marketing, product management, legal, insurance, technical support, and so on, to avoid major problems with customer callbacks.

Allowing agents to make time-driven commitments for third-party callbacks is clearly undesirable, particularly when those parties operate outside of the scope of the call center. Service agreements can alleviate this problem and help to avoid irate customer callbacks relative to missed commitments. In general, however, the more the system can track responsibilities and escalate missed commitments immediately, the more manageable the task will be for the call center.

Risks:

- High volume of repeat calls from customers due to missed commitments

- Routing and notification rules and functions that do not adequately track all ongoing commitments and escalate as appropriate

4. An ability to automate routine tasks such as fax, outbound correspondence forms, and so forth. Although clerical resources may provide an interim solution, allowing agents to create, send, and receive these items from the desktop is clearly more desirable.

Risks:

- Even with clerical support services, there will be an increase in after call work as agents personally handle urgent faxes and written correspondence, which requires physically leaving the workstation.

The One-Step Development Syndrome

It is usual for systems developers to use business requirements in order to gauge the feasibility, duration, and cost of the development effort. While this is a logical approach, problems arise when these requirements, which are often a relatively unpolished manifestation of customer care needs, are used as the only development resource throughout the entire design cycle. This phenomenon may be referred to as the *one-step development syndrome*. For example, it is relatively common for management to compile a wish list of requirements and basically "throw it over the wall" to the mysterious world of systems development. Meanwhile, the processes and analyses that should have provided the impetus for translating the business requirements into systematic tasks are virtually ignored.

Ideally, senior management recognizes customer care requirements as a critical conduit to realizing the company's goals of world-class customer interaction, rather than as a potential stumbling block to meeting arbitrary internal deadlines. Rather than asking *why* the call center needed a particular function, for example, systems developers would be committed to discovering *how* best to support those whose job it is to interact with demanding customers. No functional change would be made and no design iterated, without the prior approval of call center representatives. Without this approach, the optimization of the customer care environment through systems development is highly unlikely.

Some of the most revealing interaction between the customer care management team and the development group takes place after an initial statement of work is received. The management team, who may have solicited several potential system development resources, may want to know, for example, whether the cost of development includes retraining expenses and disaster recovery contingencies, and whether or not the new technology is compatible with the old system. Most of all, those involved in composing the business requirements will want to know how close the new system will be to fulfilling all of those requirements. At this point, the development team may convey understandably abstract descriptions of the final product and its relative capabilities. Sometimes, the marketing process is glamorized by the production of a "proof of concept" prototype. Typically, the proof of concept is an attractive user interface depiction that attempts to demonstrate that the prospective development group already has a good idea of what is needed to produce a usable computer system.

As long as the technical explanation is relatively plausible, or unless the management team is cognizant enough to discern the relative merits of different approaches to systems development (or has already made a strategic decision to contract with a particular group), the project will most often be awarded to the lowest bidder with the most aggressive development schedule and, to a lesser extent, the most appealing proof of concept prototype.

The System Release Process

The system release process often describes what is considered to be the optimal way to design, develop, and deploy the system in what is considered a timely and cost-effective fashion. Most system development groups will adopt a slightly different approach to this process, depending upon external forces such as vendor relationships, service agreements, and management constraints. Different nomenclature may also be used to describe the phases of the process, but in general there is a standard structure of budget negotiation, business requirement review, analysis, renegotiation, design, development, testing, and deployment.

There is often a significant difference between the components and tasks of an ideal system release process as it is understood by customer care management, human factors engineers, and the development organization.

Typically, customer care management appoints a project team to gather high-level business requirements. These requirements should come from several different sources, reflecting the needs of the entire organization with regard to the customer care function. Customer care agents, for example, will be more inclined to indicate areas in which they believe that the *system* could be augmented, whereas strategists, marketing and product management will simply indicate their needs without necessarily discriminating between the system and the human (i.e., the agent). In other words, "we don't care how you do it, just make sure that customer care supports this need." This can be an important differentiator, since the agents are far less empowered (under typical system release processes) to effect system change than other business entities, with the result that the development organization may trumpet any kind of automation as a business breakthrough without ever directly addressing the needs of the customer care agents.

It is important, therefore, to understand the relative goals of the various groups who should be able to affect systems design and development:

- *Product Management*

  Input: Market intelligence requirements pertinent to customer inquiries, complaints, and suggestions relative to the product or service offering

Product management should perceive the customer care organization as a critical link to the outside world's perception of a new product or service offering. In many cases, however, robust channels of communication between customer care and product managers simply do not exist. This is often because the quality and interpretability of the market intelligence gathered by customer care is not inherently useful to product management—a situation often blamed on customer care management. A well-designed system can go a long way toward helping agents gather data that can be analyzed and disseminated among product managers. It is important, therefore, that a comprehensive understanding of product management requirements is achieved by the development organization.

- *Marketing*

  Input: Market intelligence requirements pertinent to customer demographics, complaints, and suggestions relative to the marketing environment

Similar to product management, marketing requirements for feedback from customer care need to be fully understood prior to system deployment. In general, marketing managers are interested in point-of-sale information and feedback, promotional responses, survey responses, and any demographic information that can be gathered during the course of a normal contact with customer care.

- *Strategy*

  Input: Projected functions and data elements required to support a new product or service

Strategists are defined as those individuals who are responsible for ensuring that, once a product or service has been released, the mechanisms are in place to support customer needs. This means that strategists must be able to define elements such as the scope of customer care support, budgets, necessary partnerships, competitive comparisons, and direct measures of customer care quality. From a system support perspective, strategists must understand those additional functions that will be necessary to support the new product or service. This can only be achieved through process development exercises with customer care process owners.

- *Customer Care Operations and Support*

  Input: Systematic needs relative to increasing customer satisfaction and reducing operational costs in the customer care environment

Customer care requirements engender both customer contact and intraorganizational information needs. The process for sharing information on a new sales promotion may engender a systematic link between marketing and customer care, for example. In general, the systematic focus for any customer care environment will be augmenting the ability to resolve calls on the first contact to the satisfaction of the customer, with minimal delays.

After these initial interactions between management and the development team, a commitment is normally made to more or less modify the business requirements according to budgetary and time frame limitations, and proceed with development. For most organizations, this means construing a data model and system requirements before actually coding the user interface and deploying the system itself. This data modeling may involve a subset of the user population in addition to perusal of existing systems, as it is necessary to understand all of the fields that must be present in order to fulfill the business requirements. In many cases, this data modeling exercise is the only contact the users may have with the development organization.

Data modeling endeavors, however necessary, usually lack any sense of a finished product and can become tedious and frustrating to user representatives. The data modelers, and certainly the often anonymous system developers themselves, become an enigma to the user population. Strangers show up at the call center for closed-door meetings in huddle rooms. On rare occasions these individuals sit at agent workstations, silently observing and listening to interactions with customers. The agents are vaguely aware that "these are the ones who are building the new system." Overall, there is a sense of awe and even sublimation between the users and the those who are ostensibly going to improve their working lives.

For the developer, who has to do the tedious and often difficult work of coding functions, being given carte blanche to design and develop solutions based loosely on business requirements is often an ideal, if not imperative, situation. For some developers, the less interference there is from the user population, the more chance that deadlines will be met by designing interfaces and writing code that supports basic functions.

It is common for external development groups to hire computer programmers on an "as needed" basis, often seeking talented college graduates. Any decision to use a new development tool for a project often means that even experienced developers will have to master novel programming conventions and user interface design tools. This combination of inexperience and innovation often means that the development team will be capable of producing only basic representations of user needs. Demands for more complex functions are likely to produce a strong (and usually successful) "time and money" protest from the development team.

Once the data model is relatively complete, functional specifications for the system are described and handed off to developers for implementation. Based upon time constraints and opportunities to reuse code from previous development efforts, project management may be encouraged to adjust the functional specifications accordingly. Again, negotiations take place with management and, based on the outcome, business requirements are modified as necessary.

The user interface is then developed, reflecting both the data model and functional requirements. At this point, decisions are made regarding field placement, use of color, font sizes, and various other aesthetic design decisions. Despite the fact that at this stage the system development process has passed through several phases, there has been no particular effort (apart from the initial proof of concept) to discover whether the systematic interpretation of the business requirements actually makes sense from the users' perspective.

It is an unfortunate fact that one-step development syndrome systems are deployed without due consideration of whether the progressive display of fields and functions intuitively matches the task that the user is attempting to accomplish. In many cases, users are brought into the development cycle so late that they are powerless to affect change, even when change is badly needed. After all, there is very little opportunity for argument from nontechnical individuals when a computer programmer simply states, "It can't be done that way in the available time frame."

By its time-consuming and often tedious nature, computer programming is often described as the grunt work of the development process. Yet system limitations—imposed by either unrealistic deadlines or programmers (whether because of a lack of skill, training, or initiative) who are incapable of representing the functions that are required by the user population, or a combination of both—have derailed many worthy development endeavors. Ideally, computer programming should be somewhat analogous to producing, binding, and distributing a business presentation after the critical work of developing content has been accomplished. Economic and time-conscious production people may reuse binders from a former presentation, while creative and industrious types may customize the entire presentation to exceed the customer's expectation, but either way the content will be exactly what the presentation team required. In other words, process engineering, user needs analysis, and design guided by close cooperation between management, users, human factors engineers, and system designers should be the driving force for optimal system development. Users may know nothing about the difficulty of coding functions, but they are able to describe optimal solutions for situations that the programmer could never have visualized.

After finalizing the user interface design and database structure, the development organization is ready for its final tasks prior to full-scale deployment. The new system is tested rigorously to ensure that all functions are working as described. Many development organizations describe this final phase of the project prior to deployment as "user acceptance testing." Based on what appear to be reasonable speeds of response, functional completion, and multiple-user access capacity, the system is pronounced to be a more or less complete representation of the business requirements. The training department is given copies of the system reference materials, specifications, and user documentation, and the system is finally revealed to the user population. After a few weeks spent fine-tuning the local environment, the development team begins to filter away to other projects, often leaving a small team of database and system administrators on site. Eventually, the customer care organization may undertake those duties, or continue contracting with the systems development group for the life span of the system.

At this point, barring major discrepancies, the system is considered functionally complete. Any excess development budget is quickly assimilated by the customer care organization. System maintenance is normally conducted on a limited scope which, regardless of the existence of a change request process, virtually ensures that no functions will alter prior to the next system release, which could be several months or even years after the initial deployment. In other words, there is a very significant difference between the system not working, and the system not working *the way it should be*. A system crash is a far more compelling argument for immediate maintenance than the fact that agents are spending a few extra seconds on certain tasks because they have to create workarounds or take unnecessary additional steps.

In summary, managers who tolerate the one-step development process often end up with a system that can actually impede customer interactions by increasing contact time through cryptic and counterintuitive workflows, missing or inadequate functions, and suboptimal screen designs. Conversely, those who recognize the need for proactive and empowered user involvement from the earliest formalization of business requirements to the actual deployment and maintenance of the system will reap the benefits of comprehensive user "buy-in" coupled with escalated productivity and, consequently, reduced cost and increased customer satisfaction.

User-Driven Design

In order to contrive an antidote to the one-step development process, it is necessary to investigate the tools and techniques that have separated best-in-class customer care environments from their competitors. These include the use of sophisticated graphical user interfaces, knowledge-based systems, and most of all, systems design and development driven by a methodology known as *user needs analysis*.

Graphical user interfaces provide a form of human–computer interaction that has no direct correlate in human–human communication. A graphical interface can also be intelligent over and above the extent to which it is easy or natural to use. Use of an expert system "front end," for example, allows users to query the system, supply information, receive advice, and so on. Intelligent interfaces to worksheets and databases, for example, can help end users interact with the systems more easily. This interface would aim to provide the same form of communication facilities supplied by a human expert.

In recent years, tools such as expert systems, fault diagnoses systems, case-based reasoning, neural networks, and so forth, have proven effective in the automation of customer care as well as internal help desk activities. This reflects a maturation of technology and the real benefits achieved by those pioneering companies that identified and pursued help desk applications in their search for uses of the technology.

In order to provide some assistance for the user operating in a real-world domain with uncertain data, expert systems can be designed to make use of stored information about similar problems, coupled with the user's general knowledge. Case-based reasoning, for example, provides users with options not normally available in the expert system domain. This is achieved by using reasoning based on the applicability of historical events, called cases. A case consists of a textual problem description, a set of questions and associated answers, and a resolution. The system automatically summarizes past case information, then it selects cases relevant to the current problem, providing examples and guidance from past successful solutions.

Case-based reasoning allows frontline agents to provide many answers that usually can be determined only by referrals to experts. These systems can automate and improve critical customer care tasks by capturing expert knowledge as online documentation.

The user interface for case-based reasoning systems, for example, is ideally graphical and customizable to suit the needs of the user. This is achieved by using an application (i.e., a screen design package with program links to the expert system) that lets developers add, modify, or delete icons, buttons, entry fields, windows, scroll bars, help screens, and other features. These features in turn are linked to code that directs the system to perform certain actions to achieve the desired result.

The resolution to a customer problem could take a number of different forms. Depending on the category and complexity of the problem, the resolution may be one sentence, several sentences, a graphic, or sections cut from online documentation or training modules. The agent will be able to read these over the phone, or use electronic mail or fax machines to respond to the customer.

Technologies such as online documentation and graphical user interfaces have already proven their worth in terms of improved human–computer interaction, and both are relatively easy to develop as well as being available commercially at low cost. These, however, are only the "visible" parts of a far more complex sphere of functionality. Evolving technologies, such as natural language applications, are becoming more sophisticated and less costly, giving nontechnical people the opportunity to exert an influence over the final appearance and functionality of a product.

The evolution of computer technology will continue to enhance human–computer interaction. Increased development of data "mining" applications, hypermedia, expert systems, and natural language applications will not only make computers easier to use, but will also solve the critical problem of information overload, particularly in customer care environments, making it possible to find exactly what is needed when it is needed most.

Just as customer expectations for service today are determined by exposure to best-in-class customer care environments, regardless of the industry, agent expectations for system response are driven by experience with outstanding customer care systems. For example, a state-of-the-art online troubleshooting system that takes five seconds to respond when agents were formerly used to three-second rates fosters a strong sense of dissatisfaction, regardless of the quality of the functions or content of the system. It is critical, therefore, that agents are innately involved in the design and deployment of any customer care system, in order that a personal sense of ownership and commitment to the success of that system is achieved.

In an era of technological wizardry, online customer care can be a two-edged sword. First, the product itself may be so sophisticated that the majority of *naive* users depend on explicit verbal or written instructions to perform even basic functions. Secondly, the online customer care environment itself may consist of a conglomeration of cryptic interfaces to legacy systems and powerful but poorly designed database retrieval tools that require a fairly significant degree of computer literacy. In a worst-case scenario, therefore, the customer will call because he or she cannot get the product to work, and will encounter a new agent who not only has minimal product knowledge, but also is struggling to master the online customer care system. Low pay and high turnover rates certainly combine to make this situation plausible, if not ubiquitous. The fact is that, despite remarkable technological advances, software developers are still as capable of producing an unusable system as they have always been.

The International Standards Organization (ISO) has decreed that "The usability of a product is the degree to which specific users can achieve specific goals within a particular environment: effectively, efficiently, comfortably, and in an acceptable manner." For a system to be *effective* and *efficient,* for example, a human factors engineer might decree that it is necessary that the majority of users are able to use the system for particular tasks, without error, within a specified period of time. For users to be *comfortable* with a system, they must be able to learn its functions within a certain period of time. The system must be intuitively designed so that even those functions that are not used frequently may be recalled with minimal difficulty. For a system to be *acceptable,* a certain (high) percentage of users must indicate their satisfaction with the system. If a system is found to be unacceptable for specific reasons, therefore, it is necessary that the development organization is adequately funded to rectify those design flaws that, for whatever reason, were overlooked in the first place.

A user needs analysis is the optimal way for any development organization to ensure that all of these criteria are met. Such an endeavor should be driven by a thorough understanding of those processes that evolved from business requirement analysis. Systematic user needs then become apparent through task and content analysis, rapid prototyping, and usability testing. This type of analysis should be an integral part of the overall system release process.

Conducting a User Needs Analysis

There are several interpretations of exactly what constitutes a user needs analysis. From a pure human factors perspective, for example, this endeavor might include user characterization (developing profiles and characteristics of the user population), situational analysis (situations that arise during the working day) and even cognitive testing in addition to task analysis, rapid prototyping, and usability testing. Most system development efforts, however, place such a strong reliance on business requirements and rapid application development that efforts to document details about the user population and their working attitudes and behaviors sometimes become superfluous. In other words, whatever is accomplished by the user needs analysis must be highly intertwined with ongoing development efforts. This can be accomplished only by adopting a system release process that is acceptable to both the development group and the customer care organization. Failure to establish a mutually agreeable process will almost certainly result in an acrimonious relationship between customer care advocates and developers.

The lead analyst will ideally be an empowered liaison between the user population and the developers. Not only will this individual become innately familiar with user needs by attending agent training sessions and observing and interviewing agents, he or she will also work closely with a core team of agents, supervisors, and managers to review business requirements and interact with developers. A key role in the project will be the ability to visualize user needs through rapid prototyping, and to corroborate results through usability testing. The lead analyst will usually have a background in human factors, process engineering, and user interface design, and will be viewed as a key member of the development team.

While the conduit for expressing user needs to the development organization is often restricted only to the business requirements, these describe only individual functions that need to be automated. A key to understanding user needs is process analysis. This requires working with process engineers to identify areas of existing processes that could be enhanced by automation. Furthermore, by conducting task analysis and rapid prototyping sessions with users, these functions and processes can be understood in the holistic sense of the tasks that make up particular types of customer contact. Content analysis is conducted in partnership with knowledge and documentation engineers, who can determine initial boundaries and necessary functions for the online documentation and troubleshooting systems. Usability testing can then be used to verify or rectify any assumptions that may have been made during the system design phase. The result of a complete user needs analysis should be a system that not only reflects optimal customer interaction, but which also has the support of the user population even before it is deployed—a factor that can be critical to successful change management.

The lead analyst must not only be able to translate all of this information into a practical evolution of the business requirements and logical data model, but must also demonstrate the ability to work closely with developers to negotiate a systematic solution that is agreeable to all parties.

User needs analysis, therefore, involves those who will ultimately use the computer system as early as possible in the design cycle. Just as the business requirements document is an abstraction of a desired state, user needs analysis ensures that the conceptual state is translated into a viable and useful computer systems environment. The critical components of any user needs analysis are

- Task analysis
- Rapid prototyping
- Usability testing

The following pages examine each of these components in greater detail.

- **Task Analysis**

Task analysis, sometimes referred to as workflow analysis, is ideally an examination of the critical points whereby a process can be augmented by technology, ostensibly to assist the user in performing certain tasks. Ideally, the analyst will work closely with process owners in order to understand precise retrieval, processing, and storage needs for any particular task. This will result in the production of high-level system requirements. Performance criteria, such as the required speed of system response to a user demand, can also be established during task analysis.

Clearly, once the task has been defined, it is critical that any necessary agent intervention is fully understood not just in terms of completing the task, but also in terms of comprehending the reason for carrying it out in the first place. Unlike machines, humans should be given a good reason why they should carry out particular tasks, such as gathering customer feedback or using the online troubleshooting system even when they believe that they already know the answer.

The key question in any task analysis effort is "exactly what is the agent attempting to achieve, and how can the system facilitate that task?" By conducting an exhaustive evaluation of all the tasks an agent might undertake during the course of a contact with a customer, the groundwork is set for rapid prototyping—the actual visualization of those tasks as they pertain to human–computer interaction.

In many ways, task analysis is a mixture of process development and knowledge engineering, as the human factors engineer attempts to understand the end-to-end execution of a particular event. As a relatively facile example, a customer request for a seven-month-old bill copy may involve several discrete agent tasks, such as confirming the customer's identity using the contact tracking system, going to the archives to locate and copy the bill, composing a cover letter, attaching the bill to the letter, handwriting the customer's name and address on an envelope, stuffing the envelope, taking it to the mail room, and finally logging the contact and subsequent agent actions in the contact tracking system.

The human factors engineer will analyze each of these tasks and look for opportunities to streamline the process by using the computer, such as enabling the agent to retrieve, for example, up to twelve months of bills directly from the billing system, creating an automatically populated online cover letter for bill copies, enabling the agent to fax or e-mail the bill and cover letter directly from the desktop computer, and/or providing a window envelope that correlates to the printed customer address. By conducting a cost/benefit analysis of these proposed enhancements based on volume and time studies, the human factors engineer can optimize business requirements for the ultimate system design.

There is often a profound difference between simply fulfilling business requirements and deploying a system that provides outstanding support for the user population. Table 7.2 contains some other examples of system enhancements that may be realized through task analysis.

Task analysis, therefore, is a crucial first step in the human–computer interaction model. By conceptualizing ways in which computer systems can enhance the performance of humans, the human factors engineer can augment the work of process developers and knowledge engineers, thus facilitating a practical bridge between the often disparate worlds of process, technology, and content development.

TABLE 7.2.   System enhancements through task analysis.

Business Requirement	Baseline Function	Suggested Enhancement
The system will enable the identification of an explicit reason for the incoming call	Provides a 3-character field into which the user may enter one of 250 codes	Suggests an abbreviated list of call types based on user interaction
The system will capture notations relevant to each customer contact	Provides a 273-character notes field	Automatically captures notations based on user interaction
The system will provide product information in order to resolve customer inquiries and complaints	Provides textual references to general product information	Provides a fully integrated troubleshooting and online documentation system
The system will display a record of previous contacts from a particular customer	Displays date and time of previous customer contacts	Dynamically links previous contact record with former troubleshooting scenario
The system will facilitate outbound correspondence	Provides a facility for storing form letters	Auto-populates templates for e-mail, fax, and postal; can attach nodes of online documents

• Rapid Prototyping

Rapid prototyping is widely recognized as an effective and efficient means of conveying user needs to the development organization. The use of rapid prototyping can ensure that a user interface design *approved by the user community* is made available in a timely fashion. Problems are identified much earlier in the design process, and the visual presentation of the interface ensures that improvements can be described in "real time."

Long before the first rapid prototyping tools were available, designers were visualizing user interfaces on chalkboards and notepads. The availability of "front-end" object-oriented design tools, however, means that screens can be designed and scripts quickly written to create the look and feel of an entire application, rather than leaving actual screen designs and navigational paths to the user's imagination.

A group of users, human factors engineers, and systems developers working together for two or three days are certainly capable of producing a prototype that could ultimately involve several weeks or months of development work. This situation continues to cause controversy, however, as it means that design decisions that were historically left to the development organization's discretion may now be driven by those who have simply mastered a user interface design tool, rather than a complex programming language.

User interface design is often perceived as the most desirable role in the development process, as the designer can help users visualize what is considered the optimal system interaction, whereas the programmer is often "relegated" to the difficult task of actually making the designer's concepts become reality. However, unlike the rather cryptic world of computer programming, user interface design is a discipline that is open to intense scrutiny from virtually every individual who uses the system. After all, the interface is the most tangible evidence of months or even years of project work. Regardless of whether the user interface designer is a computer scientist, human factors engineer, or graphic artist, the best designers display not only creativity and business acumen, but also a strong willingness to understand the needs of the user community. The traits of outstanding user interface designers include

- A comprehensive knowledge of the business requirements for the new system
- A strong empathy with the needs and concerns of the user population
- An ability to correlate existing and anticipated business processes with systems functions
- Extensive familiarity with the user's everyday workflow through task analysis, questionnaire responses, observations, attendance at training sessions, focus groups, etc.
- A commitment to leading the users in iteratively creating the optimal user interaction
- Knowledge of an industrial design standard (such as the IBM common user access principles)
- The ability to quickly envision and construct intuitive navigational flows
- The ability to quickly create aesthetically pleasing screen designs

- An understanding of developmental constraints based on interactions with project management and the development team
- The flexibility to work with developers to improve or change the user interface design as necessary to meet project deadlines or improve usability
- The ability to create, conduct, analyze, and act upon regular usability tests with pilot groups from the user community

In many cases, however, it has been surmised that restrictions of the rapid prototyping tool can actually limit the user's capability to envision the optimal solution, or that the prototype is creating unrealistic user expectations (a common failure), or that the lead prototyper is an unskilled user interface designer. Each of these legitimate concerns emphasizes the difficulty of creating a user interface that is acceptable to both the user community and the systems development group. The subjectivity of opinions on "good" and "bad" design can lead to a power struggle that places the user interface designer in a perilous position, particularly if the designer is not closely aligned with the development group.

The absence of design principles, inflexibility on the part of the designer, and inadequate prototyping tools can certainly lead to a suboptimal system, while the most elaborate and user-friendly prototypes are often implausible even to the most skilled computer programmer. Striking a balance between these extremes should be the goal of any user interface designer. It is a tightrope that demands diplomacy, strong user support, and outstanding project management skills.

Rapid prototyping is a powerful but necessarily sensitive endeavor that can reveal both gaps in processes and previously unidentified data elements, functional requirements, and logical screen flows—as well as validating and substantiating business requirements. Involving an iterative process of design, review, modification, and validation, it enables developers to commence work on one functional aspect of a system even while users describe another. For example, in the case of a customer care environment that supports a consumer product, the development team may reuse an existent design to produce a store locator module while the design team works on an innovative prototype for product identification.

Of course, not all systems development efforts are suitable for a rapid prototyping approach. A business requirement for an intelligent troubleshooting system, for example, may result in the selection of an off-the-shelf product or even the development of a customized tool, neither of which facilitates design sessions with users. It is rather more likely that users will be consulted on the structure of the problem-solving information that should be accessible via the system, while the development team will observe and interview users in order to determine the optimal troubleshooting approach. A decision may then be made by senior management as to the economic viability of the proposed solution. The first glimpse the users get of the new system may be only after the initial knowledge acquisition and engineering is complete. In the case of a custom-built system, a pilot group of users will typically participate in usability tests to determine the viability of the interface. Based on feedback from these tests, the development team may iterate the design in order to accommodate the needs of both novice and expert users.

Ideal candidates for rapid prototyping include those business problems that are unique to a particular environment. Call center managers handling multiple types of internal referral, for example, will need to describe the escalation and call-back processes for each referral in order that the user interface designer can model the necessary interaction. Complex processes such as these are often verified by the users and depicted to the development team through rapid prototypes.

• **Usability Testing**
User understanding of the process by which an automated component does its job is a major determinant of how far the operator will trust the system. The system, therefore, should appear to perform tasks in a way that is consistent with how the agent would complete them. After all, if the agent cannot comprehend the logic behind a task sequence, performance will be impaired. For example, a basic tenet of effective human–computer interaction is to rely on recognition rather than recall. One reason why graphical user interfaces are so successful is that users need only to recognize icons instead of recalling complex typewritten commands.

The practice of usability testing may be considered one of the most important contributions to the system design process, mainly because of its ability to identify some otherwise unpredictable problems, as well as its ability to allow designers to witness users having difficulty with certain aspects of the system.

Usability testing is usually the last step in this process cycle, which may be repeated several times prior to actual system deployment, depending upon time and budgetary constraints. Ideally, the participants of a usability test will include a representative cross-section of the agent population (i.e., experienced, intermediate, and novice agents, and computer-literate and relative newcomers to graphical user interface conventions). Obviously, the greater the level of participation the better, but from a logistical standpoint, one or two groups of six to ten participants are generally manageable. The test itself should take no longer than two hours, including a fifteen-minute break.

Preparation for a usability test involves creating step-by-step scenarios that are relevant to the types of customer contact the agent will generally receive (usually between 10 and 20 scenarios involving various levels of complexity are contrived). Each scenario is followed by a series of questions that ask the agent to assess the relative complexity of the task just completed. Secondly, a dozen or more high-level exercises that do not include step-by-step instructions are created. The objective of these exercises is to assess the ease-of-use and intuitive nature of the system. Unlike the initial scenarios, a human factors engineer should observe the agents during this segment of the test. In human–computer interaction laboratories, this is most often done via video camera, and may include keystroke monitoring and other considerations. The third element of the usability test involves the presentation of screen designs along with questions that enable the agent to suggest improvements based on their knowledge of optimal customer interaction.

Having completed all of the tasks, the agent should then be asked to complete a "usability study checklist," which considers various elements of the current system design, including *comprehension* (e.g., "Is the information on the screen easy to read? Does the use of color help to make the displays clear? Was it clear where information should be entered on the screen?" etc.); *task match* (e.g., "Is the information presented in a way that fits your view of the task? Are the naming attributes used on the screen—e.g., field names, pushbutton titles, window headings, etc.—easy to understand?" etc.); *relevance* (e.g., "Is it clear what actions you can take at any stage? Are the messages displayed by the system relevant?" etc.); *navigation* (e.g., "Is it always clear what part of the system you are in? Do you think the system is well-organized?" etc.); and *functionality* (e.g., "Does each screen contain all of the information you feel is relevant to a particular task? Does the online help facility address the tasks which you perform?" etc.).

Each checklist is designed to encourage the user to enter any commentaries that may be necessary to elaborate on their views. After the completion of these elements, the user may then be asked a series of questions relative to overall system usability. These questions attempt to summarize the areas of usability that are of most cause for concern.

In summary, usability testing is the most critical aspect of user needs analysis because it is often the only opportunity to elicit unbiased system feedback from a representative cross-section of the user population. Task analysis is often excluded from the system development process, ostensibly because of rigorous time frames, but most often because its relevance is obscured by functional designs that are extrapolated directly from the business requirements document. The opportunity to involve users in rapid prototyping sessions depends largely upon the bias of the project manager. In general, the greater the level of concern for the user, the more likely it is that the development process will include a complete user needs analysis. Managers who are more concerned about realizing long-term gains in productivity and customer satisfaction through user-driven system design, however, are often obscured in an era of shrinking budgets and aggressive deadlines.

Given that systems design and development may be the largest investment a company will make in its customer care operation, it is crucial that there is no ambivalence between preconceived management expectations and the capabilities of the development group. The relative novelty and rapid evolution of the computer, however, means that many contemporary managers are reluctant to challenge developers on matters pertaining to system design. Instead, there is a tendency to focus on those "comfort zone" areas that enable management to retain a modicum of control—time and money. In so doing, management tends to wash its hands of the development process, and hence any expression of dissatisfaction with the final product invariably leads to development group complaints of inadequate funding and unrealistic time frames.

User involvement can do much to assuage this common gulf between management and system development. User needs analysis, therefore, is a form of "sanity check" that can keep management in touch with ongoing development activities, while also enabling the development group to iteratively demonstrate system enhancements and potential opportunities for improvement.

Finally, it is important to consider that even with the most sophisticated online customer care system, users have to be given a good reason to stop what they are doing before they will accept any significant change. New systems are viewed with distrust and skepticism by those who have been coping quite well with their own workarounds on customer contacts, for example. Experienced customer care agents are the first people to criticize a new system, and their word can be a very powerful influence in a consolidated call center environment. Therefore it is important that such individuals are targeted by those involved in the design and development of any online customer care system.

Integration Relative to Content

In order to understand systems integration requirements relative to content, it is first necessary to decide what type of information will be provided to agents or customers. Typical examples would be as follows:

- User instructions ("how to" instructions relative to a particular product or service)
- Policies and procedures (instructions to agents on how to deal with particular customer scenarios)
- Troubleshooting (expert assistance in solving particular customer problems)
- Response templates (predefined responses to particular customer queries)
- Interactive voice response scripts (audio scripts for customers' self-help)
- Online help (field-level help that helps new users understand system functions)
- Online scripts (context-sensitive prompts to users that may be activated based on comfort level)
- Computer-based training (online training modules)
- Contact categorization (agent-selectable lists to define reason for customer call)

These functions are often performed by several different groups within an organization. For example, user instructions and policies and procedures may be produced by a documentation team, troubleshooting scenarios by a knowledge engineering team, interactive voice response scripts by the call center management team, and the computer-based training modules by the training team. In many cases, online help, online scripts, contact categorizations, and response templates may be initially produced by the development organization. (It is worth noting that functions such as online help are often overlooked completely during system deployment; one call center had been using a multimillion dollar system for over a year before someone discovered that a double-click on the right-hand mouse button initiated the help application.) As a result of this widespread distribution of what are in many cases self-assumed responsibilities relative to the information retrieval system, it is quite possible that several functions will become neglected or even provide conflicting data. The next chapter explores the facilities for providing and maintaining reliable online information retrieval systems.

8

Information Retrieval Systems

Overview

Advances in automatic call distribution, computer-telephony integration, interactive voice response, predictive dialing, and workforce management software are a common theme of contemporary customer care publications and conferences. These technologies are considered important because tangible metrics such as average speed of answer, abandonment rate, and average talk time are the focal point of day-to-day operations for call center managers. It is interesting, however, that while most of these technologies serve as useful media through which an inquiry or problem may be handled, these do not actually *resolve* a customer contact. The resolution of a customer call is often a work-intensive and potentially costly endeavor because it often requires a human agent to provide expert assistance on a wide and dynamic range of topics.

There is no shortage of literature on how an agent should *behave* when dealing with particular types of customer, but there is far less focus on the elements required to efficiently resolve an inquiry or problem on the first point of contact. For example, how does a new agent resolve a cryptic product usage problem without having to transfer the customer to a more experienced resource? How does the agent know when company policy on a particular issue has changed? How do agents keep in touch with the latest promotional offerings? In some cases, the answer could be as simple as a few "Post-it" sheets stuck around the perimeter of the agent's desktop monitor, whereas in others it could mean conducting a rapid search of an elaborate database. This latter endeavor is facilitated by dozens of highly competitive software applications, yet is for various reasons one of the most neglected areas in contemporary customer care environments.

Many call center managers are evaluated on their operational prowess, rather than more nebulous metrics surrounding, for example, the number of *repeat* calls from customers (i.e., callbacks on problems which were not resolved during the first contact with an agent). Also, it is often far easier to quantify the return on investment for an interactive voice response unit (e.g., "Ten percent of all callers used the IVR to access account information") or computer-telephony integration (e.g., "The screen pop function saved fifteen seconds on 30 percent of all calls"), than it is to quantify productivity and customer satisfaction gains realized as a result of implementing information retrieval systems that are often used only at the discretion of the agent.

It is evident, however, that the availability of information systems that actually assist the agent in resolving a customer contact can have a far more pronounced effect on customer satisfaction than those technologies whose sole purpose is to minimize the amount of time a customer spends on the toll-free network. It also stands to reason that if the customer's inquiry or problem is efficiently resolved every time, even by the most inexperienced agent, then repeat calls will become negligible and service levels will automatically rise. One-high volume consumer products call center, for example, discovered that a well-maintained, consistently accessed information retrieval system reduced overall talk time by almost 50 percent, in addition to increasing resolution on first contact by almost 20 percent. Because this system took several months to implement, however, it required a shift in management focus, whereby satisfying the customer meant more than just answering and completing the call within a certain time frame, but also tracking whether or not the agent was able to easily access consistent, accurate, understandable and complete information that enabled rapid resolution of the customer's inquiry or problem.

Yet there is no point investing in software for online information retrieval unless there is a strong management commitment to the *continuous* provisioning of easy-to-access, understandable, and complete online information for agents (and customers, as in the case of the World Wide Web and interactive voice response). The first step in any content implementation effort, therefore, is to introduce the processes that will define the boundaries of the data-gathering and maintenance effort. Resources to support these processes, such as documentation and/or knowledge "engineers," will need to be appointed. Regardless of whether management has decided to invest in an information retrieval system or not, the necessary data need to be documented in logical realms, such as policies and procedures, customer instructions, and decision trees for problem solving. Essentially, the goal of this endeavor is to baseline available information in a hard copy (paper) format that is acceptable to the user population.

The decision whether or not to implement an online information retrieval system depends largely upon the complexity of the product or service offering, coupled with considerations of agent ability and turnover. In the case of an inbound call center environment, with a robust training curriculum, a well-educated, stable, and empowered workforce, and a mature product or service offering, there may be no need for such a sophisticated solution. Conversely, centers catering to dynamic marketing and product offerings, and staffed by inexperienced agents who are prone to quit within the first six months of employment, are ideal candidates for carefully maintained information retrieval systems. Moreover, in the case of multi channel customer care (i.e., the provisioning of direct customer access to information via the World Wide

Web or interactive voice response), agents must all *at least* have online access to the same information sources as the customer.

There is a potentially large volume of more or less consolidated information available to every call center agent. This could be in the form of a several-hundred-page handbook, or a dozen one-inch binders sitting in the corner of the agent's workspace. Obviously, this information is prone to change, and there must be some form of maintenance process that ensures that the agent always has access, for example, to the latest marketing initiative or business policy change. There must also be a feedback process whereby the agent can advise the content engineering team that certain information appears to be missing, inaccurate, or incomplete. Finally, the content engineering team must ensure that any changes being made are synchronized with the training department, World Wide Web site and interactive voice response unit content provisioners. If these processes are not implemented correctly, even the most sophisticated information retrieval system will fail to realize productivity gains.

Typically, customer care management appoints a core team of subject matter experts to develop business requirements for an information retrieval system. Such requirements may include an overall goal of increasing agent productivity and resolution on first contact by a certain percentage (often both figures are higher than 20 percent), and be composed of elements such as the ability to

- Rapidly problem-solve complex product or service problems
- Use partial or even misspelled words in conducting a search for information
- Integrate with the contact tracking system
- Establish online links between associated nodes of information
- View graphics or compressed video images
- Easily index and maintain online documentation and troubleshooting information.

When the business requirements are completed, it is then usually up to the systems development group to determine the most appropriate and cost-effective functional match to these requirements. This activity may take several weeks or even months, as various off-the-shelf systems are evaluated. In the meantime, the content engineering team should be fine-tuning their data-gathering efforts by observing agents using available hard copy documentation to resolve customer inquiries and problems. At this stage, the content engineers should also be meeting regularly with a training representative and designated subject matter experts to evaluate daily customer contact reports and agent feedback on available information. This quality-improvement process will ultimately dictate the relative success of the information retrieval system.

Although for obvious reasons it is rarely easy to obtain detailed information about competitive systems development endeavors, customer care organizations, by their nature, tend to be forthcoming about the reasons why they should be considered "world-class" for a particular industry. Many prominent companies even arrange guided tours of their customer care facilities, or allow benchmarking groups to interview managers and observe system usage. Also, consulting companies who have implemented integrated information retrieval systems are an outstanding resource who will use as much nonproprietary information as possible in order to educate potential clients. Third, conference presentations and white papers published with increasing regularity on the World Wide Web can provide an excellent source of information for the latest online information developments. Last, the abundance of companies who actually market products that are touted as information retrieval systems provide the most obvious resource to prospective customer care environments. It is extremely likely that these companies were able to develop their product as a result of a previous engagement with a customer whose budget was voluminous enough to facilitate full-scale customized development. The question is for which industry was the product originally developed? A fault-diagnosis system built for the consumer electronics industry, for example, would probably not lend itself well to a mortgage assessment application (although this is not always the case, as differences between certain troubleshooting products are often imperceptible).

Intelligent Troubleshooting Systems vs. Online Documentation

Information retrieval systems, properly implemented and maintained, can represent a quantum leap in productivity for fast-paced customer care environments who have had to rely solely on classroom training and offline reference materials. In general, information retrieval systems for customer care environments consist of *intelligent troubleshooting* and *online documentation* systems. Troubleshooting systems are designed to assist the user in identifying the resolution to a particular problem by "intelligently" interacting with a knowledge base triggered by one or more user inputs, whereas online documentation systems normally employ search engines and hypermedia interfaces to either resolve a user inquiry or elaborate on a proposed troubleshooting system resolution by providing procedural instructions. Many customer care environments, especially those with more complex products and services, use both these approaches in concert, while others rely only on the online documentation system to resolve both inquiries and routine complaints.

A key systems development decision, therefore, concerns whether or not to implement *both* the intelligent troubleshooting and online documentation systems. Companies often decide that it is more cost-effective to implement only the online documentation system, even though customers may be calling in with relatively complex problems. In effect, this means that either the decision makers believe that the online documentation system facilitates troubleshooting (which is rarely the case), or that users are adept enough to figure out the cause of the problem on their own (thus necessitating access only to procedural or generalized information such as can be found in an online documentation system). The reason that the online documentation system does not facilitate troubleshooting, especially for inexperienced or inadequately trained users, is that the nature of troubleshooting usually involves *dynamic interaction* with the individual who is experiencing the problem. Such interactions demand a degree of reasoning not facilitated by online documentation systems (whose function is to respond to search words, rather than dynamically assess the probability of a particular solution being correct).

Intelligent troubleshooting systems interactively and intelligently diagnose and resolve a technical difficulty as perceived by a customer, or provide support by advising the customer on optimal solutions to particular issues or scenarios. Certain industries, such as banking, manufacturing, insurance, and high technology, are more prone to using these intelligent troubleshooting tools in order to facilitate customer interaction, whereas others, particularly noncomplex product or service environments, are less likely to need such elaborate online mechanisms to deal with customers.

Intelligent troubleshooting systems often use rules or preexisting cases in order to problem-solve. Based on the initial user input (normally described as *symptomatic* of the problem) and consequent user responses to a series of questions related to the cause of that symptom, the troubleshooting system will recommend a solution to the customer's problem. This solution is often based on probability levels. Fault diagnosis, neural networks, case-based reasoning, and automated data-gathering tools all strive to present users with a variety of options in solving a particular problem. This multifaceted approach sometimes requires a significant amount of training and lends itself more to controlled environments, such as call centers, if not always to universal availability via the World Wide Web. Other tools may simply use rules that present questions and potential resolutions in a logical sequence.

The relative value of an intelligent troubleshooting system is proportional to the amount of effort that the knowledge engineering and maintenance team put into emulating the types of problems and terminology that are generally applied to a particular product or service. If this goal can be achieved, then the tool can be deployed not only to frontline customer care agents, but also directly to the customer via mechanisms like the World Wide Web or even interactive voice response facilities. Of course, achieving such a goal often requires long-term management commitment, not just to the deployment of the tool, but to the ongoing maintenance of the knowledge base. It becomes a question of *readiness*—how complete must the knowledge base be prior to full-scale deployment? Releasing a knowledge base at anything less than 50 percent readiness risks losing the confidence of users before the maintenance process has even begun. Attempting to achieve complete readiness, however, is often tantamount to sending a manned spaceship to the nearest star—customers are apt to discover limitless nuances, particularly with complex products.

A knowledge engineering team that demonstrates a rapid turnaround on new problem resolution will enjoy the support of the user community. The *maintenance interface* to intelligent troubleshooting systems is a key to this endeavor. Most of these systems do not require any kind of programming expertise for maintenance of the knowledge base. Instead, many knowledge maintenance engineers have no background in computer science whatsoever. Using plain English interfaces, the engineer will formalize and test cases before deploying them to the working environment. The same individuals will define links from the troubleshooting cases to the online documentation system.

There are many business reasons supporting the implementation of intelligent troubleshooting systems. These tools not only augment agent training and help to offset the effects of high turnover, but are also suitable for direct presentation to the customer via the Web or other media. By decreasing escalation rates, these tools also relieve the human expert of mundane problem-solving tasks, allowing specialists to focus on more challenging work. A key factor in deployment of these systems is that they facilitate better distribution of expertise, as expert knowledge is available to the entire customer care environment at all hours of the day. Consistency in decision making is ensured because of the endorsement of the knowledge that is contained in the intelligent troubleshooting system. The resolution of errors, therefore, becomes more immediate as the tool recommends specific actions and typically justifies its recommendations. Intelligent troubleshooting systems can allow users to inquire why a particular question is being asked, or why a particular decision was reached. This provides an on-the-job training tool to help those less-skilled users to become more expert at a task over time.

The second major element of information retrieval systems, *online documentation,* may be described as an attempt to deploy a conglomeration of user manuals, job aids, policies and procedures, promotional fliers, organizational announcements, and all other customer care-related information into a comprehensive and relatively consistent online format. In customer care environments that utilize troubleshooting tools, online documentation is usually tightly integrated with actual content of the troubleshooting system. This means that, if a customer asks for a more detailed explanation of a particular scenario or resolution, the system will facilitate selection of a

---

Case In Point: A Failed Information Retrieval System

One customer care organization spent over three million dollars internally developing a new system, and fired a third of its customer care agents just after deployment in order to cost-justify the original business case. As it transpired, many of the system functions did not correlate to the customer-agent transactions, resulting in a plethora of "work-arounds," which in some cases even increased contact times. To make matters worse, search mechanisms on both the online documentation and troubleshooting systems were cryptic and time-consuming, and neither application contained even a third of the necessary information. The million dollar CTI endeavor, which in another environment might have reduced contact time by as much as thirty seconds a call by proactively retrieving customer records, actually added several seconds to each contact as it fruitlessly searched the database for customers who rarely called from the same originating number. With a miniscule maintenance budget, it took months to effect any changes to the system design, and the customer care environment had no processes in place (much less resources) to improve the online content. As a result, the remaining agents were allowed to resort to the tried and trusted paper documentation around their desks, using the system only to log contacts and create trouble tickets. As a result of escalating calls in queue, call center management was finally allowed to reestablish previous workforce levels, and the much-touted state-of-the-art system became a very expensive contact tracking application.

node of text or a graphic from the online documentation system that relates directly to that issue.

Sophisticated intelligent troubleshooting tools such as case-based reasoning or "expert" systems are programmed to *interactively* decipher user input in order to achieve contact resolution. This means that onus is on the system, rather than the user, to extrapolate and interpret data in order to reach a solution to a problem. All that the user has to do is to enter the problem symptoms and respond to any prompts for more information. Online documentation systems, on the other hand, are more useful for *augmenting* this process by providing procedures linked to resolutions, rather than being suited to help users troubleshoot product or service problems.

Just as experienced agents may be able to surmise the nature of a particular customer problem based on verbal interaction, intelligent troubleshooting systems attempt to emulate the expert by using *inference engines* to come up with the probable solution. Online documentation systems, no matter how cleverly contrived, are not designed to interactively troubleshoot problems. Instead, they are intended to facilitate rapid information access through powerful search mechanisms and logical, designer-driven linkages to other relevant information.

It should be noted that, although online documentation systems do not necessarily facilitate troubleshooting, the troubleshooting system is usually intertwined with the online documentation system in order to provide detailed procedures and user instructions relative to a particular solution. Therefore, while management may decide to implement only an online documentation system, it is rare for a troubleshooting system to operate as a stand-alone endeavor.

By attempting to realize the notion of the paperless environment, and thus significantly reduce contact time, maintaining both the intelligent troubleshooting and online documentation systems can be complex and time-intensive endeavors. Regardless of the difficulty of ensuring authentic content for both of these systems, it is apparent that the user interface must be as intuitive as possible in order to allow the user, whether that person is a customer or an agent, to navigate easily through potentially massive amounts of information (see Table 8.1, Requirements critical to an information retrieval system).

Given the rapid evolution of information retrieval systems for customer care during the latter part of this century, it is hazardous to suggest that one approach may work better than another. The current marketplace contains hundreds of tools purporting to help resolve customer problems. Rather than delving into specifics about tool differences, it is perhaps better to examine the philosophy of intelligent troubleshooting technology and how it pertains to customer care.

How Intelligent Troubleshooting Systems Work

The first troubleshooting systems were generally referred to as expert systems. As mentioned, an expert system relies on an inference engine in order to draw conclusions based on user input and the information contained in a *knowledge base*. Inference engines, which evolved during the 1960s, were outstanding feats of reasoning and programming that attempted to emulate human knowledge using *heuristics*, or

TABLE 8.1.   Requirements critical to an information retrieval system.

Online Documentation and Intelligent Troubleshooting	Search facility	• Availability of a sophisticated search engine (e.g., wildcard, full text via trigram matching, synonym search) to enable agents to quickly locate necessary information
	Maintenance interface	• Availability of an intuitive maintenance interface to enable rapid revisions to existing information and facile creation of new troubleshooting and content
	Recreate pending scenario	• Ability to recreate a troubleshooting scenario at the point at which the associate last suggested a resolution to the customer
	Linkages	• Ability to link directly from the intelligent troubleshooting system to the online documentation system in order to view details of a suggested resolution
Customer Contact Tracking	Auto-notations	• Provisioning of an auto-notation capture facility within the case management tool (e.g., tracking agent access points and interactions) to facilitate postcontact root cause analysis
	Call history	• Ability to visually associate reason for current contact with historical customer calls (i.e., customer callback relative to previous troubleshooting issue, etc.)
	Initialize troubleshooting	• Ability to use the case management contact history component to "kick off" a previous troubleshooting scenario
	Create commitment	• Ability to quickly create and allocate (i.e., refer to branch, etc.) a callback commitment to a customer, together with system notification capabilities for due commitments, and exception reporting to team leaders on overdue commitments
	Feedback Process	• Ability for agents to systematically notify content maintenance staff of any erroneous, misleading or incomplete information within the troubleshooting or online documentation system

"rules of thumb." An example of heuristics would be the decision as to how much water to bring on, for example, a sixty mile bicycle ride. Scientifically, this decision might be made based on a formula which considers the duration of the ride, the temperature, the terrain, the weight of the bicycle, the relative fitness of the rider, and so forth. After considering these inputs, a recommendation as to the exact amount of water to carry could be construed.

Normally, no one goes to this extreme because it is far more timely to simply make the decision based on personal experience or the advice of others who have undertaken this endeavor. Such *rules of thumb,* though imprecise, might include: If the weather is hot or the terrain is hilly, then bring an extra quart of water, otherwise bring one quart. Other "rules" would define the relative meanings of "hot" and "hilly" in order to reach a meaningful conclusion. The first knowledge engineers determined that, provided the scope of the problem being resolved was relatively narrow, that expert systems could augment or even replicate the decision-making process of the human expert.

The major difference between expert systems and traditional computer programs is that algorithms (an explicit sequence of coded steps required to perform a function) are replaced by nonsequential rules that are "fired" by circumstantial data, such as user input, and which use "IF . . . THEN" statements to draw conclusions—rather like human logic.

Case-based reasoning, one of the more successful approaches to intelligent troubleshooting used in customer care environments, uses expert system technology to decipher the applicability of "cases" to a particular customer problem. A case consists of a textual problem description, a set of questions and associated answers, and a resolution that is triggered by a certain sequence of user answers to those questions. The process of entering a problem description and answering questions to reach a resolution is known in artificial intelligence circles as "forward chaining." Forward chaining is most useful to those users who need step-by-step guidance in determining the solution to a problem. Conversely, some systems allow the user to suggest a resolution first, and then answer a series of questions that will confirm that their suggestion is correct. This process is, not surprisingly, known as "backward chaining," and is extremely useful to those who prefer to explore "hunches" and wish to eliminate what might be extraneous questions from the resolution process.

Based on the user's problem description, the case-based reasoning system will explore all of the stored cases in the database in order to select those that appear to be relevant to the current problem. By answering some or all of the clarifying questions, the user will assist the matching process.

Because the troubleshooting system analyzes a problem based on user input, it is considered far more effective than using an online documentation system to problem-solve. Instead of scanning hundreds of lines of text, the user simply responds to the system prompts. Used *in conjunction* (e.g., hyperlinking the proffered solution to a particular user instruction), it can be a powerful tool for reducing contact time and increasing customer satisfaction. Some tools offer this integrated capability, whereas others depend upon application programming interfaces (APIs) in order to link specific questions or remedies to relevant documents and images. Many tools also provide integrated contact tracking capabilities, which are particularly useful to internal help desk operations, though they are not generally as effective for the market intelligence and root cause analysis needs of the customer care environment.

Some companies now provide *adaptive learning* troubleshooting tools, which automatically capture user input in order to augment an existent database, with the ultimate goal of eliminating the need for knowledge engineering completely. This approach is viewed with some skepticism by those who have spent months or even years constructing and testing large knowledge bases. While the notion of sharing knowledge across an organization in real time has obvious merit, many dismiss the claim that this knowledge can be presented in a structured and unique way without the intervention of human experts. Visions abound of frustrated agents scrolling through dozens of seemingly similar "cases" that have been separated by the use of slightly different semantics. Redundant or confusing information can virtually guarantee the failure of these systems.

Well-designed and maintained intelligent troubleshooting tools are capable of reducing contact time by more than 50 percent, particularly when they are used by new agents. In general, the narrower the scope of knowledge required and the more explicit the problem description, the more likely that the agent will quickly resolve the customer's problem. The biggest obstacle to outstanding troubleshooting systems remains the search mechanism. Despite years of concerted efforts to introduce a "true" natural language interpretation mechanism, the artificial intelligence community continues to wrestle with the semantics of the English language. As a result, troubleshooting tools must either limit the user to selecting from a predefined list of problem symptoms, or use pattern-matching techniques to interpret a free-form text input. The latter of these approaches may also use synonyms, antonyms and libraries of "noise" words to try and match the user's input with cases in the database. This usually means that the system's inference engine will actually retrieve cases for perusal regardless of the user's input. In other words, if a user entered "supercalifragilistic" as a symptom, the system would actually respond with a series of clarifying questions and even some probabilistic solutions.

Other companies use scripts and decision trees in order to enable their agents to interact more efficiently with customers. It is fair to say that both these somewhat limited approaches originally provided the impetus for contemporary troubleshooting systems. The philosophy is that, by scripting the interaction between an agent and a customer relative to a particular inquiry or complaint, the less experienced agent can significantly reduce contact time. In order to achieve this goal, expert agents (who in highly pressured customer care environments are often identified by their ability to resolve a customer contact more quickly than anyone else) are observed and interviewed in order to derive a set of questions that they typically use to resolve a customer's request. Those questions are then coded and presented as online decision trees to the entire workforce. Based upon the answer to each question, ideally, the agent is able to follow the branch of the tree to a logical conclusion.

Sophisticated troubleshooting systems *automatically* assess resolution probabilities based upon the customer's response to a particular question. That is because knowledge engineers have already created rules or cases for the troubleshooting system's inference engine based on possible response patterns. Each question is therefore expected to be presented logically and intuitively, and the onus is no longer on the agent to follow complex decision paths, but rather to let the system figure out the solution. It is worth noting that the automation of troubleshooting scenarios has been proven not only to reduce contact times, but also to contribute significantly to decreased agent turnover.

The first hurdle to stand in the way of a successful information retrieval system is that of accessibility. In other words, how easy is it to initiate and use the system, and how quickly does it respond? *Speed of response* is the criterion for measuring the effectiveness of the system and database design, and is normally the principal element of concern for development organizations. Without an acceptable speed of response, an information retrieval system is bound to fail, no matter how wonderful the content.

Accessibility also depends upon *ease of use*—a term normally applied to the human factors issue of making the system intuitive to a user. For the purposes of an information retrieval system, this would involve elements such as user search, information structure and presentation, and automatic data capture. A poorly designed information structure can completely negate the advantage of an outstanding speed of response. Similarly, a cumbersome user interface can cost precious seconds at the agent level, and is especially detrimental at the direct customer interaction level (e.g., the World Wide Web), where it can easily result in calls that might otherwise have been resolved by the customers themselves. Yet in an environment in which users are essentially a "captive audience" and must use the system regardless of the user interface (which is typical of an internal development effort, as opposed to a commercial offering), the user interface is usually of secondary importance to the development organization, and often becomes a forum for heated exchanges between user representatives and developers.

It is far easier to measure the effectiveness of speed of response than what are often perceived as subjective views on user interaction, however, and users frequently have no choice but to accept what they are given. Management support for user requirements and the results of rapid prototyping and usability testing sessions must obviously be tempered by budgetary and technological constraints, but it is critical that developers negotiate solutions that are acceptable in the context of everyday interactions with the customer.

User Interaction with Information Retrieval Systems

Unlike many straightforward database retrieval applications, such as customer demographics, contact tracking, ordering, and billing, it is important that user interfaces for information retrieval systems are not designed simply by manipulating the position of certain data fields. Rather, it is an endeavor that demands significant attention from a consortium of human factors engineers, designers, developers, knowledge engineers, documentation engineers and, of course, the users themselves. After all, it is not enough to simply retrieve relevant information—that information must be structured and displayed in such a way that the user can easily interact with the system and assimilate its content virtually at a glance. This also means that the user should not have to worry about the mechanisms for retrieving information from the database; the ability to simply enter search criteria from the outset, and have the system react instantaneously and intuitively, is certainly a key to the user acceptance of any system.

Ultimately, those with the deepest insights as to the viability of the interface design are the users themselves. It is a basic premise of any worthwhile design that the *users are given what they need* in order to accomplish a specific task. This involves exhaustive prototyping and usability testing. The presumption with an off-the-shelf solution is that the manufacturers have given user needs careful consideration in their standard interface design, in addition to facilitating customization of the user interface to accommodate industry-specific needs. Unfortunately, the same cannot be said of many "home-grown" systems, which often contradict their apparent cost effectiveness with counterproductive functionality and poorly designed user interfaces.

The user interface for an intelligent troubleshooting system is significantly more complex than that of an online documentation system. A troubleshooting system is designed to interact dynamically with the user, providing a plethora of functions, whereas at a basic level the online documentation system simply consists of a search field and a window that displays mostly text and graphics. While it is true that an online documentation system that attempts to provide troubleshooting support can become quite complex for the documentation engineer, such systems lack the inherent processing power that lies at the heart of every troubleshooting system. For example, most troubleshooting systems determine potential solutions to a problem based on user input. The user input may initially be a problem statement or "symptom" that results in a series of clarifying questions and potential solutions being retrieved from the knowledge base. Subsequently, the user may choose to answer one or more of the questions in order to increase the probability of a particular solution being correct. The user may also choose to display more information about a particular question or remedy (usually by linking directly to specific nodes of text in the online documentation system), volunteer more information about the symptom, change the answer to a previous question, view all of the questions in the knowledge base and select those that seem pertinent, and even suggest a cause or remedy by retrieving only those questions that are directly associated with that suggestion. All of these functions require far more sophisticated reasoning than can be provided by an online documentation system.

Many hypermedia-oriented online documentation systems give users appropriate prompts and controls that can immediately clarify a particular node of information, including the ability to retrace previous actions, view a high-level informational map, provide context-sensitive help, relevant examples, and the like. Others use familiar metaphors in order to present the user interface, some of the most popular being representations of books or folders. Consideration of color is also important: Users generally prefer the use of dark text on a light background, perhaps because it is most reminiscent of printed matter. Font size can also improve legibility, although there is obviously a usability trade-off between the amount of information that can be comfortably conveyed without scrolling and the actual size of the font being used.

If the online documentation system is part of a multifaceted windows environment that includes troubleshooting, contact tracking, customer profiling, ordering, and so forth, then the documentation engineers must consider the fact that most users will see only a fraction of the document unless they choose to maximize the window. Most customer care agents prefer this overlapping approach, as it allows them to quickly switch to other applications without interrupting the flow of the customer contact.

The online documentation system might also be capable of displaying several windows at the same time (i.e., allowing the user to request new information without necessarily losing the data already displayed). This can be important when an agent concludes a call, but has no time to complete after call work before dealing with another contact. It does, however, quickly clutter the screen and can be a distraction, especially to less-experienced users. Allowing users to manipulate the windows as part of screen management is considered essential in such cases.

The online display of information is considerably smaller and less visible than the printed page. It is therefore necessary that the user interface is as intuitive as possible. This means using familiar metaphors, appropriate colors, legible text, and carefully designed screen displays to help the user quickly find and assimilate information.

Database Design

Information retrieval systems are expected to do much more than simply attempt to satisfy the concept of the paperless office. Taking manuals and other reference materials off the desktop and putting their contents into a computer database is possibly one way of making a customer care environment *look* more efficient, but it may not have a positive effect on productivity, particularly if the agents are used to referencing documents of various shapes and colors in order to resolve particular problems and inquiries. Obviously, the database needs some sort of "front-end" user interface in order to communicate its contents to users in a way that fits their paradigm, or at least is intuitive enough to enable them to capably find the information they are seeking. Usually, this requires a search field, into which the user may type a query, or populate by selecting from a list of predefined search criteria.

Most search fields for both online documentation and troubleshooting systems require users to enter key words in order to retrieve data. Using Boolean logic for multiple key words (usually the conjunction AND, as in "Natural (AND) Language," which will retrieve only those instances where both words occur sequentially in the database), the system will then attempt to match the precise characteristics of the user input with the contents of the database. Any misspellings, or in some cases failure to match upper and lower case, will result in an erroneous match or no match at all. More sophisticated search mechanisms use language parsers and multiple permutations of characters in order to enable the user not only to type in a complete phrase or sentence, but also to misspell words without being penalized. On the other end of the scale, some search mechanisms constrain the user to select from a predefined list of possibilities, thus ensuring that the data are always matched. The problem with this approach, of course, is that the user must scroll through a potentially lengthy list of options and choose the one that seems to fit the inquiry or complaint.

From the system designer's perspective, a key question is whether or not to partition the database in order to make the search facility not only more *responsive,* but also more apt to find matches that are *relevant* to the user's particular needs. For example, it seems to make sense that a company with twenty products would want twenty partitions in the database in order to make a search for information on a particular product more efficient. If, however, several of those products share similar traits, then some consideration might be given to sharing the information across the entire database, rather than repeating it for every product. Similarly, an information retrieval system for a service that deals with several different types of information, such as user instructions, policies and procedures, error messages, and the like, might also require a partitioned database.

The decision whether or not to partition a database is clearly going to impact the user interface. Somehow, the user must indicate the product or aspect of the service upon which he or she would like to conduct a search. This additional task (which may be accomplished by online selection from a predefined list, or, in the case of computer-telephony integration applications, by a caller via the interactive voice response unit) may be so cumbersome as to negate the positive impacts of the partition. In general, it is fair to say that a user does not want to have to worry about whether or not he has chosen the right subject matter or she has keyed in the right product number prior to conducting a search. In other words, partitioning should be avoided if at all possible.

Unfortunately, the decision to partition a database is often made long before the first customer contact. It is also a decision that, once implemented, is highly unlikely to change. Regardless of whether or not it is ultimately determined that there was really no need to physically separate user instructions from policies and procedures because searches on both subjects are almost always mutually exclusive, the database design, for reasons of time and money, will almost always remain immutable.

It is critical, therefore, that database design decisions are not made unilaterally by the development organization. Input from knowledge and documentation engineers is clearly a prerequisite, but more importantly, test cases should be built to ensure that any consideration of partitioning will not only facilitate the database administrators, but also reward the users in terms of ease of use, speed of response, and relevance of search.

Empowerment

Agents rarely have the decision-making ability to resolve *every* customer's request on the first point of contact. This has long been a divisive issue in voice-to-voice customer care environments, where the agent must often make an "on-the-spot" decision based solely on company policy rather than a judgment call based on any extenuating circumstances described by the customer. As such, inappropriate company guidelines can cause havoc with customer care service levels, as agents attempt to transfer callers to empowered internal help desk specialists, or are forced to create customer callback commitments. Furthermore, if the agent perceives that the company guideline is unfair or biased in any way, it can greatly affect job satisfaction and on-the-job stress levels. As such, agents who handle voice-to-voice calls need timely support mechanisms and feedback channels to present "cases" of what they perceive as unfair or restrictive practices to management. Those who handle inquiries and complaints through alternative media, on the other hand, have the comparative luxury of being able to pursue a resolution to each customer communication without having the customer waiting impatiently on the line.

One of the most important reasons for usage of online tools in high-tech customer care environments is the fact that when an agent discovers a new problem, the only way to share that information with the rest of the customer care team is through a commonly used system platform. The ultimate solution will be lost on 99 percent of the customer care population unless it is universally shared through a troubleshooting system, and in turn linked with related user instructions in online documentation.

There is a concern that mandatory usage of online tools can cause the agents to become unthinking slaves to technology, incapable of using their own initiative to resolve a customer problem. Yet it can also be argued that there are so many new connotations, configurations, and interpretations that the agents will be grateful that they have a robust support tool in the form of an information retrieval system. The key to customer care management buy-in to this approach is the ability of the knowledge and documentation engineers to turn around new problems and solutions in a short period of time.

It is worth considering the following:

- Training can only cover a small percentage of troubleshooting issues.
- Online documentation systems will never substitute for an intelligent troubleshooting tool—these are most powerful when used in conjunction/support of such tools.
- If these tools are not available, agents will use individualistic and inconsistent workarounds.
- Agents need a robust feedback channel to challenge online tool accuracy/completeness.
- Requisite maintenance and provisioning of online tool solutions will necessitate additional resources.
- Separate and fully staffed teams are needed for new and existing service knowledge engineering endeavors.

It can reliably be surmised that, if agents do not use the online tools for virtually every call, the maintenance infrastructure will rapidly degenerate and these tools will be obsolete within a short period of time. This will result in higher escalation rates and increased talk-times. Furthermore, the agents need to know when a particular type of customer inquiry is beyond the scope of customer care, or when a certain call must be escalated to an internal help desk. The help desk solution to an escalated call should, wherever possible, then be provided to front line agents so that the same escalation is avoided in the future. Online tools represent the only way to ensure this in a high-volume, geographically dispersed customer care environment. Compulsory usage of an integrated expert system and online documentation solution will ensure consistency of response to all customers.

Cost/Benefit Analysis for an Information Retrieval System

Before making any decisions on system implementation, it is worth considering two perspectives with regard to the cost and benefit of online information retrieval systems. The first concerns the potential costs of *not* having an online system, and the second concerns the cost of having a poorly implemented and maintained system. From these scenarios, a model for the ideal information retrieval system emerges— one that gives users rapid and intuitive access to relevant, clear, complete, and accurate information, and one that automatically captures useful market intelligence and customer contact data.

Case Study: *A customer care environment without an information retrieval system:*

Take the example of a call center where a 900-page general reference manual is placed on every agent's desk. The manual contains virtually everything an agent needs to know in order to respond to a routine customer call, including contact criteria for every call type (such as handling complaints, misdirects, callbacks, etc.), pricing plans, repairs, distribution channels, troubleshooting information, user instructions, addresses and telephone numbers, and billing information, all neatly partitioned by colored tabs. Updates are issued each month in a shrink-wrapped package. There are often in excess of two hundred pages of updates, which results in a process whereby the agents are expected to remove outdated sheets and replace them with the new ones. Coupled with a "sweatshop" atmosphere in which the low-paid agents are responding to a continuous stream of telephone calls with virtually no permissible after call work or downtime, it is hardly surprising to observe several unopened packages in agents' desks and filing trays. In addition to this "handbook," agents also reference a series of job aids, newsletters, and other printed materials, such as vendor manuals. Television monitors are placed strategically around the call center, enabling agents to observe the latest product codes, price changes, and promotional activities. This facility is the closest the agents can get to real-time information sharing, the only problem being that they cannot control the way the information is presented on the screen, and often have to rely on scribbled notes or memory to recall that the price on a particular product had changed the previous day.

Scenario

• New agents receive eight weeks training, one of which is devoted to troubleshooting product or service problems.
• Agents reference the general manual in order to resolve customer inquiries and complaints. This manual contains information on policies and procedures, simple troubleshooting procedures, billing inquiries, product listings, promotional information, codes, forms, and useful names and addresses.
• The manual is updated on a monthly basis, at which time between 50 and 200 shrink-wrapped pages of revisions are distributed to every agent for insertion into various sections of the general manual.
• Any customer-affecting changes that occur during the month are dynamically displayed on monitors situated through the call center.
• Complex troubleshooting procedures are contained in a separate technical manual compiled by product or service engineers.
• New agents tend to escalate difficult troubleshooting contacts or ask their peers for assistance rather than use the technical manual.
• Agents refer to cheat sheets and other job aids for information that is not contained in the manuals, but is occasionally needed by customers.

• Agents reference individual customer information booklets in order to describe procedural instructions for products or services to customers. These booklets include graphical depictions of more complex procedures.
• Agents use an online contact tracking system in order to select one from a predefined list of 115 reasons why the customer contacted the company and to personally create more detailed notes about the nature of the contact.
• A weekly newsletter advises agents of any ongoing administrative activities and events.
• There is no online database of information available to customers via the World Wide Web, and the call center handles 100 percent of all customer contacts.

A hypothetical, though not exceptional, depiction of this scenario (which is used purely to demonstrate the high cost of information in offline environments dealing with relatively complex customer contacts) could be represented as follows:

Relevancies

Average daily contacts:	13,645
Average speed of answer (ASA):	1 minute 26 seconds
Average talk time (ATT):	6 minutes 12 seconds
Average after call work (ACW):	1 minute 45 seconds
Resolved on first contact (ROFC):	85%
Total agents:	242
Occupancy (8 hours)	85%

Average contact times by agent category

Expert agents (> 18 months experience):	3 minutes 10 seconds/ 15% of the workforce
Proficient agents (6–18 months experience):	4 minutes 35 seconds/ 28% of the workforce
New agents (< 6 months experience):	8 minutes 23 seconds/ 57% of the workforce

Call distribution

Billing Inquiry:	40% (92% ROFC / 4 minutes 10 seconds ATT/ 45 seconds ACW)
Troubleshooting:	29% (71% ROFC / 10 minutes 24 seconds ATT/ 2 minutes 03 seconds ACW)
General Inquiry:	18% (88% ROFC / 7 minutes 10 seconds ATT/ 1 minute 56 seconds ACW)
Other:	13% (86% ROFC / 3 minutes 12 seconds ATT/ 32 seconds ACW)

Continued

| Repeat calls: | 8% (customer callbacks due to outstanding problems, erroneous information, etc.) |

Potential Savings

Based on these metrics, it is apparent that although troubleshooting calls constitute only 29 percent of all customer contacts, these calls are *more than twice as long* as the majority of other contacts, which accounts for many of the long hold times experienced during peak hours. They are also considerably less likely to be resolved on first contact than other types of calls. These figures suggest that most agents, particularly new agents (who constitute more than half of the workforce), are having considerable difficulty locating, assimilating, and conveying troubleshooting information. The excessively long after call work for troubleshooting calls also indicates that agents are spending a lot of time creating trouble tickets (almost one in every three troubleshooting contacts is escalated) and inputting a detailed explanation of the customer's problem. General inquiry contact times also indicate a problem with immediately locating information and conveying it to the customer.

Further investigation of these contact times reveals the following:

- New agents are putting customers on hold one or more times during the course of a call in order to solicit peer feedback or scan manuals for problem resolutions.
- Expert and proficient agents are less apt to reference the general manual for updated information, resulting in customer callbacks due to erroneous information.
- The troubleshooting manual is used only by appointed technical specialists, who have more time to peruse its content.
- New agents are commonly escalating contacts for routine problems, thus overloading internal help desk resources and necessitating customer callbacks.
- Expert agents are using their own workarounds to resolve customer problems.
- All agents are spending excessive amounts of time verbally explaining step-by-step procedural instructions (e.g., product installation) to customers.
- All agents are spending between 30 and 165 seconds of after call work to compose notations relative to troubleshooting and general inquiry calls.
- Agent notations use inconsistent language and hinder useful root cause analysis.
- All agents are prone to incorrectly classify customer contacts or to select "Other" as a contact category.
- Some agents had several *months* of unopened updates on their desks.

It is evident that improvements in any or all of these scenarios would realize significant time savings, hence a reduction in cost per contact. Given that customer care management has determined a *cost per contact* of $3.95 (budget divided by the number of contacts, including prompts, transfers, contacts via voice mail, e-mail, fax, and letter) for the average 6 minutes 12 second contact and 1 minute 45 seconds of after call work, it can be surmised that the average troubleshooting contact is costing more than $6.00, while the average general inquiry contact is costing approximately $4.50. The question is how to affect the bottom line by reducing the time taken to deal with both troubleshooting and general inquiry contacts.

If an information retrieval system were to give all agents the ability to answer contacts *at expert levels,* and management decided to target a 20-second average speed of answer, the overall metrics would look something like this:

Relevancies

Average daily contacts:	13,645
Average speed of answer (ASA):	**20 seconds** (down from 1 minute 26 seconds)
Average talk time (ATT):	3 minutes 10 seconds
Average after call work (ACW):	0 minutes 28 seconds
Resolved on first contact (ROFC):	**95%** (up from 85%)
Total agents:	**121** (down from 242)
Occupancy (8 hours)	93%

It is not inconceivable that an outstanding information retrieval system could surpass what are perceived as expert levels by sharing information that would not normally be readily known to *any* agent, such as special promotions, upcoming release dates, recently discovered problems with new products, etc. This type of useful intelligence can ensure the success of the system by convincing even expert agents that it is always worth double-checking to ensure the veracity of their responses.

The above figures indicate that the average speed of answer has been reduced to an acceptable level, while the number of agents required to handle contacts has dropped by 50 percent. If each agent were paid $25,000 per annum on average, for example, the total *unloaded* salary cost savings for the customer care environment would be in the region of $3 million per year. Coupled with increased customer satisfaction and greater market intelligence through system-facilitated root cause analysis, it could be surmised that the return on investment for an outstandingly well-planned and maintained information retrieval system could be extremely rapid. Realistically, it can take several months for some users to become extremely comfortable with the paradigm shift from paper documentation to information retrieval systems, although the ubiquity of the personal computer is doing much to allay this transitional period.

Continued

Example—Initial Reductions in Customer Contacts

The previous metrics indicate that even a reduction of one minute in trouble-shooting and general inquiry contact time for new agents would realize significant savings. This *should* be capably achieved by any information retrieval system that has been integrated with the contact tracking system and populated with useful and understandable content, purely by way of automatically capturing contact data and sharing information that would not normally have been available to new agents.

The underlying premise with the following example is that even at a relatively high level (i.e., not considering the reduction in talk-time as a result of an information retrieval system), delays and repeat contacts for troubleshooting and general inquiries can be significantly reduced or eliminated. Such a system should be viably expected to reduce or eliminate all of the following costs, including

- Contacts placed on hold after reaching an agent
- Routine escalations
- Customer callbacks due to the conveyance of inaccurate or incomplete information
- Erroneous contact classifications
- Excessive amounts of time spent on after call work, such as notations

All of these cost-affecting factors could therefore be classified as potentially *unnecessary* overheads, particularly in the case of new agents, who constitute 57 percent of the workforce:

Relevancies

Average daily troubleshooting contacts: 3,957* (29% of 13,645 total contacts)

    * Expert agents (593)
      Proficient agents (1,108)
      New agents (2,256)

Average daily general inquiry contacts: 2,456* (18% of 13,645 total contacts)

    * Expert agents (368)
      Proficient agents (688)
      New agents (1,400)

- Average time customer is placed on hold *after* reaching an agent (agents requesting peer feedback, looking up information in paper documents, etc.):

	Troubleshooting	General Inquiry
Expert agents:	5.2 secs (3,083 secs)	2.0 secs (736 secs)
Proficient agents:	10.5 secs (11,634 secs)	5.1 secs (3,508 secs)
New agents:	19.5 secs (43,992 secs)	10.3 secs (14,420 secs)
Average Daily Totals:	58,709 secs	18,664 secs

- Repeat customer calls due to inaccurate or incomplete information (agent failure to update manuals, attempting to troubleshoot problems using documentation, etc.):

	Troubleshooting	General Inquiry
	7.5% (297 calls)	2.3% (56 calls)
Average Daily Totals:	220,968 secs	30,240 secs

- Repeat customer calls or callbacks due to offline escalations (cryptic troubleshooting scenarios, internal help desk overwhelmed with escalations, etc.):

	Troubleshooting	General Inquiry
Escalations :	29% of 3,957 calls	12% of 2,456 calls
	(Total: 1,147 calls)	(Total: 295 calls)
	15.1% (173 calls)	7.8% (23 calls)
Average Daily Totals:	128,712 secs	12,240 secs

- Overall totals:

	Troubleshooting	General Inquiry
Agent hold times	58,709 secs	18,644 secs
Inaccurate/incomplete	220,968 secs	30,240 secs
Callbacks	58,709 secs	18,644 secs
Daily Totals:	338,386 secs	67,528 secs
	94 hours	**18 hrs 45 mins**

These figures indicate that *even without considering reductions in actual talk time,* an effective information retrieval system could save this customer care environment as much as 112 hours of contact time each day. That is not to suggest that all escalations can be eliminated by an information retrieval system, but rather that the goal should be to first feedback company-approved policies and solutions to frontline agents, and secondly to eliminate the need for such contacts by feeding back critical product or service data to product management and marketing.

Also, the emergence of the World Wide Web as a viable medium for direct customer-to-information retrieval system interaction will continue to reduce the number of human-to-human customer contacts. Each of these cost saving

Continued

practices might be applied to further reducing the average speed of answer or necessary agent positions.

Another cost saving facilitated by deploying an information retrieval system is that of materials. It is far easier to make a simple online change than to distribute potentially hundreds of pages of updates in paper form each month. Instead of agents having to insert these updates into various locations in their reference guides, the changes are made directly into the database. This can realize thousands of dollars in materials savings as well as avoiding unnecessary and time-intensive labor for the agents (who have to insert sometimes hundreds of pages into bulky general reference manuals each month).

While the preceding example attempted to demonstrate an ideal cost/benefit for implementing an information retrieval system, there are obviously significant expenditures involved in both implementing and maintaining such a system. The following case study illustrates both the specific benefits and potential costs realized as a result of full-scale deployment.

 Case Study: *A customer care environment with a functionally outstanding and well-maintained information retrieval system*

Although the call center cited in the previous case study had implemented a superb eight-week training curriculum for new agents, low salaries and high stress contributed to a yearly turnover rate of almost 40 percent. With average talk times in excess of six minutes, and calls to the 242-agent center expected to reach six million (a two-year increase of 30 percent) due to new product releases, management decided to implement a complete online solution, including an information retrieval system. The cumulative result was not only a reduction of 50 percent in talk times, but also a 28 percent drop in agent turnover. A critical contributor to the success of the implementation was the management decision to support the switch to the information retrieval system by involving the agent population from the outset.

A core team of highly regarded supervisors was chosen to work full-time with the system designers and developers, while pilot groups of agents were involved with usability testing and focus group sessions. Agent feedback from these sessions was posted prominently at the call center. Designers and human factors analysts attended new agent training sessions and spent several days observing agents interacting with customers. Teams of in-house knowledge and maintenance engineers were trained by the development organization to ensure a smooth transition of content maintenance after deployment. The initial prototype design was explained and demonstrated to every agent and manager in the organization.

Overall, such a universally positive attitude was cultivated toward the new system that by the time it was deployed the critical management decision to make its usage *mandatory* for all agents met with no resistance. Robust maintenance processes and agent feedback loops ensured that missing or erroneous information was quickly rectified. Agents were encouraged by the fact that they could see the results of their feedback incorporated within forty eight-hours. If the feedback was invalid, the agent was advised by a peer chosen to attend the quality improvement team's maintenance sessions. No supervisors were involved in these sessions, to encourage full agent participation.

From the customer care perspective, the new system not only lowered talk-times (and consequently improved call center access), but also ensured a consistency of response that deterred unnecessary callbacks and escalations. Any escalated calls were analyzed and classified as agent training issues, content issues, or unavoidable. Processes were put in place to deal with all three scenarios. Overall, the system successfully achieved the business drivers of customer satisfaction and cost reduction.

Contingencies for an Outstanding Information Retrieval System

- Customer care management fully supports and advocates usage of the system for all agents.
- Agents are recognized for providing critical feedback on system functionality and content accuracy.
- A modified version of the system is deployed on the World Wide Web to offload routine customer inquiries and complaints.
- Some of the most common customer questions are scripted on the interactive voice response unit to further offload customer contacts.
- The system is designed and developed in collaboration with the user community through task analysis, rapid prototyping, and usability testing.
- The system is easy to use and responds to user requests within an acceptable time frame.
- The troubleshooting system and the online documentation system are integrated in order to enable users to access procedural information after resolving a problem.
- The online documentation system is linked with e-mail and fax applications to facilitate the electronic delivery of information to customers.
- Relevant data from user interaction with the troubleshooting system and online documentation system are automatically captured by the contact tracking system.
- The system facilitates root cause analysis by reporting contact information in a consistent and reliable way.
- Embedded applications, such as online help, system messages, and context-sensitive scripts, are written and presented in a way that users can easily understand.

Continued

- Knowledge acquisition for the system is limited to the scope of customer care support as defined by management.
- Knowledge engineering of system content is subjected to continual user feedback and testing.
- Documentation engineers work closely with users to determine optimal information presentation from the perspective of relevance, structure, style, and vocabulary.
- Erroneous or missing information is identified from reports and user feedback and rectified by a team of maintenance engineers within 24 hours.
- Training issues are identified on a daily basis by a quality improvement team.
- Robust informational links exist between the maintenance engineers, customer care management, marketing, product management, and legal entities.

Costs

Implementation costs for the system described above can vary significantly. A customized troubleshooting and online documentation solution, for example, can take months or even years to develop and may cost millions of dollars, whereas an off-the-shelf system costing considerably less may simply require high-level integration in order to meet the needs of the customer care environment. Obviously, it is more desirable to build a customized solution that fully meets the needs of management and users, which is unlikely to be the case with a loosely integrated off-the-shelf software approach.

One customer care group spent over four million dollars to revamp their outdated and inadequate troubleshooting system in order to implement a sophisticated knowledge-based system, which a vendor developed from scratch. While the end-product produced the desired effect (i.e., reducing troubleshooting contact times by over 50 percent), a number of similar products were already available in the commercial marketplace, a fact that was not fully exploited during the initial negotiations. In retrospect it is not inconceivable that customizing some of the functions of an existent product might also have produced the same result faster and more cost-effectively. In other words, although management made a decision that realized a rapid return on investment, it was unable to make an *informed* decision based on the facts that were made available.

It is fair to say that, with dozens of off-the-shelf, customizable intelligent troubleshooting tools available today, that there is probably a solution that could be applied to any customer care environment. There is also an abundance of online documentation systems available, although the difference between the high- and low-end systems is significant. Some of these tools are extremely sophisticated and lend themselves well to integration with other online systems, whereas others operate best simply as stand-alone applications.

Specific examples of requirements that would affect the cost of implementing an information retrieval system are as follows:

- *Direct links between the information retrieval systems and the contact tracking system for both management reporting and historical purposes*

Useful reports are the bane of most customer care environments. Large amounts of valuable market intelligence often go virtually unnoticed because contact categorizations and notes failed to adequately capture the true nature of the customer contact. In such cases, root cause analysis is, if not virtually impossible, at least extremely time-consuming and work-intensive.

Failure to integrate online content and contact tracking systems can also present a significant problem when customers call back concerning a previous contact. It often means that an agent must virtually recreate the former scenario before being able to adequately assist the customer. Next to long queue times, this can be one of the greatest causes of customer dissatisfaction. When coupled with an already irate customer due to a perceived failure of the product or service, the effect can be disastrous for both the agent and the company image.

In this case the system must provide information to the contact tracking system, which describes specific elements of the user's interaction that may be considered essential for reporting and tracking purposes. For example, for contact tracking purposes the system may capture the fact that the user utilized the troubleshooting system for a particular product at a particular time and date. The system may also allow the user to later reconvene an incomplete troubleshooting session by initiating the session directly from the contact tracking application.

For reporting purposes, the system might also capture the reason for the troubleshooting session (i.e., the problem statement as indicated by the user) for root cause analysis purposes. This would preclude the user from having to enter the problem statement twice, that is, once in the troubleshooting system itself, and once in the contact notes field.

Highly integrated systems will track user activity in an information retrieval system in order to suggest the most appropriate categorization for a particular contact. This is especially critical as more systems migrate to direct customer–database interaction media, such as the World Wide Web. By automating contact categorization in this way, management can obtain more accurate reports on customer complaints and inquiries. In agent-mediated environments such as call centers, this can preclude the agent from having to painstakingly search potentially hundreds of options for the correct category.

Another key area that can be facilitated by information retrieval system–contact tracking system integration is that of notations. One of the biggest problems in conducting root cause analysis for particular customer contacts is the inconsistency or nonexistence of explanatory notations to support the overall contact categorization. By automatically capturing the title of a particular node of text from an online documentation system that was visited by a user, for example, the system can capture notes that are consistent and immediately useful in conducting analysis.

• *A direct link from specific questions or answers in a troubleshooting system to a specific node of text in an online documentation system*

It is important to remember that troubleshooting systems, whether regarded as expert systems, decision support systems, case-based reasoning systems, and so forth, are intended only to suggest solutions, not to give a detailed description of a procedure that might be associated with a particular solution—that is the task of the online documentation system.

If, for example, a troubleshooting system suggested a particular solution based upon user input, the user should be able to link from that solution to a node of text that explains in more detail how to implement the suggested solution. This requires some form of dynamic link or exchange to be described between the two applications.

• *Rapid conveyance, facilitated by the online documentation system, of procedural information to a customer via alternative electronic channels, such as e-mail and fax*

There are few tasks more time-consuming for the customer care agent than trying to verbally describe a complex procedure to a customer. This process can easily add several minutes to any call as the customer scribbles down the procedure or even tries to effect a solution while the agent is on the phone.

The proliferation of home computers and telecommuting employees has also meant that more and more people are capable of receiving information via modem or fax. Optimally, customers who have subscribed to emerging customer care platforms such as the World Wide Web will also have the facility to receive e-mail and fax correspondence.

By affording the user the capability of automatically attaching a node of documentation to a preformatted e-mail or fax that has already populated the customer's name and number, an information retrieval system can immediately relieve an agent of a significant chore, while also eliminating any verbal misunderstandings that may occur during the course of information transfer.

• *Real time information retrieval system reports to facilitate root cause analysis and content provisioning*

A fully integrated information retrieval system could also serve as a powerful medium for real-time root cause analysis and content provisioning. Typically, customer care managers whose agents handle thousands of contacts each day cannot immediately identify any new problems. Instead, it may be days or even weeks (if at all) before anyone notices that an unusually large number of contacts were made regarding a particular aspect of the product or service on a particular date. A call center suddenly receiving multiple calls about a particular problem, for example, should be able to use real-time reports from the information retrieval system to pinpoint nodes of text that are experiencing an unusually large number of "hits" at that particular time. This can result in efficient crisis communications between the call center and the rest of the organization. Product management can be immediately alerted that a new product batch may be deficient, for example, and a policy decision can be made and conveyed to customer care immediately. This type of communication not only enhances the status of customer care in the organization, it also ensures that customers are treated equitably in the event of an unforeseen problem.

- *Automatically created trouble tickets and, if necessary, schedule callbacks, for escalated troubleshooting contacts*

When a user decides that the troubleshooting system does not contain the resolution to a particular problem, it is usual either to escalate that contact by means of a direct or online transfer to an internal help desk group, or to conduct an offline escalation by either creating a trouble ticket and scheduling a callback (in the case of an agent), or by creating and sending a trouble ticket directly from a World Wide Web site (in the case of a customer).

Escalated contacts can often mean a significant amount of work for agents. The agent has not only to make notations in the contact tracking system, but also to create a separate trouble ticket, complete with notes and other necessary data, which is then sent to internal help desk support. If a customer callback is required, the agent may open a stand-alone "tickler" application and schedule the time, date, and reason for the callback.

In many systems, even if the trouble ticketing application is somewhat integrated with the contact tracking system (e.g., transfer of customer name, contact number, date, etc.), it is usual for the tickler system to be completely isolated, which makes it easier for agents to scribble a note about a customer callback than to bother with the system.

While these requirements clearly involve some challenging and potentially expensive systems integration work, the price of ignoring them can be extremely high. Due to the complexity of molding several customer care systems together, it is not unusual for most of these to be classified as next-generation "nice-to-have-if-we-ever-have-the-money" tasks. Instead of a seamless operation, agents are most often forced to use each system as a separate entity, resulting in significant amounts of redundant work, erroneous contact categorizations, inconsistent notations, and convoluted mechanisms for sending data electronically to customers.

Apart from systems development and integration, another major cost consideration of an information retrieval system is that of content provisioning and maintenance. Unlike paper documentation, which requires technical writing and editing skills, the tasks of creating content for both troubleshooting and online documentation are multifaceted. These tasks involve (1) careful analysis and design in addition to writing and editing, (2) in many cases knowledge of a high-level programming language, (3) collaboration with systems developers, and (4) constant monitoring and stringent upkeep. Those who perform these tasks are called knowledge and documentation engineers, and it is their job to get relevant, understandable, accurate, and complete information to the user whenever it is requested.

The factors effecting the size of the knowledge and documentation engineering team include consideration of the domains requiring support, the rate at which the company intends deploying new products or services, and whether or not the company expects an initial knowledge base release with, for example, 100 percent readiness (i.e., all known problems and inquiries included) in concurrence with the release of a product or service. If the rate of new product introduction is lower than expected, the staffing level would drop accordingly.

After new product or service deployment, the knowledge and documentation engineers shift their focus to maintenance. This involves collaborating closely with users, trainers, and systems developers to ensure that the information retrieval system is meeting the business goals of reduced costs and increased customer satisfaction. At this point, much of the budget for the new system has been exhausted, and it is not unusual for customer care managers to view the knowledge and documentation engineers as a liability, in the sense that they are often funded through an operational budget that has been developed around agent salaries, rather than content provisioning or system maintenance. Those who understand the need for continuous iteration and improvement of the information retrieval system, however, will have ensured that adequate support is provided for these critical tasks.

9

Knowledge Management

Overview

Content provisioning for online information retrieval systems (see Figure 9.1) is usually the responsibility of one or more individuals recognized for their excellence in gathering and formalizing data from several sources for the purpose of answering customer inquiries and complaints. The process of *knowledge acquisition* (see Figure 9.2), for example, is one of the first steps in gathering the information that the customer care environment will need to achieve this goal. Working within the boundaries defined by management, the knowledge acquisition or content improvement team will often interview experts as well as utilize reference materials in order to create an initial repository of information, which will later be augmented by studying the type of contacts being initiated by customers. If it is a new product or service offering, this information base may be used by trainers in parallel with content engineers who, in fairly complex environments, may split their responsibilities between *knowledge* and *documentation engineering*. Knowledge engineers, who may also be acting as knowledge acquisition specialists, are responsible for formatting the information into a structure that can be recognized by the troubleshooting system. Documentation engineers perform a similar task in order to populate the online documentation system. In customer care environments that have implemented both troubleshooting and online documentation systems, these teams will work closely to ensure that links exist between a given troubleshooting remedy and its correlating online documentation procedure.

Defining the structure of online information for customer care can be far more demanding than other disciplines. This is because the predominant form of customer care is voice-to-voice interaction with the customer, and it is therefore critical that the agent is able not only to rapidly retrieve the information being sought, but also to understand that information and convey it to the customer immediately. There is no

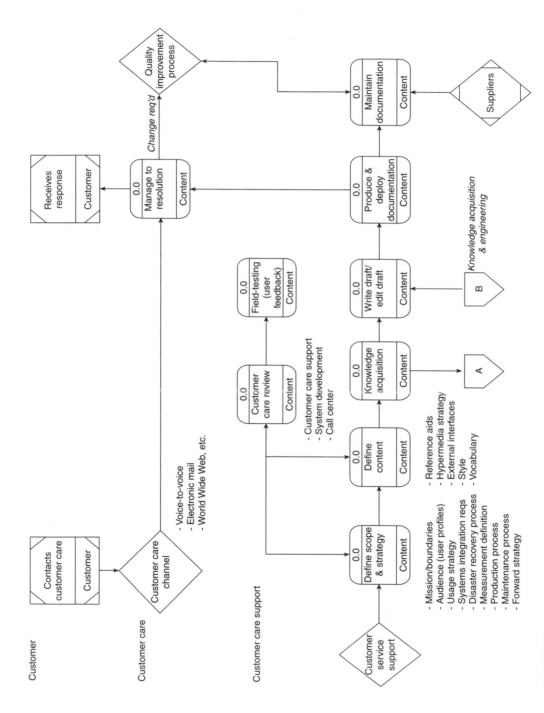

Customer

Customer care

Customer care support

■ **FIGURE 9.1** Knowledge Management

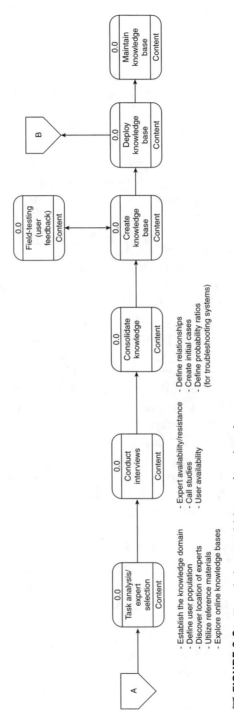

FIGURE 9.2 Knowledge acquisition and engineering

Task analysis/ expert selection
0.0
Content

- Establish the knowledge domain
- Define user population
- Discover location of experts
- Utilize reference materials
- Explore online knowledge bases

Conduct interviews
0.0
Content

- Expert availability/resistance
- Call studies
- User availability

Consolidate knowledge
0.0
Content

- Define relationships
- Create initial cases
- Define probability ratios (for troubleshooting systems)

Create knowledge base
0.0
Content

Field-testing (user feedback)
0.0
Content

Deploy knowledge base
0.0
Content

Maintain knowledge base
0.0
Content

A

B

time for the agent to ponder the functions of a poorly designed or unresponsive interface, wade through cryptic prose, or assimilate complex explanations. The information must be presented in a manner that is immediately decipherable, and any cross-references must be carefully designed to follow the normal flow of a particular customer inquiry or complaint.

After the strategy for providing content has been defined, those who specialize in the presentation of computerized information to users must define the optimal structure for that information based upon the tasks the user will have to perform. While hard copy documentation generally conforms to a linear structure, the presentation of online information is limited only by software-driven user interface capabilities.

Most online documentation packages provide hypermedia capabilities in order to present information. Basically this facilitates nonsequential user interaction. In other words, the user is able to quickly read the information contained in a *node* of text, for example, before either concluding the interaction or alternatively *linking* from that node to another node of related text or graphics. It is the job of the documentation engineer to determine exactly what should be conveyed by a specific node of text, and what linkages should exist from that node to another. However, while it may be relatively easy to change the *content* of a node, the actual *presentation* of the information, or user interface, is a strategic design decision which, once made, is unlikely to change—particularly since software *maintenance* constitutes a minor portion of most customer care budgetary allocations. Instead, users will often have to wait for the next generation of technological change to be championed by senior management.

The content structure of an *information retrieval system* clearly depends upon the purpose for which it was justified in the first place. If the system is intended to serve only as a back-up for highly trained agents, it should contain information that the agents could not normally be expected to know, such as product prices affected by the latest promotional activity, or a flaw in a particular product batch, or a recent change in company policy—in other words, changes so recent or so complex that they do not exist in the training curriculum. It is virtually pointless to include standard user procedures and troubleshooting materials in systems that users are not obligated to access; the absence of robust user feedback would render such an effort obsolete within a short period of time. It is important, therefore, to specify exactly *what* the information retrieval system will be used for, as well as *how* it will be used.

The Drivers of Content Processes

It is reasonable to assume that every content process, from systems design and development to actual online content, should be driven by *at least one* of the key properties of successful information retrieval systems. At the highest level this might be depicted as in Table 9.1.

Clearly, there are two distinct tasks involved with the deployment of any information retrieval system. The first involves the system designers and developers as discussed previously, and the second involves the knowledge and documentation engi-

▨ TABLE 9.1.   Key properties of information retrieval systems.

Process/Property	Accessibility	Integration	Relevance	Clarity	Integrity
Develop System	✓	✓			
Provide Content			✓	✓	✓

neers (see Table 9.1). In order to present a complete solution, both must actively involve the users—first in system design through rapid prototyping, usage observation, and usability testing, and secondly in knowledge management through continuous field testing.

For users, the transition to information retrieval systems rarely happens overnight. For some customer care environments it never happens at all, even when the company spends a million dollars to implement the technology. There is a distinct possibility that the system may fail from the outset if management does not vigorously advocate usage of the system, and if users are not innately involved with every decision concerning accessibility, integration, and content structure. Expert agents, for example, wield considerable power in call centers and can be one of the biggest obstacles to overall user acceptance of an information retrieval system. By collaborating with these users through the design and knowledge engineering cycle, and by listening to ongoing user feedback after deployment, an implementation team can help to ensure the success of a system. Users who have effected change need to be recognized, and their help is certainly needed in order to ensure the continuous improvement of a information retrieval system.

Documentation Engineering

In the case of an information retrieval system it is usual for the manufacturers of high-end off-the-shelf products to allow customization of the user interface using templates. This enables the creation of a standard placeholder for all information retrieved from the database, in addition to useful functional elements such as fast keys. Thoughtfully designed user interfaces for information retrieval systems in call centers, for example, require functions and displays that consider the logical flow of a typical customer contact, in addition to considerations of the optimal amount of textual information a user can assimilate while interacting verbally with a customer.

In most cases, decisions relevant to the structure of an information retrieval system may be made long before the first user interaction takes place. A development team working with an off-the-shelf application, for example, may appoint a technically focused individual to design the user interface and decide upon an appropriate structure for inputting content before deploying the application on a server, in order that the documentation team can begin their work. This is especially true when the documentation team is composed purely of technical writers, rather than experienced "documentation engineers" who specialize not only in written communication, but also in hypermedia strategies and high-level programming.

Case in Point: Potential Problems with Online Documentation

One system involved a developer who had never observed agents interacting with customers, but had been given the task of mastering the information retrieval system, developing a feasible structure, and handing off the finished product to a documentation team so that they could input the initial content for deployment at the remotely located call center. The developer was extremely proficient and was able to rapidly program the system in what appeared to be a logical online documentation structure consisting of several "books," including product information, user instructions, error messages, policies and procedures, billing information, pricing, and so forth. Given that management had decided not to implement a troubleshooting system, there was also a "troubleshooting" book. The documentation team, who were excellent technical writers but not familiar with information retrieval systems, adopted the developer's structure and slotted relevant information into each book based on data received from the knowledge acquisition team. Within six weeks, the system had been successfully tested for functional response times and subsequently deployed at the call center. Train-the-trainer sessions were conducted by the original developer, who, having completed the appointed task, was then assigned to another project. The documentation team was reduced to a single technical writer, whose job it was to input new product information as well as maintain the existing content. Both the developer and the documentation team were commended on being able to deploy the system ahead of schedule. The users subsequently received four hours of training on the new system before being requested to use it during customer contacts.

A number of significant problems surfaced when the agents began to use the system during contacts with customers. Although the initial response times were adequate, the books had been structured in such a way that it was necessary for the agent to enter their search criteria not once, but twice. The agent also had to choose the book they believed would answer their question before even embarking on the search. In most cases the agents found that their search criteria resulted in a "No matches found" response from the system. This might have been expected, given that in addition to being a new application, the content was written by individuals who had only visited the call center briefly on two occasions. Even when a match was found, the agents complained that the content rarely matched their needs. There was, however, no process in place for the agents to describe these oversights to the documentation engineer.

Those who attempted to use the information retrieval system in order to troubleshoot customer problems were observed to spend excessive amounts of time scrolling through what amounted to textual decision trees. It transpired that no one had learned how to import the graphical images that might have helped agents resolve these problems. An inherent flaw was the absence of an intelligent troubleshooting tool that would have precluded many futile and time-consuming searches, particularly by the less-experienced agents.

Continued

From a human factors perspective, the template structure was such that the content screens reminded agents of a page from a book that had been transposed online. In some cases, paragraphs in excess of three hundred words filled the screen, making it virtually impossible to assimilate the information while speaking with the customer. In others, the information structures and hypermedia linkages were so trivial that it made more sense to scroll down the screen than waste mouse clicks. There were no "speed buttons" or other visual queues to assist rapid online content. Several agents also complained that they could not read the text on the screen—white characters on a light green background—but suffice to say no one, including the remaining documentation engineer, knew how to change the color, so the problem remained.

Clearly, a feedback loop for content improvement, not to mention user interface design and overall functionality, was needed. The documentation engineer was enticed to visit the call center to listen to the agents and to observe them using the system. It was agreed that the online documentation should be rewritten based on input from call center specialists. These specialists, who were known as Tier II agents, were also being swamped with escalated calls, a situation that was being blamed on several factors, including the competence of the Tier I agents, the training curriculum, and to a certain extent the online documentation. After all, the agents were not obliged by management to use the books in the first place.

As instructed, the specialists attended several conference calls with the documentation engineer, as well as sending the engineer copies of the latest trouble ticket resolutions from escalated calls. The documentation engineer estimated a turnaround time of six weeks for this information. When this time frame was questioned, it transpired that the documentation engineer was also trying to keep up with a constant flow of information from a team of knowledge engineers, who were providing information on new product features. The obvious solution seemed to be that the company would employ additional resources to speed up the process. Unfortunately, there was not enough money in the maintenance budget to afford an expert in documentation engineering, so a promising clerical worker was temporarily promoted to assist. As a result, the turnaround time improved only marginally, the online documentation structure remained the same, and agents soon used the system only as a last resort, if at all.

Unfortunately, the relative shortage of actual documentation engineers (as opposed to technical writers) means that many well-intentioned information retrieval systems are doomed to failure from the outset. One major reason for this situation is that once a development team has decided upon what they believe to be the optimal structure for the system, the elapsed time between that decision and the actual deployment of the system in the "real world" usually makes it extremely difficult to rectify a substandard user interaction. In other words, a flawed structure that has already been adopted by a documentation team who are not technologically adept enough to know any better, soon becomes a maintenance issue that is never likely to get fixed.

The Role of the Documentation Engineer

Before information retrieval systems became a standard practice for progressive customer care environments, the task of providing information to agents and customers was relatively simple. Technical writers, whose key qualification was the ability to write well, would produce paper documentation consisting of user manuals, job aids, release notes, technical specifications, policies and procedures, and the like. Depending on the budget, this documentation might be sent to a graphic artist before being typeset and printed (or copied) and distributed as necessary. With the advent of commercial desktop publishing during the mid-to-late eighties, technical writers who adopted new skills as computer-assisted typesetters and designers became known as "documentation specialists." Meanwhile, online documentation began to flourish with new production media that used high-level programming languages and scripts to present information online. Hypertext and hypermedia finally became industry buzzwords, and online content was recognized as a most efficient and cost-effective way of distributing information to networked users. A subset of those technical writers who had become computer literate with desktop publishing now began to gravitate toward these information retrieval systems, and their proficiency with "mark-up" languages such as SGML and HTML, as well as their ability to present online information in an intuitive and user-friendly fashion, qualified them as "documentation engineers."

Many technical writers, however, found the quantum leap from written communication into information retrieval system development to be either unnecessary or implausible. As a result, documentation engineers who today are skilled in written communications and human factors engineering, and are also proficient in developing information retrieval systems, are a relatively rare breed. It is more likely that a decision to implement such a system will either necessitate the hiring of external specialists, or leave an in-house team of technical writers struggling to master hypermedia strategies while trying to create worthwhile content.

In most cases, the onus is not on the documentation engineer to actually gather information. It is rather that these individuals use their communication skills to act as a conduit for all relevant data that can be shared online with the users. In order to accomplish this task, the documentation engineer must become intimately familiar with the types of information users typically need, and how best to present that information given the environment in which it is retrieved. Highly pressured call center agents clearly have different presentation needs than those who respond to what are often more leisurely e-mail and fax requests. Customers browsing the World Wide Web, on the other hand, may appreciate a linear document that they can print easily, rather than one with several discrete nodes of text, and so forth.

Most information retrieval systems fall short of the ideal, mainly because no one takes responsibility for ensuring that the documentation engineers receive and process all of the information that is required by the end users. It is a situation that can be remedied by implementing a quality improvement team whose job it is to review daily contact reports and agent feedback, in addition to escalated contacts and trouble tickets. This kind of review process ensures that it is not long before someone realizes that the documentation engineers need robust lines of contact, not just with the knowledge acquisition/engineering team and the process owners, but also with marketing, product management, legal, partners, and vendors.

Typically, knowledge acquisition specialists and knowledge engineers will provide documentation engineers with user instructions for products and services and (in cases where the information retrieval system also acts as a troubleshooting tool) troubleshooting scenarios. Process owners provide information relative to policies and procedures, including process changes and advice on contacts that must be escalated, while marketing is relied upon to channel news of any promotional activities or price changes. Product management advises on strategic changes, partnership or vendor agreements, or new product or service offerings. Legal provides input on any company policy changes, in addition to reviewing online content for accuracy. Company organizational charts as well as internal and external contact information, such as telephone numbers, are monitored frequently for accuracy. In other words, anything that constitutes a legitimate customer care request should be catered to by the information retrieval system, and it is the responsibility of the documentation engineer to ensure that such information is reliably available when it is needed by the user.

In summary, the documentation engineer's primary focus should be designing online information in a manner that not only is *intuitive* to the user, but also enables the user to *rapidly access relevant data,* and quickly *assimilate* and *comprehend* the information that is presented on the screen. Obviously, it is critical that the information is *accurate*. However, given that inaccuracies and omissions will occur, the user must have a facile but robust and reliable way of feeding back this information to those who can effect revisions immediately. The emphasis for any documentation engineering effort, therefore, is on speed (of both retrieval and content maintenance), accuracy, and completeness.

Knowledge Engineering

Originally, the term "knowledge engineering" was used to describe the process of creating an expert system that contained a significant number of heuristics, or "rules of thumb." Twenty years ago, such systems were strictly the domain of computer scientists intent on breaking new ground in the realm of artificial intelligence. Over the years, these systems evolved into a proliferation of commercially available packages that provide what could be referred to as "content shells." In other words, these applications provide easy-to-use means of entering data that can later be used to troubleshoot problems. What this means is that today's "knowledge engineer" is generally more concerned with modeling information than developing software. In fact, many contemporary knowledge engineers have little or no programming background. Instead, these individuals employ outstanding interviewing and analysis skills to become "pseudo experts" for particular products or services.

Customer care environments that rely solely upon online documentation systems (as opposed to troubleshooting systems) in order to resolve customer problems may refer to those who formalize the information as "knowledge engineers." Yet, unlike troubleshooting systems, online documentation systems cannot be engineered to perform "interactive" or "intelligent" problem-solving sessions with users, therefore this task is more akin to documentation engineering. Regardless of the system limitations, however, the actual task of extracting knowledge and engineering it so that it can be inherently useful to nonexperts can be extremely difficult. Prior to deployment, relevant knowledge must be identified, assessed, designed, evaluated, redesigned and reevaluated. In other words, it can never be successfully transferred from an expert to a novice via an online system without rigorous intervention. It would, however, be foolish to imagine that any knowledge can be deployed in a 100 percent complete state. A decision must be made to deploy a "knowledge base" when it has reached an acceptable level of completeness. The rest is up to the quality improvement process.

The first task of any knowledge engineer is to understand the goal of acquiring the knowledge in the first place. Front-line customer care environments require access to knowledge that can be easily assimilated and conveyed to a customer. Highly competent customer care specialists (who often become the focal point for knowledge engineers) may require knowledge in a more detailed format, so that they can reach their own conclusions on a particular customer problem, rather than being hand-held through a troubleshooting scenario. Familiarization with both the scope and the audience is therefore one of the most important (and time-consuming tasks) of the knowledge engineer.

Knowledge engineers must then acquire information that belongs within the scope or "knowledge domain" that has been defined for a particular product or service. This task, which is known as *knowledge acquisition,* may involve observations, interviews, case studies, and the analysis of voluminous amounts of data. While it is often more time-consuming than anything else to actually gather content material, it is often extremely difficult to extrapolate data that can ultimately form the nucleus for meaningful troubleshooting and other online content mechanisms. This is because, unlike human experts, information systems are bereft of intuition or other subconscious processes: These systems rely on information that can be manipulated in certain ways in order to respond to user actions. Engineering information within the logical boundaries of these systems is therefore a task that requires continual testing and validation. The more information about a particular product or service that is entered into a troubleshooting system, for example, the more likely it is that, without stringent maintenance, the outputs will become convoluted and inaccurate.

Every outstanding knowledge engineer possesses a mixture of strong organizational skills, the ability to minimize fear and hostility on the part of the expert user, tact and diplomacy, persistence, and most of all empathy with the needs of the user community. By becoming cognizant of existing and potential customer problems with a particular product or service, the knowledge engineer strives to effect a quantum leap, rather than simply an incremental improvement, in user productivity.

Information Retrieval

Once the user has retrieved the information requested at the search level, it must be determined whether or not it is relevant to the inquiry or complaint. For example, a word search may retrieve multiple matches in a database, depending upon how the information is structured. In the case of an "intelligent" troubleshooting system, potential remedies may be accompanied by a series of clarifying questions, and the user may quickly choose what is considered to be the most relevant question based upon the known symptoms. An online documentation system, however, generally lacks the software-driven reasoning capabilities and singular purpose of the troubleshooting system, and therefore may present the user with a more cryptic challenge in establishing relevance. For example, an online documentation system with a completely open structure (i.e., a database that has not been partitioned to force the user to select a relevant area, such as policies and procedures, before conducting a search) may return matches in several nonapplicable areas, thus leaving it up to the user to determine relevance *after* the search. An open-ended search on "Installation," for example, may retrieve several matches in both the "Policies and procedures" and "User Instructions" sections of an online document. It would then be up to the user to determine which section to examine based on the context of the inquiry.

Obviously, a key consideration in establishing relevance is whether or not to compel the user to select a particular product or aspect of a service prior to conducting a search. This is a decision that requires rigorous analysis and cannot simply be made based on the fact that it was deemed most appropriate for another customer care environment. Factors such as database size and capacity, shared elements across products and services, mutually exclusive terminologies, and user sophistication must all be considered.

The following pages discuss the critical considerations behind every successful content provisioning endeavor. These include setting the boundaries or *scope* of the information to be made available to the agent and/or the customer, as well as the ability to quickly *search* for and retrieve relevant information. Other considerations include:

- Defining the *audience* structure and needs
- Determining the *usage strategy* for the information retrieval system
- Deciding the optimal visual *presentation* of online information
- Establishing an appropriate and consistent *vocabulary and style* for all content
- Ensuring the *integrity* of information being presented
- Verifying the *completeness* of the information
- Validating the *accuracy* of the information.

Scope

It is often far easier to broadly define what the customer care environment should support, rather than what should *not* be supported. This is a particular problem for agents who provide support for high-tech services, where the scope of support is much more difficult to establish. The natural tendency of the agent is to try and answer the customer's inquiry or complaint as quickly as possible, even if it appears to have a somewhat vague relationship to the service provided by the company. Inadequate training and supporting documentation can often mean that an agent will spend twenty minutes or more trying to resolve a problem that should have been referred elsewhere. While 80 percent of all customer questions may be perfectly legitimate, it is the remaining 20 percent that, in the absence of clear directives to agents, can wreak havoc with productivity.

It is critical that those who define the scope of customer care support, such as service strategists and product managers, work with customer care management in order to clarify service agreements with other companies and partners, and to define which type of contacts should be referred or escalated. This information should then be conveyed to trainers and knowledge engineers for inclusion in training curricula and online documentation. While it is unreasonable to assume that every contingency will be covered, both these media can be updated regularly by a stringent knowledge maintenance process. This methodology is particularly pertinent to online documentation, where agents can receive precise instructions on how to handle a particular type of contact. Similarly, customers using the Internet can be advised on potential resources for handling a inquiry or complaint that is beyond the scope of the customer care offering.

Failure to define the boundaries of the customer care offering from the outset can have ramifications that are felt for the entire life cycle of a product or service. For example, one service provider advised a team of knowledge engineers that customer care would support contacts on the usage of several products manufactured by other companies—the rationale being that the customer might need to use these products in association with the service offering. The knowledge engineers then began the process of acquiring knowledge on their assigned products and conveying their findings to the team assembled to produce online documentation. Six weeks later, during beta testing of the service, agents complained that they could never find relevant information by using the information retrieval system. The knowledge engineers retorted that they needed more time to complete the acquisition process. It was only when the training team, who had been developing their curriculum in parallel with the knowledge engineers, began examining the online documentation that they realized the majority of information had little relevance to the types of contacts the agents were receiving during beta testing. The reality was that the knowledge engineers, operating without boundaries or specific guidance, were attempting to document virtually every aspect of the products they had been assigned to research. It was estimated that for some of the more complex products a *further* four months work would have been required to complete the assignment. In the meantime, the agents would continue to struggle with volumes of irrelevant information, the obvious outcome being that the information retrieval system would be abandoned as useless long before the work was complete.

Without knowing the types of problems or inquiries customers may encounter with the rollout of the service, knowledge engineers must use their best judgment to determine the relevance of available information. Without being given guidelines as to scope, this can become a voluminous exercise in futility. In the absence of feedback, the knowledge engineers may be lulled into an erroneous assumption that the more information they can provide, the greater the chances that it will be of some relevance to the user.

It should be mentioned that in many organizations, knowledge engineers (like most systems developers) have no direct accountability to customer care management. Instead, they may work for a remote organization that rarely interacts with the customer. Their impetus, therefore, is not necessarily to be limited by discussions of scope, but rather to produce megabytes of information. This is precisely why the same knowledge engineers must be responsible for maintaining the veracity and relevance of their product by interacting directly with agents through a quality improvement initiative.

Searching

The most important aspect of any information retrieval system is the ability to interpret user input in order to retrieve relevant data. It is fair to say that the search mechanism is potentially the greatest bottleneck in the entire online customer care environment. After all, users may have ten or more different ways of formalizing a particular customer inquiry or problem. Not only are some search engines overtly clumsy and arcane, but the failure of the knowledge or documentation engineer to anticipate user syntax, coupled with the absence of adequate maintenance processes, can lead quickly to outright condemnation of the entire system.

Stated simply, many search facilities require case-sensitive, correctly spelled queries *that correspond precisely to those chosen by the engineer* in order to retrieve a *potentially* relevant node of text. The relative success of this situation depends largely upon the complexity of the product or service that is being supported. A high-technology service that is dependent upon several variables in order to function, for example, can be extremely difficult to support systematically. The user might search on one of a dozen symptoms, and even when a match is found the degree of relevance to the actual problem may be very low.

Some search mechanisms attempt to enable the user to use "natural language" type queries in order to construct a search. In other words, the user can type an entire sentence that describes the nature of the inquiry, and the system will attempt to retrieve useful data. Some of these mechanisms even allow the user to misspell words, use partial words, or even transpose an entire phrase. Most are not "true" natural language search engines, however, and rely on predefined synonyms, antonyms, noise words (i.e., words contained in a sentence that have no relevance to the actual meaning being conveyed, such as pronouns, articles, etc.), and matching sequences that enable the computer to scramble alphanumeric characters in a way that negates mismatches from typographical errors.

True natural language search mechanisms remain something of an enigma to the computer industry today. Although there are literally dozens of patents that describe the usage of natural language in computer systems, most require a great deal of time-consuming scoping and database predefinition in order to respond satisfactorily to users queries. Even then, the semantic quirks of a complex language like English, coupled with regional nuances, continue to make effective natural language interpretation the "holy grail" of the modern computer world.

Other search mechanisms force the user to select his or her search criteria from a predefined list of problems or inquiries. This precise methodology ensures relevance, but initially can be extremely cumbersome and time-consuming as the lists are searched for the word, term, or phrase that seems closest to the need being described. Some applications show the number of matches a particular search term would retrieve, which may help users to decide whether or not to pursue a particular avenue. Also, menus are sometimes used in place of long lists, thus enabling users to "build" a query. Unlike natural language type queries, both lists and menus are subjective and reflect only the engineer's interpretation of what constitutes valid search terminology.

Commonly, Boolean expressions ("and," "or," "not") are used to enable users to include certain key words or eliminate others from a search. Properly used, this approach can significantly improve the relevance of the system response. Wildcard queries can enable users to find partial matches for words and phrases, which can also help in narrowing the search focus. Other search mechanisms enable users to fine-tune a search by specifically matching upper case letters or even assigning emphasis or "weight" to certain words in a text string. Some systems keep a record of the most recent searches performed by the user, which can be especially useful in customer care environments where agents are assigned to specific products or service segments.

Audience

Another critical element in successful information retrieval systems is the cognizance of audience. There is no point in presenting the majority of customers with a direct transcript of the technical specifications for installing an upgrade to random access memory, for example. Nor does it make sense to preclude users from finding information because they used familiar jargon or dialect. Agents using online systems are normally "dual processing"—listening to the customer while concurrently trying to assimilate the content of the information that appears on the screen. Even if the agent is technically adept, it is difficult to both placate the customer and interpret cryptic information at the same time. Similarly, if the customer is given direct database access via the Internet in an effort to divert calls to customer care, it is important that the content presentation is written in a concise and easy to understand fashion. On the other hand, a documentation engineer who is writing a procedure for a technical specialist may adopt a much more detailed approach.

The rule of thumb with regard to the deployment of online information is to make the content as easy to read and understand as possible. The documentation engineer who has no customer care background should be given every opportunity not only to sit with the agents and listen to customer calls, but also to actually take calls and use the system to resolve problems and inquiries. Knowing the audience and appreciating their needs is key to producing usable content.

Clarity

Online information demands greater clarity than voice-imparted direction. Agents who are not making themselves understood can always attempt to repeat the same information in a different way. Documentation engineers, on the other hand, have just one chance to convey their message in an online medium such as the World Wide Web, before the customer picks up the phone and calls an agent. The contemporary irony is that even the customer who calls a toll-free number may get an agent who will ultimately search for, read, and interpret the same information that the customer just abandoned.

In an attempt to make online information more intuitive and useful to users, many off-the-shelf information retrieval systems incorporate hypermedia capabilities. Hypermedia-driven applications, properly designed, can improve the clarity of an online document by presenting users with discrete information linked to other relevant facts. Maintaining a hypermedia document in a dynamic environment, however, can involve a tremendous amount of work, which is why the documentation engineers for many customer care information retrieval systems would have been more effective if they had never attempted to implement this approach in the first place.

As stated, many documentation engineers are also driven by management goals that imply the measure of their worth is the *quantity* of information available online. Properly formatted, even the most nonsensical and cryptic technical writing can look adequate at a glance. In many cases, the documentation engineers themselves may have no real understanding of the information they are inputting. Tight deadlines and an absence of user testing can reduce the art of online documentation to an exercise in futility. Procedures that may contain a complete response to an inquiry are often so poorly written that they are never used. The pervasive attitude in some customer care environments is that as long as the information is correct, it does not matter if it's hard to understand. This situation generally guarantees the rapid demise of the information retrieval system.

Successful online documentation depends a great deal on the degree of empathy between the writer and the user. The best documentation engineers make it a point to "live" with their users, understanding the environment, becoming more familiar with the product or service and the type of jargon adopted, and requesting continuous feedback. Knowing the audience can be a significant driver of style and design. Just as it is difficult for developers to understand usability problems with a functionally outstanding application, it is easy for documentation engineers to become alienated from the true needs of their users. By testing and observing users and by listening to their comments, the documentation engineer is capable of allying many calls to customer care, and helping to resolve those calls that are made by providing clear and understandable documentation to the agent.

Usage Strategy

There is little doubt that an information retrieval system should be far superior to using paper documentation in a customer care environment. Yet many agents find it easier to use an assortment of cheat sheets, job aids, reference manuals, brochures, and marketing fliers scattered around their desks, than to try to find the answer to a customer inquiry or complaint using the information available on the computer. The proliferation of yellow "stick-it" sheets on the periphery of an agent's monitor are metaphorical tombstones that testify to the failure of an information retrieval system. There is no doubt that carefully designed, implemented, and maintained systems result in a response rate that surpasses any hard copy reference material. It also ensures that every agent has access to the same information. The success of these systems, however, is directly proportional to the significance and credibility that management affords them, and subsequently the commitment and expertise of those who maintain them.

Many customer care environments do not compel agents to refer to information retrieval systems when resolving a customer's inquiry or complaint. One good reason is that the system is often so poorly maintained that it doesn't contain any useful information. Even if a strong commitment to integrating, maintaining, and improving the system is made, some customer care managers consider obligatory usage of online systems to be synonymous with reducing the agents to mindless automatons, incapable of rationalizing a customer problem. Instead, the agents are given free reign to use their own judgment and recollection on any contact. If the agent needs a memory jogger, then it is his or her prerogative to conduct an online search to see if any information is available. The agent then makes a notation as to the nature of the contact and the proffered solution, and systematically closes the contact.

Conversely, some customer care managers insist that agents refer to the online documentation for every type of contact, regardless of whether the agent is highly experienced or otherwise. There are several contingencies associated with this strategy, yet properly implemented it makes a compelling business case. Again, there is no point in obligating agents to use the information retrieval system if it is poorly maintained. For the system to be truly useful, there must be a rapid rectification process on missing or erroneous information. This is normally achieved through a quality improvement team that has robust links to both customer and agent feedback. The information must also be meticulously engineered so that even the most inexperienced agents can rapidly find what they are seeking and convey it to the customer in a clear and concise manner. Finally, the system platform must support rapid information access. Even if all of the information is available and it is easy to find, a gap of ten seconds waiting for the system to respond can seem like an eternity to any agent. Poor system response invariably causes many information retrieval systems to fail.

Compelling agents to use the information retrieval system ensures a consistent quality of response to the customer. If the agent or the customer consider the response inadequate, then the content should be marked for assessment by the quality improvement team. In the interim, it leaves no one in any doubt about company policy, and can dissuade disgruntled customers from contacting the company repeatedly until they receive the answer they are seeking. If the customer becomes irate, the agent does not need to feel intimidated or pressured into giving a different answer and can escalate the call without any sense of failure. For example, one center handling six million calls per year discovered that implementing and stringently maintaining a sophisticated information retrieval system not only reduced contact time by more than 50 percent, it also reduced agent turnover by 28 percent. The latter improvement was attributed to the fact that the agents were both able to find information rapidly and also confident that management would not only support them for using the system, but also reward them for making suggestions on how both the system and its contents could be improved. Expert agents were recognized for pointing out errors and inconsistencies, and those who were particularly adept were given rotations on the quality improvement team. Far from being reduced to robots, the agents realized that the online system was a way in which they could effect change across the entire customer care environment.

Integrated information retrieval systems provide even more compelling reasons for obligatory usage. A customer care system that tracks user activity can preclude the need for voluminous after call work. It is a concept clearly embraced by forward-looking technologies such as computer-telephony integration. Based on mouse clicks or keyboard inputs, the system can keep a running track of user interaction, using application programming interfaces in order to create an association between the customer, the current contact, and the types of problems or inquiries that are involved in that contact. This can obviate the need for agents to create elaborate notations in an attempt to describe the nature of the contact, and instead create an easily interpretable record of the contact for reporting purposes.

Last, nonobligatory usage of online documentation virtually ensures that the system will be rendered obsolete within a short period of time. If highly motivated and knowledgeable agents have no compulsion to use the system, for example, it is fair to assume that the process of discovering what is missing or erroneous will virtually grind to a halt. Feedback to the quality improvement team will be negligible, and knowledge engineers will never be educated as to the veracity of their work. Even when information is updated, agents may continue to espouse the policies and procedures they learned in training (for example, unless they happened to be present when the billing manager verbally announced that the company now accepted American Express credit cards). Giving the users the ability to comment or complain about the structure of an online documentation system is a critical step in resolving innate weaknesses that may not be evident to the knowledge or documentation engineers. This feedback, which may be achieved via shared or "public" annotations on the system itself, written forms, or even verbally, is an integral part of the improvement process described earlier.

In summary, the decision whether or not to implement an information retrieval system demands careful consideration of the resources management is willing to commit to maintaining the content of the system. The success of the system is contingent upon the level of confidence users have that they will find relevant information immediately. This requires constant maintenance, which can only be achieved by a robust connection between users and those responsible for the integrity of the information. If the commitment is made, the decision whether or not to integrate the information retrieval system with other customer care functions should be driven by management's need to reduce contact time, lower costs, and produce useful customer contact reports. The final decision whether or not to compel agents to use the system should be made on the basis of the company's desire to provide consistent and accurate information to the customer.

Presentation

Once the user has conducted a search and retrieved relevant information, the next consideration is how to present that information so that it is inherently useful, that is, easy to assimilate and understand even in a time-intensive customer care environment and capable of conveying a complete answer to a particular inquiry or complaint. Clearly, these two contingencies for best in class customer care are a significant task for any knowledge or documentation engineer. First, making content easy to assimilate and understand can be difficult under any circumstances, notwithstanding a highly pressured customer care environment. Every call center agent knows that ten or twenty seconds of silence while he or she attempts to find and understand a particular piece of information with an impatient customer waiting on the line can be a stressful experience.

Poorly conceived document design can be caused by the failure of management to explicitly define the scope of a particular customer care offering. Again, if the individuals responsible for knowledge acquisition are given no clearly defined boundaries for a particular product or service, it is extremely likely that the knowledge and documentation engineers will be given unstructured information which, over a period of time, may result in a confusing tangle of linked text nodes and multimedia representations. Stringent planning and testing is required to ensure that every concerned individual understands the limits of the customer care offering, and that the associations between major categories of information make inherent sense. Elements within these major categories need to be defined and represented as a network or hierarchical structure.

The fact that most users of a customer care–oriented information retrieval system, especially agents (as opposed to customers accessing the system directly from the World Wide Web) want information in a hurry, should preclude any documentation engineer from allowing line after line of verbose text to appear as a result of a query. Users want the facts stated simply and precisely, not a paragraph that includes several associated concepts that do not explicitly answer the original inquiry.

Hypertext (now referred to as "hypermedia" as a result of the availability of digital graphics, sound, and video in addition to text), a term coined by Theodore Nelson in the sixties and a concept described over fifty years ago by Vannevar Bush, is a critical function of most information retrieval systems. By attempting to emulate nonlinear, associative thought patterns, hypermedia-enabled applications allow documentation engineers to provide users with singular facts linked to other predefined relevancies. If the user desires to explore a particular "node" of associated information, then that option is immediately available. Hypermedia, therefore, represents an online effort to present discrete facts that will satisfy a user's need in a way that is easy to understand at a glance. In a way, it is the antithesis of the prose that fills this and other paper books in a traditional linear fashion. The difference, of course, is that this book was not written as a real-time informational medium for agents or impatient customers.

A successful hypermedia application in a customer care environment depends largely on the ability of the documentation engineer to understand the type of questions customers are likely to ask, and to represent the answers in a way that facilitates rapid resolution. This is an extreme challenge for documentation engineers who have never taken a customer call, or who depend entirely on knowledge engineers to pass along pertinent information. In other words, the documentation engineer must become a "power user" by spending as much time as possible with the user population observing, using, and testing their outputs in the real world. It is crucial that management encourage this type of collaboration between users and engineers; failure to do so will virtually guarantee a significant rift between those who *produce* and those who *use* the end product.

One of the principal design decisions an engineer has to make concerns the actual structure of the hypermedia document. Do customer inquiries lend themselves more to a linear sequence, grid, hierarchical, or networked structure? Many customer care environments use online documentation primarily to access what can be termed as *user instructions* or procedures that explain how to perform a particular task using the company's product or service. This type of interaction lends itself well to a *sequential* approach, that is, a linear set of instructions read sequentially. A *grid* structure is useful for instructions that invariably can contain the same attributes, such as a set of commands containing properties, notes, and examples. In this case, the online document can be constructed in a way that hypermedia links are represented by pushbuttons aligned horizontally across the screen. A *hierarchical* structure can be employed when the user does not need to see all of the information at once. Instead, the most relevant information is initially displayed, with other necessary facts revealed progressively at the command of the user. Some customer care environments use this in place of a more elaborate troubleshooting system by formalizing decision trees as part of the online documentation system. A *networked* structure, which, due to its potential complexity and the aptitude of the user to become "lost in hyperspace," is rarely used in a fast-paced customer care environment, allows free and unstructured movement between various nodes of information, some of which may be more closely related than others. This approach is similar to the semantic networks employed in cognitive psychology and artificial intelligence.

Vocabulary and Style

For many technical writers, making the transition to online documentation is a natural consequence of the information age. Many writers, however, attempt to apply the traditional techniques of technical writing to the more rigorous arena of online documentation. While all the rules of good writing still apply, online documentation requires a far more precise and carefully planned approach in order to succeed. First, to facilitate rapid interpretation by the user, the language must be simplified and any ambiguity of meaning must be removed. Jargon, if considered necessary, should be limited to those words and phrases that are innately familiar to the user community, whether by virtue of regional dialect or terminology specific to the product or service being supported. This can be most valuable when an agent attempts to search for information using localized terms. However, given the trend for companies to migrate information retrieval systems to the World Wide Web for direct customer access, it is even more important to avoid any kind of specialized language unless absolutely essential. A compromise is to include specialized terms as "pointers." In other words, these terms may constitute part of the same node of text as the more conventional terminology (perhaps as an unobtrusive list beneath the main body of information), thus enabling agents to use specialized terms or jargon without being penalized by a "No matches found" response from the system.

There are several ways in which a documentation engineer can enhance the usability of an online document. For example, most online documentation systems enable engineers to emphasize particular words or phrases using color or text attributes such as italics and underlining. Sometimes, this treatment indicates that a hypermedia link exists, while on other occasions it is used to simply emphasize the importance of a word or phrase. Using these kinds of visual prompts sparingly can help the user to quickly comprehend the message. Consistency is also a critical factor in the documentation engineering process. By using the same terminology throughout an online documentation system, the engineer can avoid confusion and save valuable time. Other common pitfalls to avoid are references to previous text, long paragraphs and sentences, nonstandard spellings, and cryptic error messages.

Integrity

An information retrieval system that boasts an intuitive user interface design, rapid response times, outstanding integration, and relevant content and clarity of expression must also provide complete and accurate information if it is to meet the needs of its users. Nobody can expect the knowledge and documentation engineers to get all of the information right the first time, so there has to be a process that ensures that any information found to be missing or erroneous is rectified as quickly as possible. This maintenance process normally involves a composite team of subject matter experts (usually one or more expert agents) together with the knowledge and documentation engineers who have been assigned to maintain existing content, a training representative and a customer care advocate who represents the needs of the users to the development organization.

It is critical that the users are confident that their feedback on any missing or erroneous information will result in some reaction from the quality improvement team within a short period of time. Some customer care environments strive to validate user feedback and make any necessary changes to the information retrieval system within 24 hours. Others—especially those dealing with regular new product or service support in addition to maintenance of existing information—often find that limited knowledge and documentation engineering resources preclude any kind of rapid response to user feedback. In fact, many such environments tend not to actively solicit user feedback, and focus more on provisioning than maintenance. The end result with these types of endeavors is usually that the information retrieval system is perceived as unreliable and that users are better off seeking answers from some other source.

The availability of complete and accurate content depends largely upon the company's commitment to the maintenance of the information retrieval system. Failure to allocate sufficient knowledge and documentation engineering resources to this task can virtually ensure the rapid demise of the system.

Completeness

Ideally, from a customer's perspective, a company will provide access to all available information which may enable the resolution of a particular inquiry or complaint. Up to quite recently, that has meant either searching product packaging or literature that may have come with the product or service, or calling a toll-free number that may or may not be easy to locate, depending upon the company's attitude toward customer care. Today, it could also mean going online and exploring a website.

From a business perspective, it makes economic sense to put as much information online as possible. There are, however, certain types of information that the company will not make generally available to the public. This includes proprietary information, such as product schematics, design specifications, customer and billing database records, and the like. There is also other information, such as significant flaws in a product or service, that will not be considered for inclusion at a website. After all, it's unlikely that a company will readily admit that 60 percent of all its products don't work quite as well as they should because the factory in Taiwan was poorly managed. Instead, the company will deal with such problems on a one-to-one basis, preferring to wait for the customer to send an e-mail message or call before discussing any form of replacement or remuneration. It's a form of damage control that ensures that agents will never be replaced entirely by customer-accessed online services. It also gives the company a chance to rectify the problem before the word gets around. The trouble is, of course, that the very existence of the Internet enables the word to get around hundreds of times faster than ever before.

There are varying forms of *completeness* when it comes to online customer care. The agent should, of course, have the most up-to-date information available online in the form of policies and procedures, troubleshooting and general information, customer records, and user instructions. The website should also include all of this information with the exception of policies and procedures, customer records, and those "dirty skeletons in the closet" discussed earlier.

From the outset, completeness depends upon the close collaboration of management with customer care strategists,—those responsible for defining the scope of the customer care offering. This generally involves areas like marketing and product management, who must clearly indicate the type of contacts customer care is expected to handle, and those related to the product or service being supported, but which should be directed elsewhere. This critical information must be conveyed to a team of knowledge acquisition specialists who are responsible for gathering all information within the boundaries defined. This usually involves defining suppliers (such as subject matter experts, existing documents, partners, vendors, etc.) and handing off relevant information to a knowledge engineering team, who may be responsible for building the troubleshooting scenarios, and a documentation engineering team, who will define the content of the online documentation system.

A robust feedback and maintenance process is the only way to ensure that the information retrieval system is as complete as possible. Any missing information can be quickly identified not only by analyzing contact report and trouble tickets, but also by encouraging users to directly report difficulties encountered trying to locate a particular procedure, instruction, reference, and the like. Direct user feedback to a quality improvement team is also an excellent way of identifying training issues, missing keyword search terms, system usability issues, and inaccurate content.

Accuracy

A close ally of completeness, accuracy also demands rigorous user feedback channels. Given that a user has accessed an information retrieval system, conducted a successful search, and is ready to act upon the seemingly complete information presented, the only question remaining is whether or not the information displayed is accurate. For example, a troubleshooting system may suggest a particular remedy based upon the initial symptoms described by the user, together with the answers to several clarifying questions. If the suggested solution is found to be completely incorrect, it indicates either that the knowledge engineer was given erroneous supplier information, or that the engineer made a mistake in actually entering the data. Either way, there needs to be a mechanism for correcting the error as quickly as possible.

An inaccurate response to a customer contact will lead either to an online escalation, or to a repeat customer contact, depending upon how soon the error is discovered. It is important, therefore, that escalated contacts or repeat contacts receive particular attention in order to determine whether these events occurred as a result of inaccurate or incomplete information.

The process of correcting inaccuracies or populating missing data in information retrieval systems needs to be driven by careful assessment of the time frame involved. For example, it is reasonable to surmise that, if the information does not exist online or is erroneous, the customer will nevertheless ultimately receive a response from an individual, whether agent or specialist, that is satisfactory. If the customer care processes are working correctly, that response will be documented either in the contact notes, trouble ticket, or direct feedback from the user to the quality improvement team. If the response comes from a specialist, management may choose to assume that, because specialists are also subject matter experts, the answer is correct until proven otherwise, and therefore instruct the documentation or knowledge engineering team to format the information immediately. This approach can work very well in environments that enjoy robust links between agents, specialists, and the quality improvement team, by ensuring that, even if the answer is occasionally incorrect, it will be quickly discovered and rectified. In other cases, management may insist that the knowledge engineering team first validate the information through independent research, and even have it approved by the legal department or product management, before allowing it to be put online. The success of the latter approach depends largely upon resource availability and the existence of reliable intraorganizational feedback channels. This can be extremely detrimental in fast-paced customer care environments that rely on rapid content maintenance in order to resolve customer inquiries and complaints.

If user feedback or the study of reports indicates an *unknown* issue to the quality improvement team (i.e., the result of *incomplete* information), then further knowledge engineering is required in order to provide the necessary content. This may involve the knowledge engineer contacting a vendor or other supplier to acquire the missing content.

Other changes to the information retrieval system may not require knowledge engineering, but instead may necessitate revisions to available search words (e.g., adding a popular search word or phrase to a particular node of information in order to ensure a user "hit"), changing or adding general information (such as promotional events, names and addresses, organizational changes, etc.), format, grammatical, or punctuation changes, and so forth. All of these types of changes or additions can be quickly made by the documentation engineers.

When a change or addition is made to the system, it is necessary to alert agents reactively. This may be accomplished via the information retrieval system itself (i.e., a particular online document that displays any changes to content), or some form of broadcast application. Each change should be date stamped online, so that users are in no doubt about the time frame of the last revision to a particular node of documentation or troubleshooting scenario. It is important that users do not become complacent about the content of the system, and that they are fully aware that the maintenance process is designed to effect dynamic improvements.

Disaster Recovery for Content

Once the commitment to utilize an information retrieval system has been made, existing documentation tends to become rapidly dispersed or discarded. Individual agents may keep whatever paper references they have found to be most useful, but in most cases no one is actually given the task of archiving the available information in a hard copy format.

The key question for managers of highly automated customer care environments is how to deal with system outages and still gather customer data while maintaining normal service levels. While the primary focus will continue to be customer satisfaction, the question is how much must be sacrificed in terms of contact management during the outage. Contingency plans for disaster recovery even at the content level must be formalized and understood.

In customer care environments that support highly complex products and services, for example, management may determine that, in order to avoid long hold times and disgruntled customers, agents will forgo all after-call work, such as notations and call categorizations. Complex troubleshooting scenarios will be immediately transferred to predetermined agents who have been trained to use regularly updated hard copy troubleshooting scenarios and user instructions. In so doing, management attempts to ensure that internal help desk specialists are not overwhelmed by escalated contacts.

In order to ensure that agents are dealing with the most recent iterations to any information, management must designate an agent or documentation engineer to be responsible for the upkeep of all available hard copy documentation. In some environments, such as large call centers, this may even require a full-time librarian position. Not only does it ensure that agents always have access to the most recent information, but it also means that any changes to existing information may be detailed separately (perhaps on a weekly basis) and provided to agents as a special bulletin, preferably online or if necessary in paper form.

Minimizing the effect of system outages is clearly a priority for any call center manager. Information access is an integral part of any disaster recovery scenario and should be given strong focus in order to avoid unnecessarily long contact times.

An industry-leading service provider determined that in excess of 3,000 daily accumulated minutes of system downtime for their 700 agents (i.e., about 45 minutes per agent) was unacceptable. If any part of the system is down, the manager responsible for the problem area is immediately notified. The longer it takes to fix the problem, the less likely that manager is to achieve the "quality indicator" of 99 percent availability. Compensation is tied to these indicators and they are monitored daily.

Other Forms of Online Content

Computer-based training (CBT), is often considered too expensive a proposition to implement in a customer care environment. Instead, most call centers rely on instructor-led training classes in order to educate agents. This approach works well in centralized call centers with low turnover rates and predictable product or service support strategies, whereby management may hire several agents simultaneously in order to meet forecasted demand. Conversely, distributed customer care environments with high turnover rates should provide the impetus for CBT applications. Rather than having an overwrought training group traveling all over the country, giving multiple classes to one or two new hires every few days, the customer care organization should be able to cost-justify the development of a computerized training program that not only assists new agents, but also provides a useful refresher course for existing staff.

In many cases, basic computer-based training modules are produced in order to supplement classroom training. The plethora of rapid prototyping tools available on the market today means that basic applications can be produced relatively economically. A three-person team of subject matter expert (usually a trainer or expert agent), writer, and designer can produce a basic CBT application relatively quickly. One call center commissioned a one-hour-long, 127-screen CBT application to be delivered in under three weeks. The application, which was produced by an external company specializing in online documentation, cost under $30,000 and was estimated to have saved over 500 classroom hours of annual training time. At a cost of approximately $150 per hour for facilities, trainers, and agents, it was considered a worthwhile expenditure. Of course, more elaborate authoring tools involving complex CBT functions can take far longer to develop.

There are several types of CBT application, including guided tours, tutorials, simulations, and integrated or embedded training (a relatively rare approach whereby the CBT application is actually a part of the customer care system). The most common CBT applications are tutorials, whereby the user completes training modules at his or her own pace, usually answering a series of questions correctly in order to proceed to the next module.

In summary, potential applications for CBT in customer care environments are often neglected, due either to budgetary constraints or tight development time frames. In terms of systematic priority, CBT ranks well below the development of user instructions, policies and procedures, and online help. It is considered a "nice to have" add-on to the customer care system platform, but like online scripting (see Figure 9.3, Online script development), it is not an area that generally gets a lot of attention from the customer care support team.

Another example of online content is the provisioning of assistance for agents who are unfamiliar with certain system functions. This is often referred to as online help. It is remarkable how many customer care systems lack adequate online help facilities (see Figure 9.4, Online help development). This is because, for many development groups, the provisioning of system help is often a chore that occurs after all of the "hard" work has been accomplished. Customized applications, particularly those developed internally, are usually the biggest culprits in this regard, whereas off-the-shelf applications by commercial necessity contain adequate help facilities.

Context-sensitive online help is most useful in a customer care environment, where new users of a system may wish to be quickly reminded of the purpose of various functions and fields. There are few agents who have time to read paragraphs of online help documentation with a customer on the line. That sort of presentation is best saved for computer-based training, where the agent is given adequate time to complete various assignments.

Reference topic help facilities provide indexing and search facilities that give the user explicit instructions on how to complete a particular task. Another common function built into customer care systems is the provision of *online scripts* that, based on the user's active window, give general instructions on how to proceed.

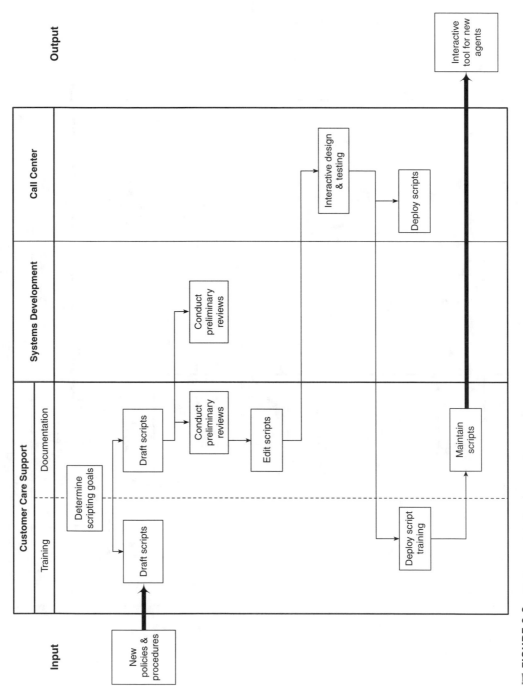

Input

New policies & procedures

Customer Care Support

Training | Documentation

Determine scripting goals

Draft scripts

Draft scripts

Conduct preliminary reviews

Edit scripts

Deploy script training

Maintain scripts

Systems Development

Conduct preliminary reviews

Call Center

Interactive design & testing

Deploy scripts

Output

Interactive tool for new agents

▨ **FIGURE 9.3**   Online script development

177

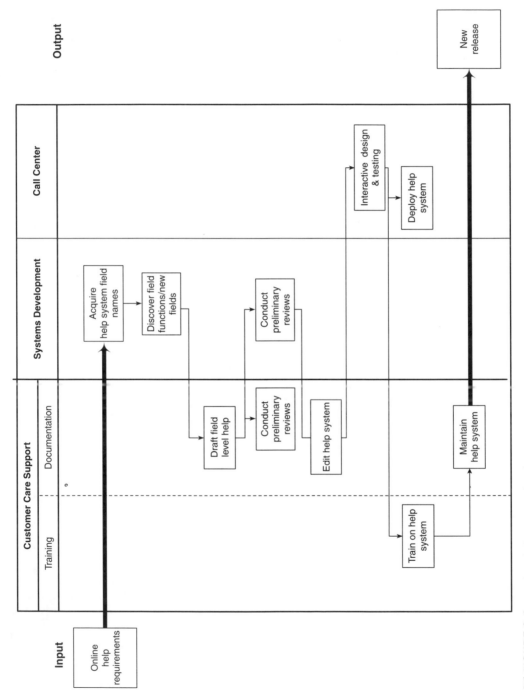

FIGURE 9.4 Online help system development

System messages may also be classified as part of online help. These messages pop up on the screen when there is some problem or delay that merits explanation. The trouble with most of these messages is that the explanation is often impossible to interpret, sometimes leaving new users with the impression that they must have done something wrong, and more experienced users shaking their heads and bemoaning the fact that "the system is down again." System messages are embedded in the actual application itself, which usually means that they are composed by a developer who, in the context of the programming environment, may believe that the message makes perfect sense or that anyone with the technical manual would know what it meant in a matter of seconds. Some are well-structured, but many lack the subtlety of communicating cryptic information to a nontechnical audience. All system messages should be reviewed for clarity by a documentation engineer prior to deployment.

Some applications provide context-sensitive help on a message bar at the bottom of the screen, whereas others use a variety of pop-up windows, F1 keys, right-hand mouse clicks, and so forth. Users are often given the option to disable context-sensitive help, an event that usually occurs when they are familiar with the application. Customer care systems, because they usually involve several different applications such as contact tracking, troubleshooting, ordering, and the like, often end up with multiple ways of accessing help. Users may have to press the F1 key on the ordering system, click the right-hand mouse button on the troubleshooting system, and use a menu command on the contact tracking system. It is important that this sort of inconsistency is avoided wherever possible. Two development groups working on disparate customer care applications, such as troubleshooting and online documentation, using two programming languages (as is often the case) does not imply that the way of accessing help is *necessarily* different in both cases. As with any worthwhile integrated system, collaboration is needed to ensure a "seamless" interface wherever possible.

Some online help facilities allow the user to enter field-level data as part of the online document. This is especially useful when the user is uncertain whether the data they are entering are in an acceptable format. Instead of reviewing the help facility and returning to the application, the user can simply complete the original operation from the help window. This technique, often referred to as *passthrough*, demands greater attention from the development organization during the system design phase than any other form of help.

Online help continues to be the poor relation of most customized applications. As a carefully designed and populated part of any application, it can diffuse user hostility and confusion. In a customer care environment it can significantly augment user competence and the likelihood that every function and data-gathering mechanism is used to its fullest advantage.

CHAPTER

10

Electronic Mail

Overview

Many of the issues involved in handling electronic mail (e-mail) can be broadly categorized under *Interpretation and Response,* which deals with the ability of the customer care environment to provide a timely, accurate and complete response to an inbound communication, and *Maintenance,* which deals with a company's ability to quickly identify an existing customer.

From the customer care perspective, it is often difficult for an agent to interpret exactly what the customer is looking for from an initial e-mail message. In worldwide customer care environments, for example, it has been found that the foreign customer who does not feel comfortable describing his or her needs verbally to an agent will compose an e-mail message instead. In many such cases, the agent may be unable to interpret the e-mail and tries to call the customer, who may be unavailable, leading to a string of costly follow-ups and a potential loss of customer confidence.

Enabling the customer to convey his or her needs electronically to the receiving agent is clearly a major issue. In the case of a troubleshooting scenario, for example, it is critical that the response to a customer does not suggest a resolution that the customer has already attempted. In one sense, the flashing cursor on the blank field (traditional e-mail transmits virtually no nonverbal cues) is the purest commercially proven form of human-computer interaction today. In another, it is a recipe for misinterpretation, which is why many companies are adopting a customer-constraining electronic forms interface. Regardless of the approach, an inbound e-mail could become a problem for a customer care environment for any or all of the following reasons:

- *The customer did not provide enough information.*
- *The customer mentioned several disparate issues.*
- *The receiving agent did not provide an adequate response.*

181

- *The system did not facilitate the response.*
- *The customer sent the message to the wrong department.*
- *The message was written in a foreign language.*

Each of these problems may be elaborated as follows:

- *The customer did not provide enough information.*

Customers currently have two generally recognized ways of sending e-mail messages to a customer care address. The first is to acquire the address and send a message via the Internet. Normally, this will be a plain text message with no attachments. In other words, the entire context of the inquiry or complaint will have to be derived from the customer's words. This often necessitates a callback to the customer because the nature of the message is unclear. Fortunately, widespread usage of the World Wide Web and the subsequent proliferation of web-centric customer care facilities should encourage most customers to take a different route. The ideal scenario is for the customer to always visit the website first, to see if the answer resides there before sending an e-mail message asking for help. For example, in appropriate cases (such as a high-tech problem-solving scenario) those who have searched a database or consulted a knowledge base on the Web have left behind an audit trail that could be automatically stored through an application programming interface with a subsequent e-mail. This way, the receiving agent could interpret the customer's need far more easily, and possibly preclude the necessity of a callback. It is recognized that such an approach, however, is expensive and often subjective. In other words, there is rarely a guarantee that the Web page from which the customer generated an e-mail message is directly related to the problem or inquiry being conveyed. In any event, a contingency for success with regard to this strategy is that the customer care environment on the Web is sufficiently developed to encourage customers to conduct an inquiry or solve a problem on their own.

- *The customer mentioned several disparate issues.*

The customer who mentions several disparate issues, some of which may or may not be relevant to customer care, presents the most time-consuming case. In the interests of outstanding customer care, each issue should be dealt with individually, and those that do not pertain to customer care should be easily channeled to the correct party. In the event that a portion of a message is redirected, the customer needs to know who it was sent to, and when to expect to receive a response. Given this scenario, the receiving agent needs a potentially large amount of supporting information to be readily available, as well as some time-saving system functions. Ideally, the receiving agent should be able to forward all or selected portions of the e-mail text, quickly explain why this action is being taken, select a listed receiving agent (such as a marketing manager), send a copy to the customer with an *automatically retrieved* time frame of response from a particular receiving agent, and append the customer record accordingly. This concept of automatic retrieval of time frames to response is another area that requires particular attention. Such an approach implies the existence of mutually acceptable time frames through the implementation of service agreements between disparate departments—not a facile task in high-volume e-mail environments.

• *The receiving agent did not provide an adequate response.*

This problem is of particular concern to management. Unlike voice-to-voice communication, where the agent is basically a "captive audience" who may be closely monitored and who must be careful not to alienate the customer, e-mail is a one-way communication that enables the agent to interpret a message anyway he or she pleases. An agent who is quantitatively measured by the number of e-mail responses generated each day will be far more apt to adopt erroneous or ill-considered conclusions. The customer has no immediate way of clarifying the situation, so the probability of repeat contact (this time by telephone) is high. It is important, therefore, that management recognize the value of creating a separate job description for those who handle inbound e-mail. Apart from outstanding written communication skills, this agent must be a proven analyst and subject matter expert, with a track record for outstanding customer care. It is also critical that management set appropriate guidelines and time constraints for responding to e-mail messages.

• *The system did not facilitate the response.*

Outbound correspondence, whether postal service, fax, or e-mail, is an extremely time-consuming process for many customer care environments. Postal service correspondence is certainly the least efficient of all. It is not unusual to witness call center staff handling outbound postal service correspondence by first typing the contact details onto a prewritten form (or sometimes having to compose an entire response), printing the letter remotely on plain paper, handwriting their return address onto a window envelope (or worse yet, having to also write the customer's name and address on a plain envelope), photocopying the plain paper onto company letterhead and discarding the original printout, folding all the contents into the envelope and finally sealing and placing the envelope in an outbound mail tray before going back and commenting the customer's account.

In the ideal scenario, the system would provide templates for all standard responses. Any customer information would be automatically loaded into the template for further editing as required. The agent would be able to access any relevant online documentation, such as troubleshooting procedures, and attach it to the template. The customer contact record would be updated automatically. If a customized response was required, the agent would be able compose his or her own and, in predefined circumstances, channel it to a senior editor for approval (e.g., responses to complaints). The senior editor would oversee all customized templates and determine, based on frequency, whether one should be added or removed from the master list of templates. Agents would be immediately notified of any changes to existing templates.

• *The customer sent the message to the wrong department.*

This problem occurs when the customer is provided with several choices of addressee. A consumer products company, for example, may route customer contacts based on mutually exclusive product lines. In this circumstance, the company may put the onus on the customer to select the correct department, similar to an automated attendant approach, thus increasing the possibility of misdirects. The best scenario, at least in terms of avoiding rerouting delays, is to provide the customer with just one address for the entire organization. This means that the burden of routing then becomes the responsibility of the customer care organization, thus necessitating the appointment of a routing specialist or the provisioning of cross-training to ensure that all agents are capable of identifying the correct recipient.

• *The message was written in a foreign language.*
It is critical that the interpretation software can search inbound e-mail messages for key phrases that indicate that the message is composed in a foreign language. If the volume of such messages is sufficient, the messages may be automatically routed to a translation specialist, who in turn will translate the original message and then forward both the original and the translation to an appropriate agent. A potential problem with such an approach is that, particularly in the case of emotive messages, the tone of the complaint may be lost on the agent unless the translation specialist is particularly skilled in this regard.

Electronic Mail Maintenance

Inbound e-mail, like computer-telephony integration (CTI), is a potent medium for gathering customer data even before a human receiving agent has intervened. In fact, the "hit rate" (i.e., the percentage of time an existing customer is identified) on inbound e-mail is potentially much higher than for CTI because the customer will use the same or a limited set of e-mail addresses no matter where they are located, whereas telephony contacts tend to be much more disparate. A facility for storing and displaying several e-mail addresses should therefore be facilitated in the system design. Given that a message is received from an existing customer, the database can be automatically searched, a customer contact record created and associated with the customer's profile/contact history, and the message, profile, history and record can all be available simultaneously for routing to an appropriate receiving agent. In the case of an unknown e-mail address, it is either a new customer or an existing customer who has changed the Internet provider, in which case the system must conduct a check on the customer's name. It is important that new customer profiles are not created every time an existing customer changes his or her e-mail address. Some online service call centers are known to have as many as seven profiles for the same customer. Given that the customer "churn" or turnover rate for Internet providers is expected to be in the region of 60 percent (mainly due to price "wars"), it is reasonable to assume that in the foreseeable future many customer care environments will have to deal with multiple "customer address" changes.

Contingencies

Contingencies surrounding the successful usage of e-mail in customer care environments:
    There are two schools of thought relative to customer-generated e-mail correspondence within customer care environments. The first asserts that the purest form of non-verbal communication is one that enables the customer to compose whatever comes to

mind and simply issue a command to send the message to a given address. The second advocates the use of electronic forms to lead the customer through a predefined set of input fields. This approach is clearly beneficial to the customer care environment, as categorization of data is uniform and therefore more easily integrated with other applications. From a human-computer interaction standpoint, however, constraining the customer in this manner is suboptimal. Ideally, the customer should be able to submit an inquiry or complaint in whatever way he or she chooses, and the customer care environment should be able to interpret and respond to that message rapidly and effectively. Without demeaning the increasingly widespread use of forms, which offer an adequate solution for computer-literate customers communicating directly from the Web, the following process and technology descriptions cover both Web-based and independently generated e-mail messages that require intelligent interpretation.

Contingencies dictating the establishment of best in class customer care for e-mail communications:

1. The company facilitates the creation and delivery of an e-mail message from the customer.
2. The customer care environment is able to integrate, interpret, and route the message efficiently.
3. Response to the e-mail message is timely, accurate, clear, and complete.

The following section examines each of these contingencies and their associated requirements in more detail.

Creation and Delivery

The company facilitates the creation and delivery of an e-mail message from the customer.

The first contingency requires the company to make the customer aware of its e-mail facility, and to make the process so intuitive and responsive that the customer ultimately prefers it to calling a toll-free number (see figure 10.1).

Summary

Process

- Marketing company website and e-mail addresses
- Creating and sending independent e-mail messages
- Creating and sending Web-based e-mail messages
- Defining attachments to Web-based e-mail messages
- Approximating time frames to response
- Receiving, categorizing, and storing inbound e-mail messages
- Analyzing inbound e-mail sources and frequencies

Technology
The system will facilitate:

- Integration—contacting customer care instantly via e-mail from a company website

186

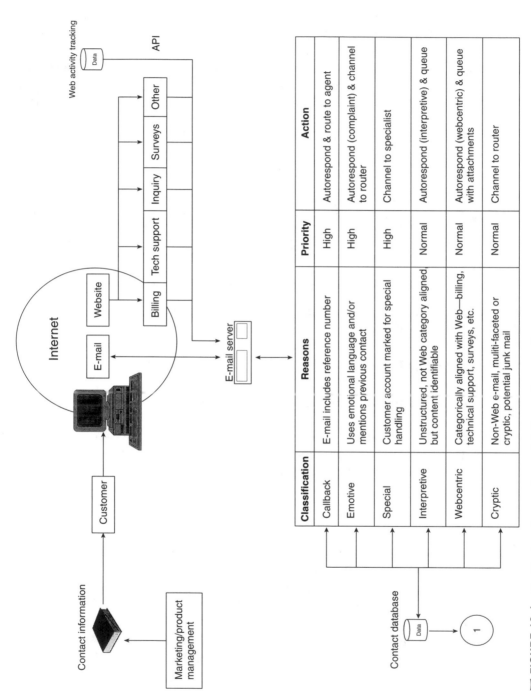

☒ **FIGURE 10.1** Facilitating the creation and delivery of an e-mail message

- Data—automatically attaching data, such as a Web troubleshooting session, to a customer e-mail
- Classification—initial categorization of an inbound e-mail message
- Auto-response—time-stamping e-mails based on classification
- Measures—purpose of the e-mail, independent vs. Web-generated e-mails, etc.

Content

- Literature and online help content
- Template and form content as defined by process owners for Web-based e-mails
- Data gathering for automatic attachment to Web-based e-mails
- Auto-response Content.

Details

Process

- *Marketing company Web site and e-mail addresses*

The first step in the process of encouraging customers to use e-mail in communicating with customer care is to ensure that they are fully aware of the facility. A logical step is to include the company Web site and e-mail addresses on all packaging and literature. Include a reminder on the toll-free number interactive voice response (IVR) unit and ensure that all agents are prepared to encourage e-mail usage.

- *Creating and sending independent e-mail messages*

Perhaps the least desirable way for a customer to contact customer care is via a message that does not clearly define the nature of the inquiry or complaint, and which may in some circumstances necessitate an immediate callback. Nevertheless, provisioning of an independent means to send an e-mail to customer care via the Internet is still less time-consuming for the customer than faxing or using the postal service. In the case of an independently generated (i.e., outside the company website) e-mail, it is important that the customer is educated where possible as to the optimal content of that message (e.g., include the product model, serial number, when purchased, nature of the problem, reference number for callbacks, etc.). Again, this type of information could be included with any product or service packaging and literature.

- *Creating and sending Web-based e-mail messages*

Regardless of where the customer is located within a company's website, the facility to send an e-mail to customer care should exist. This could involve areas such as unsolicited comments, customer surveys, troubleshooting problems, or billing inquiries. If the company has opted to use electronic forms, this process must include the content definition of each e-mail type by the responsible process owner. For example, a troubleshooting report form might include areas for the customer to enter details of the problem he or she is trying to resolve, in addition to an area for entering a reference number (for callbacks). This approach should not be confused with the increasing availability of interactive forms on the Web, where the customer attempts to resolve a problem without contacting customer care. In the case of plain text e-mail responses, hints on what the customer might mention in a message could be available from online help.

• *Defining attachments to Web-based e-mail messages*

The success of e-mail as a medium for customer care will in many cases depend upon the quality of information that can accompany a customer's message. For example, if the customer has been trying to troubleshoot a particular problem without success, the system could automatically capture a "trail" of data relevant to the customer's interaction and attach it to the message. Exactly what information should be captured for any particular Web transaction needs to be defined by the process owner and implemented by the systems development organization, based on rigorous cost/benefit analysis.

• *Approximating time frames to response*

The receipt of several types of customer-generated e-mail may trigger the dispatch of an acknowledgment that will, based on initial categorization of the incoming message, approximate time frames to response as well as issuing the customer with an appropriate "reference" number. For example, based on customer-stated expectations (direct measures of quality), volume, and resource allocation, it may be ascertained that it should generally take customer care two hours to resolve inbound technical-support e-mail messages. This time frame should be included as part of the autoresponse to the customer. Other considerations might include whether or not the customer is a "special handling" or "priority" account, or, in the case of an advanced auto response feature, whether or not the message contained any words that might involve a complaint. It has been found that customers expect almost a "real time" response to Web-generated e-mails—a condition that can be to some extent assuaged by the "autoresponse" feature described above, as well as the ability to quickly channel high-priority messages to agents for immediate response.

• *Receiving, categorizing, and storing an inbound e-mail message*

A technical process for efficient transfer of e-mails and attachments to customer care. Typical customer care categorizations would include technical support, billing inquiry, account maintenance, general inquiry, ordering, request for service, and the like.

• *Analyzing inbound e-mail sources and frequencies*

Given that the ultimate goal of the company is to eliminate all contacts with customer care, knowing where e-mails are being generated from and why may be critical to the success of the endeavor (although it can never be assumed that the source of the message, such as a particular page on a website, is necessarily related to the customer's inquiry or problem). Shortcomings in the quality of the product or service, as well as in the effectiveness of a website, can be derived from this type of intelligence. The Web facility, unlike the telephone, enables analysts to view the source of the inquiry or complaint. For instance, if the majority of e-mails were generated from a specific website location that dealt with operating a specific element of a product, or conducting a task specific to a service, then it is reasonable to assume that the customer has uncovered some vital design or operational flaw. This process should ensure that such information is quickly assimilated into the organization.

Technology

- *Integration*

A process-driven *design* for company websites must engender the possibility that the customer will want to contact customer care with a comment, inquiry, or complaint at any time. The click of a mouse button should facilitate this need. Depending on the context, this function could be labeled "Feedback" (in the case of unsolicited feedback), or "Contact customer care" (e.g., in the case of an unsuccessful troubleshooting session). Whatever the context, the function needs to be as obvious and intuitive to the customer as possible.

- *Data*

In addition to allowing the customer to quickly create and send an e-mail message from a website, the definition of context should include a facility for gathering data on the customer activities that preceded the decision to generate an e-mail. For example, any search words used or data input in the context of a troubleshooting session should be automatically captured and attached to the e-mail for further analysis by the receiving agent.

- *Classification*

Classifications of inbound e-mail could include "Callback" (the customer includes a reference number alluding to a previous contact), "Emotive" (the customer mentions a previous contact and/or uses language that indicates a complaint), "Special" (the profile indicates that any communications from this customer should be handled by a specialist), "Interpretive" (the customer e-mail is unstructured and unaligned with a Web category, but may be interpreted by an intelligent processor), "Webcentric" (the e-mail is categorically aligned with a topic from the company's website), and "Cryptic" (the e-mail cannot be easily interpreted or is multifaceted, requiring human intervention before routing).

- *Autoresponse*

Unlike voice, e-mail does not require both parties to communicate in concert. Any customer-generated e-mail message should invoke an immediate response confirming receipt of the message, a reference number and, based on initial classification, the approximate time frame in which a customer might expect a response. This function will do much to allay the customer's fear that an e-mail to customer care disappears into a "black hole," as well as providing a realistic time frame for response. In the case of callbacks, the message should be routed immediately to the party responsible for the original message, if available.

- *Measures*

"Why did the customer send an e-mail?" is clearly the key question. Reporting on the source (e.g., in certain cases the location within the website) from which an e-mail was generated, the categorization of inbound mail (and ultimately the precise reason for the e-mail), time frames to response fluctuations, Web-generated e-mails vs. independent, and so forth all belong under this contingency.

Content

- *Literature and online help content*

Process owners and product management/marketing should work together to determine the content of packaging and literature as it pertains to customer awareness of the company website and e-mail addresses, and the verbiage that outlines to the customer the optimal content of an e-mail message (for both literature and website online help).

- *Template and form content as defined by process owners for Web-based e-mails*

Plain-text e-mail templates normally include the customer's name and e-mail address, and the customer care address (both automatically generated), and a subject field. Electronic forms, such as are required for an integrated trouble ticketing application, are much more defined. A good example of a predefined form would be an online customer survey, where customer responses need to be uniquely categorized. Defining the content of such forms is the task of the process owner.

- *Data gathering for automatic attachment to Web-based e-mails*

If applicable, the knowledge and documentation engineers, process owners, and, in particular the agents themselves are in the best position to define the elements of a company's website that should be automatically attached to a particular type of inbound e-mail message. These requirements should be as dynamic as the structure of the website itself—an integral part of the change request process.

- *Autoresponse content*

The content of the autoresponse should be dictated by process owners and fine-tuned by the documentation engineers. Any changes to the content of this response would have to be approved by the process owners. Examples of auto-response formats might include callback, special handling, interpreted, and Web-generated message acknowledgments. These acknowledgments would include the original time of receipt, the approximate time to response, and a reference number for customer callbacks.

Integration, Interpretation, and Routing

The customer care environment is able to integrate, interpret, and route the message efficiently.

The second contingency for the successful usage of e-mail in customer care environments is the one most likely to reveal bottlenecks in the process that result in significant customer dissatisfaction. Up to this point, the message has been received, categorized, and stored. Now further analysis is required to ensure that the message is dealt with appropriately (see Figures 10.2 and 10.3).

Summary

Process

- Interpreting the e-mail message (including recognition of foreign languages)
- Dealing with cryptic or multifaceted messages

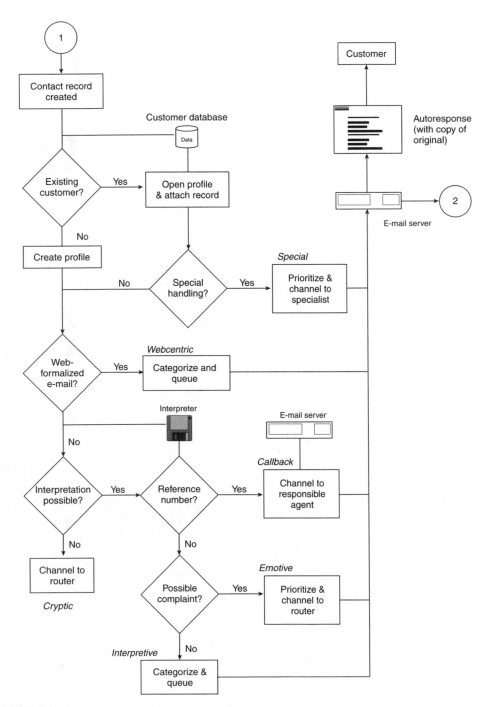

FIGURE 10.2   Classifying and autoresponding to inbound e-mail messages

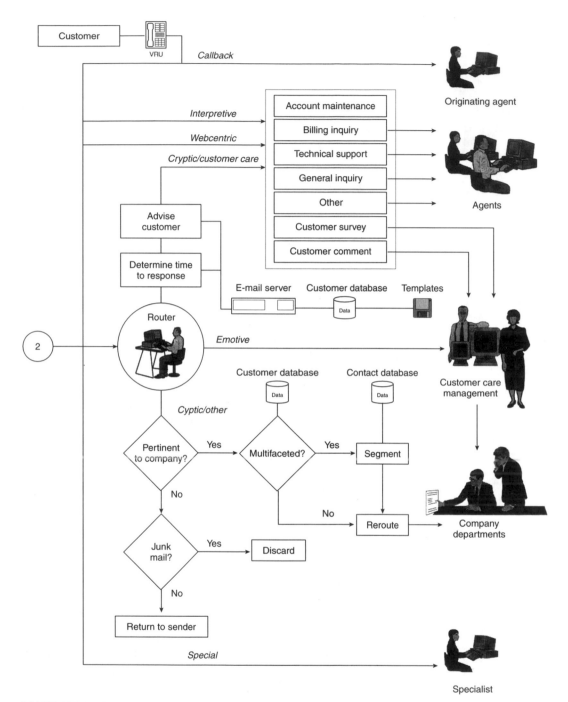

⊠ FIGURE 10.3   Integrating, interpreting, and routing the e-mail message

- Routing the message
- Handling customer callbacks
- Gathering market intelligence

Technology

The system should facilitate information extraction through

- Interpretation—assessing the context of an inbound e-mail
- Routing—selecting the correct receiving agent and transferring data
- Callbacks—associating a "callback" e-mail with the correct receiving agent
- Measures—calculating the percentage of e-mail messages handled by group and individual, and the like

Content

- Content of system-generated messages for new, special attention, due, and overdue e-mails.

Details

Process

- *Interpreting the e-mail message (including recognition of foreign languages)*

In the absence of an intelligent information extraction mechanism or predefined electronic form, human intervention is always required to read and extract relevant data from the e-mail in order to determine context. Initial categorization, as described in the previous section, may provide a springboard into this activity. At this point, the message "router" may need to determine the specific product or service that is the subject of the message, the reason for the message, and whether the message is an initial contact or a follow-up on a previous contact. Another key determination is whether or not the message contains any "emotional" words that may indicate a customer complaint and a high-priority contact.

- *Dealing with cryptic or multifaceted messages*

Some messages, while technically within the domain of customer care, must be rerouted to other parts of the organization. Depending upon the structure of the customer care environment, others may also need to be routed internally to specialist groups. It is essential that entities such as marketing and product management have agreed to specific responsibilities regarding timely response to e-mail messages that are routed through customer care. For example, product management may be involved in the creation of a template that applauds the customer for a new product suggestion, or the legal department may agree that a 24-hour time to response is reasonable to give the customer for any legal issues communicated via e-mail or fax. In the case of disparate messages, where the customer describes several different issues on one message, the router must be easily capable of segmenting the message and routing it as appropriate.

- *Routing the message to the appropriate receiving agent*

To this point, certain assumptions have been made from analyzing the source and context of the customer's e-mail. The next step is clearly a critical part of the process of providing a timely and accurate response to that communication. It is a relatively simple procedure—select a receiving agent and send the message or portion of the message, along with relevant attachments and notification of time to response (as indicated previously to the customer), to a particular receiving agent. While the actual routing procedure may be simple, the decision as to whom to send the e-mail message to is by no means trivial. In the absence of a routing specialist, every agent must know who should receive a specific type of e-mail message—a scenario that presents a major training issue for any organization. Any new mail should first be scanned for relevance by the receiving agent before it is automatically placed in the prioritized time queue. If the e-mail is misrouted or the receiving agent does not acknowledge its receipt within a given time frame (i.e., the normal receiving agent is unavailable), the message should be returned to the router with an appropriate explanation.

• *Dealing with customer callbacks*
In the event that the customer calls back or sends another message, he or she should be able to refer to the number that was automatically generated as a result of the initial communication. This number could be input at the IVR level (in the case of a callback) to be consequently routed via CTI to the responsible receiving agent, or read by either the router or an intelligent interpreter application (in the case of an e-mail). A problem arises here when the customer misquotes the reference number—especially when it's a valid number but not the correct one. Such a situation requires confirmation prior to customer callback that the number matches the customer's contact history. In the event that the customer cannot locate the number, all agents should be capable of bringing up the original message and checking the status. If the message response is not overdue, then the customer should be advised accordingly. In the event that the message is overdue, the receiving agent must take immediate action or the contact should be escalated.

• *Gathering marketing intelligence data*
Just as inbound customer calls represent an outstanding opportunity to gather valuable market intelligence, so too must e-mails be recognized as conduits for customer comments and complaints on the relative value of a particular product or service. Root cause analysis should be conducted on all inbound e-mails to ensure that, despite the erstwhile underestimated value of this medium, customer concerns of a critical nature should not be overlooked. By using the contact tracking or case management system as a repository for multichannel customer interactions, the customer care environment can ensure that every contingency is accounted for in the quest for viable market intelligence.

Technology

• *Interpretation*
From a technology standpoint, plain-text e-mails clearly present a significant problem in terms of any type of automated interpretation, which is why there is a proliferation of electronic forms on the market. As explained previously, Web-generated plain-text e-mails may provide a certain degree of categorization, upon which an approximate time to response can be immediately conveyed to the cus-

tomer, but in large scale e-mail environments this is simply the first step in a complex process. The entire message must be effectively interpreted in order to determine the correct receiving agent(s). For optimal accuracy, this determination should be made by human subject matter experts, but it is fair to say that for routine, noncomplex messages these determinations should be made by an intelligent processor, leaving the human "router" to deal with multifaceted or cryptic communications. In busy customer care environments, this approach would realize significant cost- and time-saving benefits. Ideally, the technology should be able to exploit visual, contextual, and sentence structure in order to process the nature of the communication. For routine inquiries, it is feasible that this technology would augment the receiving agent's task by retrieving and populating predefined templates that would appear to resolve the customer's request. Electronic forms, on the other hand, are specifically composed to convey certain types of customer contact, therefore these forms should normally present an unambiguous scenario, such as a troubleshooting problem. From a human-computer interaction viewpoint, however, the use of forms is rarely considered optimal.

- *Routing*

Based on the premise that any approximations of time frame are conveyed to the customer, it is critical that the inbound e-mail is "time-stamped" prior to routing. A routing audit trail is also necessary here to ensure that no department or agent receives the message again after receiving it once. Again, the appropriate technology can stop this from happening or invoke an exemption process through a count of the number of reroutes. If the number exceeds the number of designated reroutes, then a manager gets to see the message immediately. In other words, the customer care receiving agent of the message will be immediately aware of the customer's expectations in terms of timely response. The receiving agent should have the ability to change the time to response, but this would involve a number of functions, including an explanation of reason for reporting purposes (e.g., misroute delay, erroneous initial categorization, inadequate time allocation, absent receiving agent, etc.), an autogenerated e-mail of explanation addressed to the customer (reiterating ticket number, new time frame, and apology for inconvenience), and finally a reprioritization of the e-mail queue in the follow-up application. In the event that the receiving agent is unavailable (i.e., does not retrieve the new message within a given time frame), the message should be automatically rerouted to the router with an accompanying explanation. The "router" (or the customer care manager) responsible for routing the messages needs the ability to view the number of e-mails being handled by each receiving agent or group, similar to a call management system, and reroute the messages as necessary. It is also crucial that the system facilitates automated message forwarding for people who go on vacation or are otherwise unavailable. In such cases, both the manager or agent needs to be able to autoforward messages as appropriate.

- *Customer Callbacks*

A strong technology focus is required to prevent customer callbacks (via telephone, e-mail, or fax) from becoming a significant problem for the customer care environment. In the case of e-mail or fax, the message should be systematically read for any mention of a ticket number or for any context that alludes to a previous communication, such as a date. If one is found, the customer database should be searched and the relevant contact record retrieved for the number or other identifiers. The message should then be routed for the immediate attention of the responsible party. In the case of a telephone callback, the IVR should include a facility for the customer to enter the ticket number, which, in collaboration with CTI, should enable rapid retrieval of the e-mail in question.

• *Measures*
A facility for calculating the percentage of e-mail messages handled by group and individual, the percentage of missed follow-ups, percentage of customer callbacks, percentage of e-mails vs. telephone calls, and so forth all constitute the type of data that should be gathered and analyzed as a result of interpreting and routing e-mail messages.

Content

• *Categorization*
With the exception of system-generated messages for new, special attention (such as customer callbacks), due, and overdue responses, no content descriptions are required for this contingency.

Response

Response to the e-mail message is timely, accurate, clear, and complete.
The final contingency relative to outstanding customer care for e-mail communication is the actual response to the customer. So far, the message has been acknowledged, categorized, interpreted, and routed. Now the receiving agent must determine the most adequate response to the customer within the shortest possible time frame (see Figure 10.4).

Summary

Process

- Handling misrouted messages
- Prioritization of messages
- Changing the time to response
- Preparing to respond
- Escalating the e-mail message
- Creating an outbound e-mail message
- Editing an outbound e-mail message
- Sending an outbound e-mail message

Technology
The system will facilitate

- Integration—association with existing account, creation of new contact records, and the like.

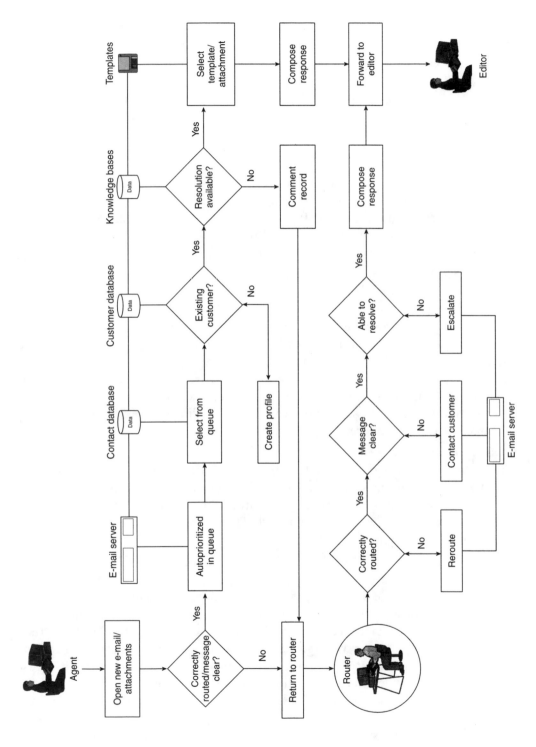

FIGURE 10.4 Responding to inbound e-mail messages

197

- Interface—ability to access templates, attach documentation, and the like.
- Misroutes—ease of rerouting e-mails
- Measures—overall contact times, types of customer suggestions, and the like.

Content

- Existence of online knowledge bases
- Creation and maintenance of online templates.

Details

Process

- *Handling misrouted messages*

In the event that the receiving agent determines that a particular message has been misrouted , he or she will either immediately return the message, together with a brief explanation, to the router for rerouting (or, if certain of the responsible party, the agent may be empowered to reroute the message directly to prevent a potential bottleneck at the router level). The router will then reassess the context of the message and reroute it accordingly, together with the original receiving agent's explanation.

- *Prioritization of messages*

After the receiving agent has initially viewed an incoming e-mail for appropriateness, it should be automatically placed in queue based on prioritization (time to respond, special handling, follow-up, message content (e.g., payment cancellation, etc.). Any message that is still in queue within, for example, thirty minutes of the conclusion of time to respond, should be automatically brought to the receiving agent's attention. Any missed time to response deadlines should be automatically escalated to prevent unnecessary customer callbacks.

- *Changing the time to response*

A receiving agent may determine that the given time to response for a particular e-mail is inadequate, in which case a notification must be sent to the customer referencing the original (together with autogenerated number), the new time frame, and the reason why it was changed. This change would then be conveyed to the follow-up system and the prioritization queue would be adjusted accordingly. Any such changes would be gathered for management analysis.

- *Preparing to respond*

When the receiving agent selects and opens an inbound e-mail message from the queue, the system will respond by opening (or creating) the corresponding customer profile and contact records in addition to the message itself and any relevant attachments, such as Web-gathered data or customer-attached files. The receiving agent will review any previous contacts (e.g., original contact in the case of a follow-up) for relevance, in addition to the attachments (it is critical that the receiving agent does not suggest a solution or provide information that the customer has already encountered). Based on all available information, the receiving agent will make a decision on the most appropriate response. In the event that there is not enough information to resolve the contact, the receiving agent may decide, based on relative urgency, whether to attempt to call the customer or send a template-driven e-mail message requesting further information.

- *Escalating the e-mail message*

Certain types of customer communications, such as complaints and highly technical inquiries or problems, are clearly beyond the scope of the frontline receiving agent's jurisdiction, and as such must be escalated. In the case of e-mail communications, which are screened by either a human "router" or intelligent processor, escalations should be more predictable and therefore may be made without the message ever being sent to the first tier receiving agent. The critical line between what constitutes a permissible escalation and a "routine" contact, however, is rarely well-defined, which leads to unnecessary and time-consuming research by the receiving agent, and ultimately a dissatisfied customer. Clearly, the online documentation for company policies and procedures can do much to clarify this delineation, and as such should be an integral and mandatory part of the process dealing with any customer contact. In the case of an escalated e-mail that is sent to the correct group (e.g., technical support) but is erroneously routed to a frontline receiving agent, the agent should be able to immediately (as in the case of a misrouted message) send it back to the human router, unless the agent has exceeded the time to respond, or the designated number of reroutes has been exceeded, in which case the message should be escalated to the supervisory level.

- *Creating an outbound e-mail message*

Having decided on the most appropriate form and content of response, the receiving agent will select an appropriate template (on which any known data, such as the customer's name, the ticket number, etc. will automatically be populated) as well as a textual attachment selected from available online documentation (such as a troubleshooting procedure, user instruction, pricing plan, store location, etc.), if necessary. A copy of the customer's original e-mail will also be automatically included. If any customization to the template is required, the system will automatically route the message through an editor prior to dispatch.

- *Editing an outbound e-mail message*

In the event that the receiving agent makes any changes to an existing template in order to respond to a customer's e-mail, the message may, depending upon the significance of the change, be routed to an editor for approval. The editor should be a documentation engineer who is proficient with company policies and procedures. If there are any grammatical mistakes or statements that may contravene company policy, the editor will adjust the message as necessary before sending it to the customer. The editor is responsible for recommending the creation of new or revision/deletion of existing templates to process owners based on the frequency with which existing templates are revised or customized responses created. The frequency of such changes should be systematically tracked using template versioning and possibly even change management software. The editor is also responsible for advising receiving agents on any changes that may have been made to their original response, as part of the feedback process.

- *Sending an outbound e-mail message*

When an e-mail response is sent to a customer, that customer's record should automatically be updated to include the title of the template and the titles of any online documentation text "nodes" that may have been attached to the response. This information should be used in order to drive the selection of the "contact category" which will be used for reporting on the nature of the customer's contact with customer care. The receiving agent or editor will be prompted to affirm the category selection before closing the contact. If the list is inadequate (leading to an "Other" selection), the quality improvement process is invoked.

Technology

- *Integration*

Any incoming e-mail messages should be associated with an existing customer account, if possible. In the event that the customer's e-mail account is not found, a secondary search should be conducted on the customer's name and any matches should be displayed to the receiving agent. If there are no matches at all, the system should automatically create a new customer account. In all of these cases, the incoming e-mail should create a new contact record for association with the customer account. The receiving agent should be able to select the new contact record in order to view the e-mail. If the e-mail was generated from the company's website, then it may include a record of the customer's transactions on the Web (if considered cost-beneficial in the context of resolving the customer inquiry or problem), which the receiving agent should also be able to view in order to further clarify the nature of the inquiry or complaint. A prerequisite should be the ability of the receiving agent to access any available online documentation and attach it to the e-mail in order to augment the response to the customer. Any action taken by the receiving agent, such as a response with an attached user instruction or procedure, should be automatically reflected in the contact record. A copy of the original e-mail should be attached to the response, and the entire response should then be accessible from the contact record (for customized responses only). None of these activities should require agent intervention (e.g., manual notations, etc.). Finally, the contact category (i.e., the reported reason why the customer called) is automatically suggested to the receiving agent or editor as the contact is closed. If the system-generated category is inappropriate, the agent is given the ability to select another category from the existing list.

- *Interface*

From a technology perspective, the outbound e-mail process described previously requires a carefully designed interaction between the human and the system, as well as a robust interaction between the various components of the system itself. In high-volume e-mail environments, the user and system interfaces represent the key to the success of the medium itself. A tremendous amount of unnecessary manual labor can be avoided, making e-mail an extremely viable alternative to voice. It should be easy to create, revise, and delete templates, and attaching text from online documentation to an e-mail message should be extremely intuitive. The templates themselves should be automatically populated, where possible. The receiving agent or editor should not have to type in voluminous notes about the nature of a contact, and manually categorize the contact from a list of 200 reason codes. In summary, there is no reason why handling e-mails cannot be as efficient, or in some cases even faster, than dealing with inbound telephone calls.

- *Misroutes*

Any messages classified by receiving agents as misroutes may, depending upon volume, be replicated and stored separately for further analysis and reporting purposes. The router, on receipt of a classified misroute and an obligatory attached explanation from the receiving agent, should be able to easily channel the message to the correct receiving agent. Again, in the case of an escalated e-mail message that was erroneously routed to a front-line receiving agent, the agent should be able to immediately send the message back to the router.

- *Measures*

Measures relevant to this contingency include number of e-mails resolved on first contact, number of outbound calls/e-mails required for customer clarification, overall "talk" (processing and response) time, types of customer suggestions and suggested action, contact categorizations, results of online customer surveys, number of messages classified as misroutes (and by whom), template usage, and so forth.

Content

- *Existence of online knowledge bases*

Clearly, the receiving agent will need access to all types of online knowledge, including policies and procedures, troubleshooting, general information, user instructions, error messages, and so forth. The upkeep of such information is of critical importance (feedback process).

- *Creation and maintenance of online templates*

Here are some of the categorizations that may involve the creation of templates relevant to customer responses:

Account Maintenance

Change account information

Cancellation

Order status

Billing Inquiry

Disputed charges

Balance inquiry

Payment history

General

Pricing

Mailing addresses

Customer suggestions

Customer comments

Request for clarification

Technical Support
Troubleshooting procedures
User instructions

Organizational Structure

As described, handling and responding to customer e-mails requires a high degree of structure, in addition to process, technology, content, and agent integrity. High-volume e-mail environments will employ not only agents, but specialist agents, routers, and editors as well (see Figure 10.5, User interaction). The most pivotal human role in this environment is that of the "router." While technology, such as an intelligent message processor, can assuage the interpretation and routing of certain inbound e-mails, the human router will always be needed to interpret cryptic messages, disseminate multifaceted messages, and channel emotive messages to management. The router will also have to appropriate times to response, update contact records, and advise customers accordingly. Additionally, the router will have to deal with misrouted messages returned from agents, as well as messages that the agents were unable to resolve. In other words, the router is the focal point of the entire e-mail operation—the one who can facilitate the success of the medium as an alternative customer care channel. Another key role is that of editor, for this individual must be not only an outstanding communicator, but also a subject matter expert who is fully aware of company policies and procedures.

In addition to the roles described above, it is also critical that the organizational structure and process engineering allows for strong communications links between customer care and the rest of the company, particularly the product management and marketing departments. Customer e-mails often provide more detailed information than can be captured during a toll-free call. It is important that this information is used to educate the company as to shortfalls in customer expectations of product, service, or even the customer care environment itself. Any information that the customer cannot easily find in marketing literature or at the website must be identified and revised if considered appropriate. All of this can be achieved only with a carefully designed organizational structure that recognizes the value of customer care as a competitive differentiator.

Significant business reasons for utilizing e-mail in customer care environments:

- Decrease in transaction costs:
  - Cost-effective usage of the network
  - Relative absence of immediate time constraints
- Decreased contact times:
  - Higher hit rate on inbound contacts
  - Reduction in time-consuming human-to-human interaction
  - Ability to capture and analyze customer interaction at website
  - Ability to attach procedural, troubleshooting, and informational data to messages
  - Ability to use prepopulated template responses (autoresponse)

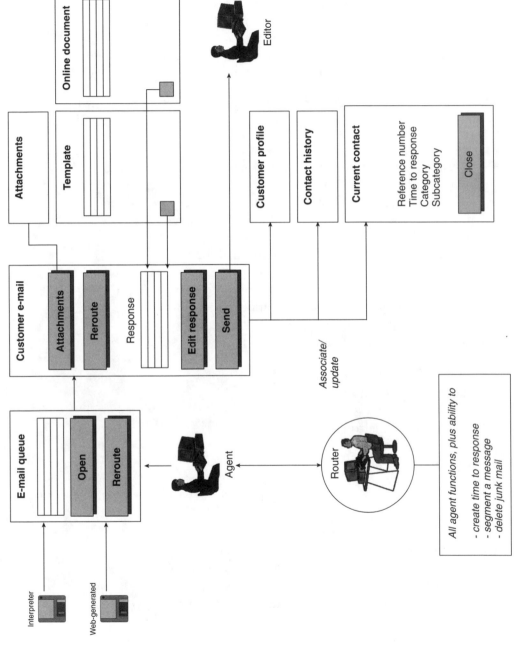

Attachments

Online document

Template

Editor

Customer e-mail

Attachments

Reroute

Response

Edit response

Send

Customer profile

Contact history

Current contact

Reference number
Time to response
Category
Subcategory

Close

Associate/
update

E-mail queue

Open

Reroute

Agent

Router

Interpreter

Web-generated

All agent functions, plus ability to

- *create time to response*
- *segment a message*
- *delete junk mail*

FIGURE 10.5 User Interaction

- ♦ Ability to customize responses with minimal effort (augmented response)
- ♦ Ability to automatically categorize contacts
- Accessibility
  - ♦ Easy, efficient, and detailed incident report tracking
  - ♦ Easy-to-target customer satisfaction surveys/suggestions
  - ♦ No "waiting by the phone" for customer care follow-up calls
  - ♦ Twenty-four hour facility for inbound e-mails
  - ♦ The customer's ability to "converse" with a particular agent, which is not normally an option on inbound telephone calls.

Implementing processes, technology, content, and costing relevant to handling e-mail communications:

- Processes
  E-mail messages are efficiently received, resolved, and reported via the following processes:
  - ♦ Marketing company website and e-mail addresses
  - ♦ Creating and sending independent e-mail messages
  - ♦ Creating and sending Web-based e-mail messages
  - ♦ Defining attachments to Web-based e-mail messages
  - ♦ Approximating time frames to response
  - ♦ Receiving, categorizing, and storing inbound e-mail messages
  - ♦ Analyzing inbound e-mail sources and frequencies
  - ♦ Interpreting the e-mail message
  - ♦ Dealing with cryptic or multifaceted messages
  - ♦ Routing the message
  - ♦ Handling customer callbacks
  - ♦ Handling misrouted messages
  - ♦ Prioritization of messages
  - ♦ Changing the time to response
  - ♦ Preparing to respond
  - ♦ Escalating the e-mail message
  - ♦ Creating an outbound e-mail message
  - ♦ Editing an outbound e-mail message
  - ♦ Sending an outbound e-mail message
- Technology
  E-mail messages are displayed to agents with
  - ♦ Customer profile and previous contact history (if available)
  - ♦ Content (actual verbiage of customer message)
  - ♦ Attachments (any Web activity/customer attachments)
  - ♦ Current contact record, including
    - ■ Time of receipt
    - ■ Time to response (hours/minutes remaining)
    - ■ Categorization (billing inquiry, etc.)

The system will facilitate the user in

- Selecting *any* e-mail in queue
- Creating a new customer profile
- Searching online knowledge bases for solution
- Opening a response template
- Attaching a solution to a response template
- Editing a response template
- Creating an original time to response (router only)
- Changing the time to response and alerting customer
- Returning the message to the router (misrouted or insoluble)
- Select from a list of reasons why the message is being returned.

The system will automatically

- Track and attach information relevant to customer Web activity
- Classify and route Web-generated e-mails based on origination (e.g., Web troubleshooting)
- Interpret, classify, and route independently generated e-mails (noncryptic/multifaceted)
- Identify special handling e-mails and route to specialists
- Create a contact record for every inbound e-mail message
- Immediately respond to certain types of customer e-mail, to include
  - Generating a reference number
  - Retrieving and generating time to response based on e-mail type
  - Populating appropriate templates based on contact type
- Associate a contact record with a customer profile (if available)
- Display the contact record, contact history, and customer profile with open e-mails
- Alert the agent when new e-mail arrives
- Display all e-mail in queue for a particular agent
- Prioritize the e-mail in queue based on time to response
- Reroute *new* e-mail messages if not opened within a given period
- Alert the agent before time to response expires
- Subcategorize the e-mail based on agent selected attachments from online knowledge bases
- Reroute e-mails when time to response expires
- Create autonotations based on agent actions
- Populate the selected response template (with customer name, e-mail address, details, etc.)
- Create an e-mail to the customer explaining why time to response has changed
- Forward completed responses to editor for approval
- Attach reasons (from agent to router) to each returned e-mail
- Reporting capabilities to include
  - The average time per contact
  - The average time in queue

- The number of customer callbacks via e-mail
- The number of customer callbacks via IVR
- The number of e-mails as a percentage of overall contacts
- The number of system interpreted e-mails
- The number of Web-generated e-mails
- The number of emotive (complaint) e-mails
- The number of telephone callbacks within 24-hours of e-mail receipt
- Categorizations and subcategorizations of all e-mails
- Autonotations associated with each e-mail
- The number of e-mails handled by each agent
- The number of e-mails redirected due to agent unavailability
- The number of missed times to response
- The number of misrouted e-mails and why
- The number of insoluble e-mails and why.
- Content
  - Template and form content as defined by process owners for Web-based e-mails
  - Data gathering for automatic attachment to Web-based e-mails
  - The company will advertise website and e-mail addresses on all literature and packaging
  - Company literature and website help will describe the optimal content for customer e-mails
  - Existence of online knowledge bases
  - Categorization of online templates
- Costing

  The extent to which e-mail automation will be applied is based on factors such as
  - Availability of tools to facilitate automation
  - Integration issues with existing software
  - Operational savings realized from avoiding manual labor
  - Consistency or speed required in handling a given message type.

Summary

The preceding pages described the contingencies surrounding the successful implementation of electronic mail facilities for a customer care environment. The emergence of commercially viable e-mail interpretation, response, and routing tools, together with the unprecedented success of the Internet, continues to revolutionize a medium that was formerly the domain of sophisticated business-to-business endeavors. As a low-cost alternative to customer care via the telephone, e-mail demands significant attention from cost-conscious companies.

Obviously, the successful implementation of an e-mail facility depends largely on the commitment to process excellence. While technology can facilitate such processes, a strong human resource component is required to ensure flawless execution. The customer who sends an e-mail message but is forced to call the toll-free number in order to resolve the original issue is liable to end up costing the company far more money than even the lengthiest voice-to-voice communication.

A customer care environment that can demonstrate to its customers that electronic mail messages are handled in a timely and professional manner, will encourage the development of an inexpensive and cost-effective medium and perhaps even contribute to the demise of the toll-free call as a primary means of customer support.

11

The World Wide Web

Overview

Today's customer care environment is characterized by complexity. Emerging media, coupled with disparate applications on the agent's desktop, continue to create usability issues that directly impact customer satisfaction. The emergence of the World Wide Web as a business resource, however, is encouraging many systems development managers to use standard Web graphical user interfaces or "browsers" in order to provide a consistent and intuitive front-end to users, in addition to providing both Intranet (i.e., internal to the company) and Internet contact handling capabilities. This approach is tremendously beneficial for a number of reasons:

- Real time information across the entire organization via an Intranet (e.g., the latest marketing promotion)
- Ability to track customer activity on the World Wide Web
- Intuitive graphical user interface elements that reduce the learning curve for new users
- Rapid online content delivery and maintenance
- Ability to route customer and agent feedback across the organization as necessary

The remarkable economy of placing customer care-oriented information on the World Wide Web as opposed to provisioning toll-free number voice-to-voice support makes this medium an absolute "must" for many contemporary companies. Even if the website were used only to answer the most facile of customer inquiries by a small percentage of the customer base, it can ostensibly justify its existence a hundred times over in a short period of time. As more consumers and businesses avail themselves of this facility, the role of the Web will continue to expand as a viable alternative to centralized call center operations.

From a systems maintenance perspective also, the consistent "look and feel" and intuitive nature of Web browsers make this medium ideal for direct usage by agents. Providing an "Intranet" rather than a conglomeration of disparate user interfaces for different applications is an approach that is enjoying huge success in customer care environments. Agents using Intranet browsers no longer have to contend with learning yet another graphical user interface. Instead, it becomes the job of the development organization to integrate new functions with the existent interface, thereby significantly reducing the learning curve for frontline agents.

The success of the Web as a medium for customer service depends largely upon the quality and quantity of the information that a company chooses to put into its website. Customers who are familiar with some of the best sites on the Web expect information on order status, solutions to product or service problems, up-to-date pricing plans, and online billing adjustments, coupled with the ability to indicate a need to speak with an agent, send an e-mail message, maintain account information, or share ideas and information with company employees and other customers (see Figure 11.1, Webcentric customer care). This expectation cannot be underestimated from a competitive point of view, and companies who are thinking of investing in a customer care component for their websites have the novel advantage of being able to easily investigate the level of sophistication provided by their rivals.

Toll-free number support continues to be the most significant customer care differentiator between one company and another. Today, however, a customer may decide to access the World Wide Web in order to gauge the relative support available in this regard. This notion, albeit anathema to those companies who provide outstanding voice-to-voice customer care but have yet to venture onto the Web, is nevertheless becoming a solid litmus test for many customers. It is also fair to surmise that although the Web has become a ubiquitous term in everyday dialect, it has yet to realize its full potential as a customer service medium. A comparison might therefore be drawn to the era when simply having a toll-free number was considered somewhat of a competitive advantage, whereas today the measure of differentiation depends upon several variables, such as hold time, agent empowerment, and instant access to information.

Unlike voice-to-voice communications, customer care on the Web does not currently rely upon courtesy or empathy as measures of customer satisfaction. The contemporary website is overtly impersonal, unbiased, and impervious to anger. It does not, however, preclude a customer from venting frustration via a well-placed electronic mail facility or even linking directly into a company's automatic call distributor queue in order to speak to another human being. A well-designed website that provides in-depth information may therefore be viewed as a powerful customer satisfaction device. The onus is on the customer to initially discover an answer to his or her problem or inquiry. Any failure to achieve this goal should be viewed as an opportunity for improvement and handled accordingly. In other words, a customer who sends an e-mail or calls an agent from a website can be a valuable resource for improving the level of online customer care.

Presenting online information directly to the customer is not without risk. If that information was cryptic and poorly organized in the view of a trained call center agent (and it often is), it will almost certainly not help the customer quickly resolve

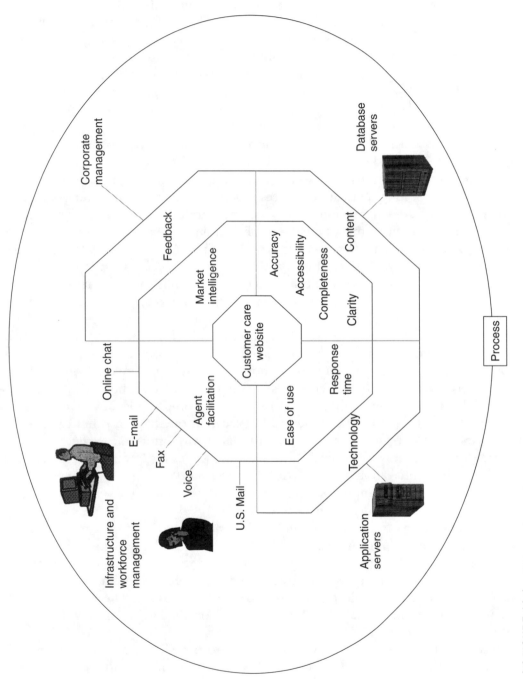

FIGURE 11.1 Webcentric customer care

211

an inquiry or problem. Secondly, the process for acquiring, engineering, and maintaining information in multiple locations must be established. Finally, even if a company has the most exhaustive information available online, the user interface itself may preclude the customer from accessing the data in an intuitive manner.

In the not so distant future, transactions with Web-enabled customers will perhaps be akin to face-to-face conversations. Digital technologies have already made their way into consumer households, enabling rapid transmission of data from the Web. Today, online "chat" sessions enable customers to exchange "real time" information on the Web—a capability that is augmented by emerging voice capabilities.

The beauty of the Web from the customer care perspective is the fact that it has promised a simplicity of content provisioning and maintenance that is not interrupted by developmental issues. The website maintenance team should be a cohesive blend of knowledge engineers, marketers, software developers, artists, and documentation engineers. Overall, companies must make a wholesale commitment to content provisioning on the Web by allocating adequate resources to knowledge acquisition and documentation engineering. As with voice-to-voice customer care turnaround times on inaccurate or missing information must be fast—ideally within 24-hours of discovery.

Even the most rudimentary website would be incomplete without a facility to rapidly convey a message to the company. Most often, this is provided in the form of an electronic mail address. For the call center manager, this means that resource(s) must be allocated to respond to any customer e-mail messages. A somewhat more complex function would involve responding to a customer who selected the "Call me" option, which in most cases would result in a callback to the customer within a given period of time. A third approach is being adopted by companies who take their customer care website investment even more seriously. This involves integration between a Web function often described as "Speak to a Rep" and the call center automatic call distributor. Essentially, this means that a customer exploring a website can initiate a telephone call to the center, and be placed in queue with other calls. Taking this function a step further is to provide the agent with information regarding the Web page the customer was perusing when making the call, or even a complete history of customer interaction on that particular website visit. This capability clearly involves fairly rigorous computer-telephony integration, often at a price that raises doubts about potential return on investment.

Today, customers "surfing" a company's World Wide Web site can choose to speak directly to an agent using features like "WebPhones." This means that the customer does not have to install a second telephone line in order to conduct voice-to-voice communications with an agent. Instead, the customer clicks on an icon installed at the company's website, indicating a desire to speak to a human. The "call" is placed in queue via the automatic call distributor, whereupon the agent can identify it as a Web-generated interaction.

A critical strategic decision is whether or not to put all available customer care information on the Web. From a competitive standpoint, it doesn't make sense to open corporate databases to the world at large. Some information, such as payment history, usage, and account information obviously should be accessed only by individuals using personal passwords, whereas other information, such as troubleshooting, could be universally available to registered users or (depending upon the proprietary nature of the content) perhaps all website visitors. It may well be that the company will not want everybody to know about particular product or service nuances, in which case the agents will access somewhat different databases.

A secondary—but no less important—decision is whether to charge customers for premium customer service, that is, voice-to-voice access to agents. Many companies do not provide toll-free service, for example, but expect their customers to pick up the cost of the call. Companies with massive customer bases and limited resources are already taking the extra step of charging a premium for speaking to an agent, especially if the entire knowledge base for a particular product or service has been deployed on the Web. Customers are guaranteed that they will reach an expert, rather than a novice, agent.

The following list demonstrates the power of the Web as a powerful medium for customer care:

- Order new features/products
- Check order status
- Locate nearest branch or store
- Access directories
- Check current bill
- View previous bills
- Send/receive e-mail
- Talk to a "live" agent
- Change account information
- Conduct price plan analysis
- Download software upgrades
- Participate in online chat forums
- Create trouble tickets
- View frequently asked questions
- Access documentation
- Interact with IVR functions
- Download bug fixes and workarounds
- Configure utilities
- Access online knowledge base
- Technical troubleshooting tips
- Access product training program.

User Interface Design

In the case of Webcentric customer care, the migration of powerful user interface tools to the user is completely changing the face of customer care. Standards, or lack of them, are now limited only by the users ability to manipulate relatively simplistic user interface tools in whatever way they choose. The discipline of human-computer interaction, which has been influenced so much by the availability of various user interaction widgets (list boxes, icons, radio buttons, etc.) may disappear altogether. Everyone is a potential designer now. Computers are available to more people in a greater variety of contexts than ever before. As a result, the need for accessibility, ease of use, and user engagement has grown more pronounced.

A few years ago, leaders in the field of human-computer interaction were pre-
dicting that the designer of interactive systems would have the skills of an engineer,
an artist, and a psychologist. Others predicted that a design team would consist of
many players, akin to a theatrical production. Instead, today there are potentially millions of designers working in attics, basements, universities, and offices. It is akin to
the transition of publishing from the typesetters and designers to the desktop. As
World Wide Web home page creators, these individuals also have ostensibly as much
opportunity to reach a mass audience as a billion dollar company.

Yet there is, of course, a place for visionary designers. The involvement of sociolo-
gists, anthropologists, and psychologists is required now to help the industry determine
the best way to design the functions of these models for humans who have not been
weaned on "standard" graphical user interface design. The goal is to create seamless interaction between all facets of a customer care system—the troubleshooting system, online
documentation, store and branch locations, repair tracking, contact tracking, and the like,
as well as achieving layered user interface complexity—a system built for novices as well
as experts. A key element of this endeavor is task analysis—the study of what the users do
and the ways in which they perform their tasks. Good task analysis means *continual* user
testing. It should consider the environment in which the computer will be used.

Yet, so many disparate sectors of the industry must contrive to produce the ultimate
user interface. Voice recognition hardware must reach new heights, bandwidth must
increase exponentially, a new visual standard must be embraced by the Web. After all,
how does a user with just a keyboard interact with today's hypermedia interface? Potentially, this means changing the keyboard or doing away with it altogether. A wonderfully intuitive solution to all of this won't work if the system architecture doesn't support it, or if it runs too slowly. Conversely, it doesn't matter if the interface responds
instantly, if the user can't use it. The typical user is in a rush, bored, or impatient.

Another major obstacle to the success of online customer care is the fact that users
are often fearful of destroying data, of hurting the machine, or of seeming stupid (both
to other users and even to the computer itself). In ten years, this fear will not exist
for the majority of those with the sort of buying power that interests commerce on
the Web today. Those in high schools and universities today will be the target
market of tomorrow, and they will not possess the fear that characterizes many contemporary computer users. Nevertheless, a great leap backwards is required to accommodate today's buyers, back to the purest form of human-computer interaction,
perhaps . . . the flashing cursor. With the promise of improved voice recognition and
the new generation of online expert systems, perhaps it will be possible to offload those
expensive calls from novice computer users. Finding ways to help people resolve
inquiries and problems without human intervention is the designers highest challenge.

Interactive Voice Response vs. The World Wide Web

The World Wide Web has several advantages over the interactive voice response,
including

- The visual medium is far more intuitive than following verbal
  instructions only.

- The Web gives customers the ability to print information (e.g., product usage instructions, directions, account information, etc.) directly from the desktop.
- The Web displays available options at a glance (there is no need to wait for prompts).
- Most websites provide built-in electronic mail capabilities.
- The Web allows the customer to access far more detailed information.

The interactive voice response unit, however, continues to have a role to play:

- Disaster recovery messages (the voice-to-voice telephone network is an extremely reliable medium)
- The ability for the customer to leave a quick voice mail
- No computer is required to access an interactive voice response unit.

Rapid and voluminous information resources, ease of use, and global availability are outstanding features of the World Wide Web. Slowness, difficulty of use, unreliability, and too much wasted time are also among common complaints about the Web. However, its adoption by large corporations, and the interest of the media, guarantee that it will continue to evolve rapidly.

Knowledge Management for the Web

A logical progression for any company planning to deploy a website for customer care would be as follows:

- *Describe functional and navigational considerations*
  This task would involve a graphical depiction of the entire website, indicating the name and purpose of each screen in addition its relationship with other screens. It would also involve describing the function of each graphical element placed on the screen, for example:

SCREEN 1.   General business questions.

Title	Sub Title	Current Text	
Customer Care Web Site	General Questions	"Here are some other questions that will help us assess your eligibility for our program"	

Control	Label/Title	Description	Function
Single select list box	How long have you been purchasing our product?	Allows the customer to select number of years (e.g., 0-1, 1-2, etc.).	Use only in conjunction with "Next" button: If >3 years go to screen 1a If 0–3 years go to screen 1b
Radio buttons	Do you buy our product for business or personal usage?	"Yes" / "No" selection (no default)	Use only in conjunction with "Next" button: If "Yes" go to screen 1c If "No" go to screen 2
Push button	Next	Standard CUA "OK" push button behavior	Determines user's eligibility accesses screens (1a, 1b, 1c) as per the above parameters

- *Content considerations*

The second stage of design involves populating each screen with content that either encourages the customer to explore the entire site (as in the case of companies who are not only providing useful customer-oriented information, but who are also attempting to convince the customer that their brand of product or service is better than any other), or provides the customer with a rapid solution to a problem or inquiry. Many companies use intelligent troubleshooting systems as a means of resolving customer problems, and these systems are just as viable on the Web as on an agent's desktop, the difference being that it is far less expensive to resolve customer problems directly from the Web.

- *Graphical considerations*

The last stage prior to deployment of the Web application is the actual graphical design of the site. After all of the navigational, functional, and content decisions have been made, the task of making the site as attractive as possible is usually given to an individual who is particularly skilled in that area, such as a graphic designer or even an artist.

The processes pertinent to the creation and maintenance of a customer care website include

- Security considerations, including the determination of which data the customer is allowed to access
- Communications, including providing an e-mail facility as well as the ability to speak to an agent
- Handling customer feedback and suggestions and improving the website accordingly
- Tracking customer interaction on the Web for market intelligence purposes
- Coordinating website content with training and call center information retrieval systems.

Strategic Considerations

The following strategic considerations need to be addressed relative to a customer care-oriented World Wide Web site:

- How are customers expected to access this site (i.e., via the main corporate site or via the Web search engines)?
- Who will be responsible for maintaining the screen flow, content, and "look and feel" of this site and how does this relate to the upkeep of the main website?
- What is the strategy for ensuring that content is consistent with company policies and procedures (legal issues, etc.)?
- What is the migration path to full-scale appropriation of customer care facilities on the Web, and what contingencies need to be in place to ensure that this is successful?
- In the case of deploying intelligent troubleshooting systems on the Web, will the system be capable of parsing, interpreting, and analyzing free-form text input from customers and using that information to eliminate unnecessary questions to the customer?

Using World Wide Web Features

FAQs

As potentially one of the most useful customer care functions available on the Web, frequently asked questions (FAQs) demand particular attention. Using quantitative data gathered from customer interactions via the toll-free number, coupled with expert answers from the existent agent population, it should be possible to define questions and answers to all types of customer inquiry. Presales (i.e., price ranges, product or service offerings, terms and conditions, etc.) and postsales (i.e., troubleshooting, account maintenance, billing, etc.) questions could be considered as separate entities that may be located in different areas of the website.

By making website FAQs comprehensive, targeted, up to date and easy to find, a company can take great strides in assuaging certain types of calls. Such a task demands considerable research and dedicated effort, however, especially in companies that constantly change marketing strategies or are dedicated to product innovation. Of particular concern from a maintenance viewpoint should be the ability to direct inquiries from any part of the website back to specific FAQs. For example, if a potential customer wants more information on a product feature, a hyperlink should bring them back to details that constitute part of the FAQ construct. In this way, the website designer can ensure that the site does not become an unruly mass of links guaranteed to lose the customer in proverbial "hyperspace."

Like any hypermedia program, a website demands extremely careful planning to ensure that all links are logical and relatively easy to maintain. Many FAQ designers use a hierarchical approach to ensure that the customer is able to navigate easily. By starting the FAQs at the highest level of the hierarchy (e.g., specific product names), the design and content delivery can proceed in a logical fashion.

Internet E-Mail

From an online customer care perspective, e-mail epitomizes the purest form of communication between the customer and the company. Most company websites provide immediate access to e-mail via aptly entitled pushbuttons (e.g., "Your 2 Cents," "Feedback," "Write Us," etc.). When the pushbutton is selected, a template automatically populated with the customer's e-mail address is retrieved. The cursor may flash in the text field, allowing the customer to simply type his or her message and select the "Send" pushbutton.

Today, a 24-hour response to e-mail messages is considered acceptable. This benchmark is likely to change considerably as customers are encouraged to communicate electronically. Some companies respond in as little as five minutes, particularly those who have availed themselves of the latest automated response technologies, while others are clearly not in a position to support the e-mail facility in any sort of timely fashion.

Forms

Easier to distribute and interpret from an administrative perspective, forms encourage customers to categorize the inquiry or complaint from the outset. For example, a company may provide one form for technical support, one for sales, and another for general inquiries. All three may look the same (i.e., problem/inquiry field, followed by identifier fields such as customer name, company name, phone number(s), order number, etc.), but will be distributed by the customer care server according to category. Some companies are encouraging customers to use forms instead of e-mail by providing the hypermedia link to e-mail only at the bottom of the form, with the caveat "If you experience any problems responding to this form, e-mail your response to. . . ," or other such comments.

Online Help

Few people who take the time to visit a website want to belabor this activity by having to access online help in order to find what they are looking for; either it's an intuitive process or it's just not worth the effort. Although not strictly a form of online help, the most common aid used by infrequent visitors to a company website is the "Search" facility. Providing an ability to search intuitively and easily is critical to the successful completion of many, if not all customer inquiries and problems that involve a company's products or services. Given the problems invariably encountered even by trained agents in attempting to search online databases, it is not difficult to imagine the damage a lethargic search engine coupled with inaccurate, incomplete, unclear, or even nonexistent information can do to a customer's perception of a company.

Ideally, a customer should be able to type (or, in currently novel circumstances, verbalize) a free form (natural language) inquiry in order to navigate around a website. This is the ultimate form of online help, but demands a level of sophistication that remains a far-sighted goal for many software development endeavors. While there are certainly tools on the market that strive to enable such communication, the majority of online help facilities continue to place the onus on the customer to figure out menu-driven or selectable list box responses to inquiries. This is a relatively acceptable approach, but combined with the ongoing response time issues on the Web, it is a step that should be avoided wherever possible.

Many online searches result in the retrieval of a plethora of cryptically named hyperlinks that are of little or no help to the customer. Others provide a textual abstract that explains the content of each item retrieved (often combined with corresponding confidence ratings). Still others attempt to narrow the customer's search by providing a selectable matrix of needs that can help to define a resolution, particularly to a product problem.

A carefully designed user interface, subject to constant usability testing and iteration based on customer needs, is perhaps the most successful form of online help. Using devices such as context-sensitivity (e.g., on-demand text explaining the function of an icon) can be extremely useful in assuaging customer needs in a timely manner. While online wizards and intelligent agents continue to infiltrate the Web, it is apparent that, for most customers, trying to resolve customer care problems and inquiries via this medium remains a tenuous replacement for dialing a toll-free number, and should therefore be treated with the utmost care from a design perspective.

Billing and Account Maintenance

Change Account Details

Providing editable account information online helps the company to ensure that a particular customer's record is always up to date. When the customer requests online access to account data, the company will often respond with a mailed letter containing usage instructions and password information, or even allow this activity to occur online simply by having the customer enter a preestablished password or security word. The customer can then manipulate logistical information, including billing name and address, credit card numbers and expiration dates, price plan subscriptions, feature additions/cancellations, and the like, using an online form.

Many service companies are allowing customers to change their pricing plans at the press of a button. This activity is usually linked to an online analysis tool that enables the customers to enter their usage data (e.g., approximate hours per month, peak times of usage, etc.) and have the tool select the best plan for them.

From the billing inquiry perspective, it is relatively common to provide the customer with a facility for reviewing current charges, as well as providing access to the past several months of billing details. This expeditious process averts the need for interaction with an agent, who may then have to print out a copy of a previous bill, for example, then fax or mail the bill to the customer.

Technical Support

Troubleshooting

If companies are seriously interested in encouraging their customers to use the Web as an alternate means of customer care, they must provide intuitive troubleshooting support. This means getting the right answer to a particular inquiry or complaint on the *first* try. Many vendors are now integrating their problem resolution tools with the Web, enabling around-the-clock support with a potential for powerful contact tracking and root cause analysis of customer problems. For example, the customer can either select from a list of known problems or type in a query. In turn, this information can be captured and analyzed, enabling a company to easily track the number of calls about a particular problem and take immediate action:

- Rapidly identify a critical flaw in a particular product or service.
- Update online FAQs to reflect a common problem.
- Recognize customer terminology and adjust online documentation accordingly.

In the event that customers are unable to resolve a particular problem online, they can easily submit their request to technical support (see forms). Some tools facilitate technical support specialists by automatically creating trouble tickets for every problem, and they even start diagnosing the potential resolution using artificial intelligence (such as natural language interpretation), as well as enabling look-up and creation of customer profiles (the customer, rather than the agent, fills in the blanks). Subsequently, customers can check the resolution status of their problems by going online and entering either their last name or a trouble ticket number.

User Instructions

If the company provided the facility, most customers had to use bulletin boards in order to access procedural and instructional documentation. Today, more companies are using the Web in order to provide customer access to this "How to" information. Documents may be listed in order of popularity or, alternatively, be accessed via the troubleshooting system as linkages to potential problem solutions.

Tutorials

An extension of the user instructions process, online tutorials provide customers with the ability to understand more complex procedures through the use of text, graphics, and even video displays. Providing this form of assistance via the Web can also help to offset calls to toll-free numbers. Some companies, particularly those who have captured niche markets, charge customers for the privilege of accessing tutorials—a strategy justified by saving the customer the bother of ordering videotapes or other forms of assistance.

Online Chat

Several companies are offering access to online chat sessions, particularly those involved in high-technology industries. Customers can exchange views and opinions online, possibly in the presence of a subject matter expert from the company, but most often as a readily available "bulletin board" for problem resolution and helpful hints. Web functions have made these sessions highly interactive and accessible to just about anybody who happens to be in the vicinity.

Q&A Forums

It is no longer unusual for the CEO of a particular company to spend several hours online with existing and prospective customers, answering questions that are posted on the company's website. Several companies have used this as a highly effective public relations endeavor, but just as toll-free numbers were once a sign of competitive differentiation, Q&A forums with senior managers are likely to become a "customer intimate" norm, which is an inevitable aspect of contemporary business strategy.

Internet-based Customer Care Technologies

Computer-Telephony Integration and the Internet

Real-time voice and fax communications via the Internet are being applied to all kinds of existing computer-telephony integration opportunities:

- Long distance telephone service
- Business phone service
- Fax delivery and broadcast
- Call centers and audio conferencing

Computer servers have already merged computer-telephony integration functionality with Internet access. These servers handle real time routing of voice, fax, and data via the Internet to remote destinations. Applications include internet call centers, unified messaging on the Internet, and Internet-based collaborative computing using real-time audio.

Internet-Based Unified Messaging

Unified messaging is traditionally viewed as the merging of voice mail, fax and e-mail so that all message types are available for access in one location. Typically, unified messaging is made available to the user's proprietary desktop client application or via a traditional telephone interface. What the Internet now brings to this market is the option of delivering all message types via an Internet client. This represents two major changes to the existing paradigm: a nonproprietary graphical interface to an Internet-enabled message server, and voice mail/fax mail at local toll charge prices.

Internet Enabled Interactive Voice Response (IVR)

Customers who access Web-enhanced IVR applications are better able to differentiate the product or services offered because the presentations include visual and audio components. Perhaps even more compelling is the ability of IVR systems to augment websites by adding large or legacy system integration.

Internet Automatic Call Distributors

Traditionally, callers interact with an interactive voice response unit to answer most of the questions about an order. When a caller leaves the IVR and is forwarded to an agent, the agent receives the information gathered by the IVR. In an Internet call center, a customer interacts with a Web page and clicks on an icon to go to an agent for help. Today, a customer can enter his or her phone number on a form, which is submitted via e-mail. The form is routed to an available agent who then queues a return call.

Integrating Websites and Call Centers

The important step of integrating a website with the remainder of customer care operations cannot be overlooked. The website may facilitate those customers who simply want general information about prices and products, but introducing automated customer care without integration with call center operations will hardly enhance productivity, increase customer satisfaction, reduce costs, or increase market intelligence gathering.

Many companies are using technologies that directly link the Web to live agents. It is worth considering the initiation of callbacks from the Web using the common, everyday telephone (with computer-telephony integration). Customers looking for technical support on the Web can choose to speak to a live agent, at which point the system may either route the call directly to an agent or automatically queue a callback request by delivering detailed information about the customer and the customer's request. A call center may use the same technology to provide length-of-anticipated delay announcements to callers. The result is that messages, not callers, wait in queue for agents.

With Internet computer-telephony integration, customers enter relevant information about the problem into a message form. The information is routed to the technical support call center along with a list of the help pages visited. This information is used to route the call to the most qualified technician, who will then research the problem and have suggestions ready for the customer.

The Protagonists' Vision of the World Wide Web

There is no question that the unprecedented rise of the World Wide Web is causing many companies to reconsider traditional customer care strategies. The protagonists vision might include the following:

- Telecommuting agents will be able to log on to both the telephone and computer networks anywhere, anytime, and anyplace as necessary to handle queue times.
- Agents will use the same systems as the customer, with the exception of proprietary databases.
- The Web will facilitate marketing and customer care entities collaborating in order to represent an "end-to-end" relationship with the customer.

Forward-thinking managers recognized the potential of the Web for offloading customer calls almost as soon as it appeared. Others are still mired in day-to-day operational problems that preclude any detailed thinking about provisioning multichannels for customer care. Putting a customer care facility on the Web, however, does not require the same amount of logistical planning that would be entailed by Interactive Voice Response, fax, and e-mail support. Website content can be developed in-house using relatively inexpensive software, and deployment is simply a matter of purchasing adequate storage space on an Internet server. A customer care Web component, therefore, can be envisioned and realized in a short period of time. Typically, a company will start by putting responses to frequently asked customer questions (FAQs) on the Web. By allocating a dedicated resource to ensure that this information is kept up to date, the company is also investing in a potential "Webmaster" (in this case an individual who is very familiar with customer care scenarios and can also exploit the capabilities of the Web as a medium for customer care). By recording the number of "hits" on a particular site coupled with any otherwise unwarranted decline in call volumes, management can begin to assess the relative impact of its initiative. It is an exciting time for website protagonists, particularly with the advanced functions that could be placed online with comparatively minor budgetary support.

CHAPTER

12

High Technology at the Call Center

Overview

Several established technologies play a significant role in the quest for world-class customer interaction. Interactive voice response (IVR), for example, together with automatic call distributors (ACDs), voice mail, fax, call management systems, auto attendants, workforce management tools, and computer-telephony integration (CTI), are now found in many contemporary call center environments. These tools offer call center managers sophisticated solutions to a variety of traditional issues, such as rapidly answering the customer call, identifying the customer, routing the call appropriately, and handling the customer's inquiry or problem without any unnecessary delay.

Tools like call management systems are invaluable to call center operations, for instance, as these are used for calculating *average speed of answer, number of incoming calls, number of calls abandoned, average talk time, average after call work time, work time not related to a specific call, average staff availability, and so forth*. Automatic call distributor features such as *expected wait time* can advise a customer on just how much longer he or she will have to wait in queue for an agent. *Information indicators* can deduce where a customer is calling from (e.g., a payphone, cellular phone, prison, etc.) and route the call according to its perceived priority. *Automatic number identification*(ANI) can be used to match an inbound call with an existing customer information file via computer-telephony integration, allowing the agent to identify the customer immediately, and so on.

Regardless of the technology, however, there is always a need for human factors consideration and most often some form of maintenance process. With interactive voice response, for example, the most important considerations involve scripting and database integration. Skills-based routing, a feature of automatic call distributors, also requires careful monitoring and assessment. The decision to implement computer telephony integration most often involves consideration of the end-to-end call handling process, while workforce management software needs stringent maintenance in order to successfully affect call center service levels. The following section is not intended to summarize the many excellent features of these technologies, but rather to examine each from the human interaction perspective.

Interactive Voice Response Scripting

Interactive voice response (IVR) scripting is possibly one of the most neglected art forms in the customer care environment today. It is also occasionally one of the most obtrusive and annoying technological solutions to emerge from the unprecedented success of toll-free telephone lines. Managers may perceive IVRs as an excellent and efficient "front-end" that screens and routes calls to the proper agent. For some customers, however, it is apparent that IVRs are viewed as impersonal and time-consuming obstructions that prevent them from reaching a human being who can resolve their problem. After all, a pleasant voice recording does not, for example, make interminable menu selections and confusing product troubleshooting scripts any more palatable to the customer. IVR *scripting,* therefore, is a critical feature of the call management process, and should be treated accordingly.

A rule of thumb for any customer care manager involved in IVR scripting is to implicitly understand the needs of the user as well as the goals of the business. If the business goal is to decrease the number of calls in queue by 33 percent, then the manager needs to understand the best way to convey IVR solutions to one in every three customer problems or inquiries in an efficient and speedy manner (see Figure 12.1, Interactive voice response strategy and maintenance). This can only be achieved by iterative design and testing through task and customer contact analysis. Customers who elect to wait in queue, for example, might be given the option to access procedural information or answers to the most frequently asked questions for a particular product *without losing their place in queue.* Caller's may also be given the option to access their account or billing information and even make changes as considered necessary. The IVR may also enable the customer to leave a voice mail message for agent callback, depending upon the call center environment. The customer should also be able to exit the IVR at any time during the call.

Speech recognition is also becoming a more commonplace feature of IVR technology. Ideally, this would eliminate the need for customers to interact via the telephone keypad (one of this technology's biggest drawbacks) or even to listen to menu selections that are annoyingly subjective. Allowing customers to "barge in" and state their needs by using synonym relationships to retrieve relevant information requires the maturity of IVR technology. Speech recognition, despite significant progress in recent years, is still imperfect, and most customers are compelled to access information in an arcane manner. The integration of the IVR with the fax machine has also opened new and useful avenues for human machine interaction. Scripting for speech recognition and fax-on-demand clearly requires extensive user evaluation as well as

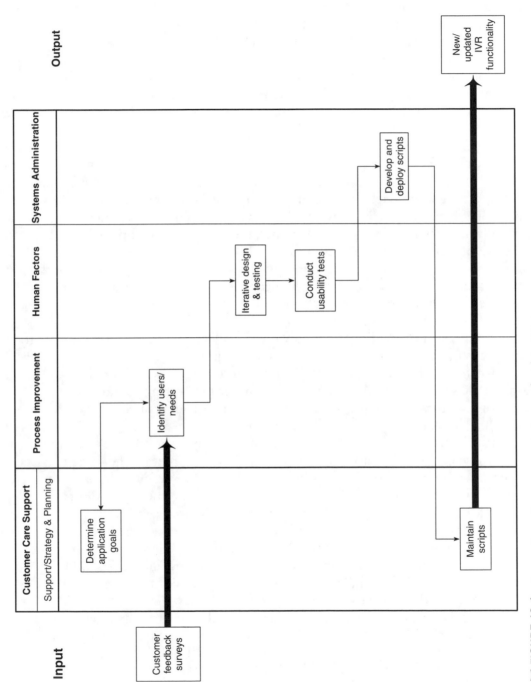

Input

Output

Customer Care Support	Process Improvement	Human Factors	Systems Administration
Support/Strategy & Planning			

Customer feedback surveys

Determine application goals

Identify users/ needs

Iterative design & testing

Conduct usability tests

Develop and deploy scripts

Maintain scripts

New/ updated IVR functionality

▧ **FIGURE 12.1** Interactive voice response strategy and maintenance

225

coordination with systems integration processes to ensure that customer requests are fulfilled appropriately.

Any IVR script should be rigorously tested with users prior to being deployed. A pilot group of customers from the target population should be chosen to test both the performance and perception of the script. Based upon these data, the script should be revised and tested again with a different group of customers, and so on until customers indicate a high level of satisfaction with the content. A mixture of field evaluations, expert opinions, and usability tests can be used to gather feedback on scripts. This type of usability evaluation not only provides data about ease of use, but also reveals flaws in assumptions about what customers need as well as providing valuable data relative to meeting business goals.

In general, IVRs cannot be used as an absolute substitute for customer care agents. Customers with complaints may become even more irate if they are forced to contend with the IVR before reaching a human. Nevertheless, outstanding IVR scripts, used appropriately, can result in increased customer satisfaction as well as improving agent productivity, while also providing useful management reports. By reducing abandonment rates and hold times, the return on investment for an IVR can be extremely high. None of these results will be realized, however, unless the IVR script is perceived as understandable, easy-to-use, and rewarding. Complaints most often occur when the script writer is someone who has little or no contact with the customer, but has been given the chore by default. Human factors engineering is rarely a consideration in such circumstances.

It is important that the IVR scriptwriter uses language that is easily understood by the customer. Many scripts sound stilted and unnatural when they are verbalized from written documents. Just as playwriting and dialog are considered art forms, so too is IVR scriptwriting. A cardinal rule is that if the verbiage sounds unnatural or confusing, don't use it. Many companies use professionally trained speakers to ensure that the message conveyed is of an appropriate tone and cadence, and that it embraces, rather than antagonizes, the customer. Using even the most resonant professional voice, however, does not help when the voice repeats the same message a dozen times as the customer waits in queue. There are several options in this case, such as alternating male and female voices, changing the message as different time thresholds are reached (i.e., the longer the wait, the more empathy with the customer, providing estimated wait times, etc.).

Just as scripts are important, so to is the logical flow of interaction with the IVR. Flow charts that outline the structure of the IVR are clearly an integral part of ensuring both an intuitive design and that the customer is never caught in an endless loop of interaction with the device.

One of the most fundamental requirements with regard to opening the call center's interaction with the customer is to present options that do not cause confusion. Clearly, the most frequent customer requests should be the first options available. Some IVRs use computer-telephony integration in conjunction with ANI in order to determine the callers' most common inquiries, and arrange the menu choices accordingly. Given that the customer is using a Touch-Tone phone, the IVR scriptwriter should be cognizant of the fact that it is easier to find numbers than letters (i.e., don't ask the customer to select "O" for "Other", etc.). Some transactions should also require a confirmation from the customer. In the event that the customer doesn't bother to select any menu choices, or persists in pressing "0" in an effort to reach an agent, the call center manager must instruct the scriptwriter whether or not to repeat the menu choices or simply transfer the customer directly into the "general" queue.

Customer education is required on the use of IVR, especially for complex transaction applications. This can be achieved by sending easy-to-follow brochures or job aids directly to the customer, explaining the IVR menu structure and functions. It is far easier for a regular customer to navigate quickly to a desired function using a flowchart. For example, a financial services customer may determine that he or she can acquire the return on investment from certain mutual funds simply by selecting a particular sequence on the keypad, such as "2,1,4,4." This type of navigational assistance precludes having to endure lengthy prompt sequences and encourages customers to use the IVR rather than wait for a human agent.

Types of Interactive Voice Response Applications

- *Supply Generic Information*

The customer calls and is given several menu items by which to select the information to be heard. Information is generic and the same for all customers (e.g., billing inquiry). All generic explanations given by the agent today could be replaced in this manner.

- *Supply Customer-Specific Information*

The customer calls and is validated via the IVR. Potential applications include sending a bill copy, compiling a fax-on-demand bill, and the like.

- *Customer Information Processing*

The customer responds to demographic questions and the IVR updates a database for reporting. This is most often used at the "back end" of a customer contact.

- *Customer Transaction Processing*

The customer calls for information and is able to create a transaction, e.g., shipment information. Customer shipments are then picked up by the freight company. Similar functions apply to other industries, such as telecommunications, where the customer can automatically add a feature such as voice mail, adjust a bill for disputed charges, or change a billing cycle, and so forth.

Other Examples of IVR Usage

- A medical company uses an IVR to enable customers to get information about invoice receipts, date of payment, and check number.
- A footwear company has applied a store locator facility on the IVR (and gives customers who use the facility additional discount coupons as an incentive).
- A bank enables customers to hear account balances, verbal listings of last five checks, and verbal listings of previous three deposits, and provides the ability to pay bills.

- A major consumer products company uses IVR to enable customers to order parts and supplies—with an intuitive script that is designed by expert call center agents.
- A restaurant chain employee benefits application handles routine benefits inquiries from employees.
- When the IVR closes a call for a telephone consumer products company, information is sent to the call management application via CTI in order to automatically update its databases.

Real time IVR monitoring is also considered a good idea; it should constitute an effort by a dedicated team to monitor the features the callers really wanted. This should ensure a high degree of scripting success. A successful IVR will actually *increase* human-to-human talk-times, as agents will have to deal with more complex issues. The IVR may also have the capability to automatically call regular customers back to advise them, for example, when an outage will be fixed. The same system is sometimes used to negotiate a payment date with a customer. Also based on customer interaction with the IVR (e.g., entering a home telephone number, customer identification number, etc.), a company may choose to identify frequent callers for special treatment using CTI. For example, a company who discovers that 6 percent of the customer base is constituting 40 percent of all calls (as is often the case) may want to route those callers to a special queue of agents who are trained specifically to discourage unnecessary repeat calls. Similarly, using this information to route "past due" customers directly to collections, or priority customers directly to a specialist agent, the IVR can help to ensure that the call center operation functions efficiently.

Computer-Telephony Integration

Computer-telephony integration (CTI) is the functional integration of telephone network capabilities with voice switching, data switching, computer applications and databases, voice processing and, of course, people. Basically, CTI attempts to facilitate the exchange of information between telephony and database products, enabling the routing of the right call to the right agent, along with immediate access to the right information.

Historically, the problem with CTI has been the high cost of retrieving customer information based on the identification of an incoming call and displaying it on the agent's desktop simultaneously while the call is being routed to that agent. This activity clearly requires a great deal of processing power, although the arrival of off-the-shelf CTI-enabled "middleware" packages now makes this a more economic proposition. Notwithstanding the obvious advantages of CTI, such as intelligent call routing and synchronized data and voice retrieval, most literature on the subject ultimately gets around to admitting that contemporary CTI implementation can be an extremely complex, expensive, and time-consuming endeavor. There is nothing simple about synchronizing the plethora of legacy systems and relational databases that exist today with advanced telephony capabilities, such as voice response, automatic number identification, agent profiling, voice mail, fax, e-mail, automatic call distribution, and other such systems.

Asking a vendor to implement CTI should be a cautious business decision. To begin with, there are a confusing number of options in terms of standards, services, and products. Many vendors are technology-focused individuals who have little or no understanding of the customer care environment. Worse yet, a vendor that lacks vision can severely limit the evolving potential of CTI. The result of such implementations can be cryptic, ineffective, and almost impossible to maintain—a potential boon for professional service organizations! It is critical, therefore, to thoroughly examine the efficiency and applicability of the customer care environment before seriously considering an investment in CTI. The bottom line is that CTI will not fix what is wrong with existing systems, it will simply augment and associate the data contained in those systems with any telephony functions utilized by the customer in order to create a more technically integrated customer contact environment—one that has the potential to produce more meaningful management reports in addition to helping agents become more productive.

The most popular application of CTI today is known as the "screen pop," where both the incoming call and existing customer data (if any) are coordinated. This is achieved by capturing the caller's telephone number through automatic number identification (ANI) and using that information to search the customer database for a match, a process sometimes referred to as "switch to host." If a "hit" is found, both the database information and the actual call are simultaneously transferred to the agent. This aspect of the technology clearly works best for companies with a relatively immobile base of customers who consistently call from the same number. Implementing screen pop functionality can be justified simply by calculating the time saved on each call.

Another popular aspect of CTI is intelligent call routing which, based on certain criteria, may automatically route calls to particular agents. This is more elaborate than skills-based routing, which is most often handled by the ACD based on the selection the customer has made from the automated attendant or IVR, coupled with the skills attributed to a particular agent. Considerations for intelligent routing decisions may include who the customer spoke to on the previous call, whether or not the customer prefers to speak with a particular agent, skillsets of available agents, and whether the customer is calling back about an outstanding request. By enabling the customer to define some information from the outset (via the interactive voice response unit, for example), in addition to using ANI (and dialed number identification service [DNIS] in the case of call centers servicing multiple toll-free numbers), the intelligent call routing mechanism can offset a tremendous amount of work for the agent, thus significantly increasing overall call center productivity. Of course, the success of intelligent call routing is often contingent on the ability to use CTI to influence workforce management systems, thus ensuring that the right kind of agents are actually available for the right kind of calls. CTI can also ensure that call transfers do not mean that the customer has to repeat an inquiry or complaint several times.

Depending upon managerial preference (and budgetary considerations), CTI can also facilitate customer callbacks by capturing customer interaction with the network (reporting the telephone numbers of customers who abandoned after thirty seconds in queue, for example), as well as interactive voice response and voice mail facilities. Additionally, CTI can provide security by determining whether a call is emanating from an approved number, and consequently providing remote access to data applications. This is useful for distributed customer care, where "work at home" agents can also take advantage of CTI capabilities. As discussed, CTI can bypass agents completely in some cases by giving customers direct access to database information, such as order status, via IVR.

Optimally, CTI can provide a single point of system control by tracking customer calls from start to finish, including measurement of escalations. This process of capturing statistics from each call's lifetime paves the way for powerful management reports that can help assuage the isolation of the call center from other company departments. A successful CTI implementation can solve a lot of cumbersome data integration problems, but a great deal of planning is required to manipulate data from multiple sources. The problem of leveraging data from both legacy systems and standard query language (SQL) server products has been around much longer than CTI, which by its goal of uniting computer and telephony functions adds a new layer of complexity to the issue.

By putting telephony functions directly on the agent's desktop, such as the ability to answer or place a call with a mouse click, view center-wide call management statistics, review the previous day's performance, and so forth, CTI can help to provide agents with a user-friendly, integrated environment. Optimally, CTI can also facilitate the presentation of fax, e-mail, and voice interaction through a unified desktop interface.

CTI is implemented by deploying software on both the switch and the computer that causes both systems to exchange messages. A CTI server can be added to this mix in order to translate messages and convert protocols between dissimilar systems. CTI programs can be written directly into the switch software, but it is more common to use application programming interfaces (APIs) as a standard means of ensuring that interaction can take place between the switch and the computer. One of the problems with CTI today is that there are so many standards to choose from in terms of APIs. Telephony application programming interface (TAPI) is the standard for Microsoft and Intel, for example, while Novell and AT&T have historically used the telephony services API (TSAPI). To further confuse matters, there are several other standards, including computer-supported telephony application (CSTA) and switch-to-computer applications interface (SCAI). As for fax and e-mail integration, a popular standard is the messaging applications programming interface (MAPI). CTI vendors often claim to support one or more of these standards, but until there is compliance on a larger scale it means that a customer care environment may make an costly investment that will later encounter compatibility problems with new software. In other words, a call center may become reliant on a particular vendor's proprietary implementation of one of these standards.

While CTI continues to evolve, there is no question that much work still needs to take place in order to get telephone switches and computing environments to work together. Today, there are more off-the-shelf CTI-oriented solutions than ever before, but given the fact that no two call center environments are completely the same, a greater or lesser degree of customization is always required. The cost and complexity of integration are often amplified by necessary maintenance. Changes to one system may render the original CTI implementation obsolete, or at least less effective than before.

A CTI implementation clearly involves many different business functions. It is, therefore, essential that the right team players are engaged from the outset. Such a team should include an operations manager, customer care systems developer, telecommunications specialist, and a financial analyst (who ensures that the implementation will really be as cost effective as the vendor has promised). In order to design intuitive call flows, it is also critical to involve agents on an ongoing basis. This team will develop processes and work/call flows, build a prototype (definitely a preferred methodology) or design the actual system architecture. It is essential to have a clear picture of the ultimate deliverable and how it will enhance the working lives of agents as well as improving customer satisfaction.

As with any integration effort, it should be anticipated that implementing CTI will require a greater degree of continuous improvement. It is important, therefore, that the budget and resource allocation reflects the need for maintenance as is necessary to stabilize the system. Financial analysis should be based on a business case that clearly states the anticipated benefits of such an implementation—such as tangible cost savings, coupled with intangibles such as improved agent job satisfaction and higher levels of customer care.

A successful full-scale CTI implementation would capture the essence of this book—a high degree of automated customer contact tracking and reporting that enables customer care environments to increase productivity and reduce costs, thereby allowing empowered agents to focus on what they do best: provide outstanding care to customers. Yet the fact remains that technological solutions such as CTI, even superbly implemented, are only as good as the processes they attempt to automate. Furthermore, poorly trained, unempowered agents who rely on inadequate information sources will still be perceived as incompetent. No CTI prescription can cure these ills.

Despite the nontrivial integration problems that surround many CTI implementations today, it is reasonable to assume that these will become less arduous in the future through the provisioning of off-the-shelf "middleware" type packages. To take this supposition a stage further, it could be surmised that CTI-driven database applications could eventually preempt the ACD as a mechanism for determining the most appropriate agent to receive a particular call. Because such databases would not be constrained by ACD functional limitations, an enormous amount of data could be used to analyze the type of caller, his or her anticipated needs, value to the company, and hence a rated list of the most appropriate agents to handle such a contact. This would represent a significant paradigm shift away from what has become a multibillion dollar ACD industry. In the nearer term, it is feasible that well-funded call center managers may start purchasing minimal ACD functionality in order to allow CTI integration with powerful external databases as a means of optimizing customer interaction.

Automatic Call Distribution

There are several publications that deal with the nuances surrounding network technology integration. For the purposes of this book, however, it is worth mentioning that automatic call distributors (ACDs) are playing an increasingly important role in facilitating not only voice-to-voice customer contacts, but also those contacts that emanate from other media. In summary, ACDs are highly sophisticated call handling tools that have evolved over the last 25 years as indispensable features of inbound call centers. Technological advances such as interactive voice response, computer-telephony integration and automatic number identification (ANI) have increased the strategic importance of the ACD as a medium for potential cost reduction and efficient call handling. Contemporary ACDs not only can hold a call in queue and route the incoming call to the most qualified agent (through skills-based routing), but also can determine the identity of the caller, collect additional data, play messages, and provide critical call data to the management systems used to monitor and control call center operations.

Some of the features included with contemporary ACDs include

- Call interrupt (the option of delivering another ACD call when the agent is already busy with a call, as in the case of an emergency)

- Call vectoring (customized incoming call handling, e.g., response to the caller with music or announcements, or automatically changing call treatment based on length of time in queue, or routing to a different split based on time of day)

- Call center networking (routing based on customer DNIS, time in queue, number of calls in queue, number of available agents)

- ISDN (Integrated Services Digital Network) - enabling the customer identification (ANI), the dialed number (DNIS), and the selected agent ID to be transferred automatically to the host computer before the agent answers the call. The host then displays the appropriate customer data on the agent's terminal by the time the call is answered (with an intelligent interface between the ACD and the host computer)

- Telecommuting (allowing agents to work at home or in a satellite business office using ISDN. Basically, the agent logs into the switch through the voice response unit and ACD calls are routed as if the agent was part of the call center. Supervisors can monitor the performance of these agents through the call management system. Integrated with CTI, the agent may conduct business as though he or she is part of the call center)

- Voice mail (a feature of the IVR that enables the customer to leave a message without waiting for an agent)

- Productivity metrics (the ability to specify current call center statistics on the agent's computer screen)

- Skills-based routing (programming the ACD based on agent's ability to answer certain types of inbound calls).

Using ACDs for Skills-Based Routing

By utilizing ACD features such as overflow groups, queuing to groups of similarly skilled agents, and routing to specific agents, as well as allowing agents to be virtual members of more than one group, call center managers can attempt to optimize resolution on first customer contact by initially allowing the customer to define the exact nature of the problem or inquiry using the IVR. This technique is known as skills-based routing. It is also a technique that requires careful consideration prior to implementation. One major telecommunications company defined no less than 600 skill groups to enable a comprehensive matching of callers to qualified agents. This represented a difficult routing scenario, however, as many ACDs limit the particular skills to be associated with a particular agent.

An important consideration prior to implementing skills-based routing is the effect on agents. There needs to be a strong correlation between agent compensation and the acquisition of new skills. Although this may sound obvious, it is not unusual for companies to overlook the fact that an agent with eight skill code qualifications should receive higher compensation than lesser skilled associates. Similarly, it is frustrating for high-performing agents who have not yet had an opportunity to acquire all the necessary skill codes to have to transfer a customer simply because a particular inquiry is not within their jurisdiction. This is most often the case when a customer asks follow-up questions on a particular contact. A common complaint among skill-coded agents is that "I'm getting six calls for every one that John takes" or "I'll never apply to be skill-coded for those type of questions!" Consider the situation in which the company offers agents incentives for cross-selling to customers. Those agents who are not skill-coded as such may have done all the preliminary work in satisfying the customer, but then have to transfer the contact to a peer to make the lucrative sale. It is a situation that can cause serious employee dissatisfaction and has caused companies to reconsider collapsing skill codes and seek "universal agent" type solutions.

If, however, a company determines that skill-based routing is a nondisruptive and efficient way of dealing with incoming customer contacts, then it is worth considering computer-telephony integration (CTI) as an efficient means of dealing with specific customer needs. For example, using CTI to investigate customer needs via automatic number identification (ANI), together with IVR responses, and then routing the contact to an agent whose detailed skills have been assessed by the CTI application, appears to be an ideal implementation of this business approach. As with any contemporary CTI application, a high degree of evolution is still required before scenarios such as these become the norm. Particularly in multimenued IVR applications, such efforts remain manually intensive and, depending upon the complexity of the customer care environment, somewhat risk-prone endeavors.

Facsimile

Manual Routing is historically the most economic, reliable, and therefore common way of handling any inbound fax in centralized customer care environments. Many call centers continue to use paper fax machines to receive inbound correspondence, whereas others use single-person workstations as a potentially more efficient means of determining who should receive the fax, before routing it electronically to a desktop computer.

A process whereby agents must leave their workstations and walk to a remote fax machine in order to retrieve a customer communication is obviously suboptimal. Yet this is a common practice in many call centers today. Such a process can cost several minutes of potential talk-time, with a consequent downturn in service levels. Some customer care managers have found it more palatable to appoint clerical support to collect and distribute inbound faxes on a regular basis.

Apart from manual handling, there are several ways in which inbound faxes can be routed to an intended recipient, including bar-code interpretation, optical character recognition, intelligent character recognition, T.30 protocol, and others. Regardless of the routing mechanism, however, the objective is clearly to treat a fax like any other customer interaction—as quickly and satisfactorily as possible.

Bar-coding requires no manual intervention, as incoming faxes are automatically scanned for routing to the appropriate recipient. The problem with this approach is that the customer must send a fax that has already been bar-coded, either by affixing a bar-code sticker or by using a fax cover sheet that has been "pre-programmed" for routing. Bar-coding of faxes remains a fairly proprietary endeavor, and usually requires special licensing.

Optical character recognition (OCR) involves scanning an inbound fax in order to convert it into readable text, determining the name of the intended recipient, and then routing the fax appropriately. This method is not always reliable, as much depends on the legibility of the inbound fax. Intelligent character recognition (ICR) is an elaboration of OCR that is generally more reliable in terms of deciphering even lower-resolution faxes. ICR is somewhat slower and also more expensive than OCR.

Other methods of handling and routing inbound faxes include the capability of allowing the customer to enter an agent extension when sending the fax. Using what is known as T.30 fax protocol, the inbound fax is automatically routed to the agent's desktop. With another option, particularly in environments where certain agents are dedicated to particular customers, the customer's fax number can be used as a trigger for routing the inbound correspondence.

Most faxes are transmitted via the public switched telephone network (PSTN). As the Internet proliferates, however, more faxes will be converted into Internet formats in order to allay the high cost of dedicated fax transmission across the PSTN. This also means that customer care environments who provide both Intranet and Internet facilities to their agents and customers will be well-positioned to take advantage of forthcoming Internet platforms. Such technological advances bode well for the future of unified messaging capabilities involving fax, e-mail, and voice mail.

The most popular automated fax implementation in customer care environments today is that of "fax-on-demand." This feature is an extension of the interactive voice response process that enables the customer to call any time of day to retrieve directions, brochures, white papers, and solutions to frequently asked questions without speaking to an agent.

Ideally, the fax-on-demand application will include reports listing the documents currently available to customers, with field-level listings for each document where required. Other reports should include a list of those customers who requested faxes, and which faxes were requested by volume. The application should also be able to generate reports on the integrity of any graphics files being sent to the customer.

In summary, fax processing, like electronic mail, has become commonplace in customer care environments today. Given the proliferation of fax capabilities within the consumer market, it is clearly a medium that can significantly reduce talk-times (e.g., in the case of providing a customer with a lengthy set of written instructions) as well as alleviating the often unacceptable delays encountered by using traditional postal mail services. By providing agents with fax receiving and sending capabilities from the desktop, as well as implementing fax-on-demand facilities, customer care managers can realize significant productivity gains by increasing the occupancy of call center agents.

Trends

The use of high technology in contemporary call centers continues to flourish. After all, there is an entire industry focused on the continuance of the call center as the principal medium for customer care. As such, improvements in the areas of interactive voice response, automatic call distribution, workforce management, and computer-telephony integration are expected to dominate the marketplace for some years to come. The rapid emergence of the World Wide Web, however, has forced several major vendors to reconsider their strategic approach to customer care. Until quite recently, for example, industry publications scarcely acknowledged the Internet as a viable medium for world-class customer interaction. Today, vendors are anxious to demonstrate how their software products can reliably integrate with customer care facilities on the Web. Whether this trend may trigger the gradual demise of centralized call center technology is a matter for conjecture. In the meantime, however, the industry will continue to espouse the premise that facilitating the receipt, routing, and handling of inbound calls is the most cost-effective way to nurture customer loyalty.

CHAPTER 13

Market Intelligence

Overview

The first step in determining the type of market intelligence data to be gathered and its relationship to management needs is to define the business requirements that justify the output of the report in the first place. Clearly, the optimal time to do this is prior to systems implementation, in which case the user interface and underlying system functions can be fully defined and cost justified. Failure to take this step up front most often leads to convoluted and meaningless ad hoc reports that require a great deal of manual root cause analysis (a task virtually impossible in high-volume call center environments) in order to justify their existence.

A useful question for senior managers at this point is "What information can our customer care operation specifically gather that will enable our company to provide a better product or service to our customers?" This is a far better perspective than the one that many companies seem to adopt by asking the question "How can we provide a low-cost customer care operation that is at least equates to those of our competitors?" This latter approach typifies the reason that many call center managers tend to focus purely on operational metrics, such as average speed of answer, abandonment rate, and average talk-time, rather than the dissemination of information that could really benefit the company. In such an environment a call center manager is far more likely to be fired for customer complaints about service levels, than to get promoted for providing reports that are useful to the company as a whole.

It is important, therefore, to define the basic goals of the reports that emanate from the customer care environment. These could be classified as follows:

1. Missed sales opportunities/account cancellations (e.g., presales inquiries, customer suggestions, competitive activities, etc.)

2. Potential product or service improvements (e.g., troubleshooting and other product or service support contacts)

3. Potential customer contact improvements (e.g., telemarketing complaints, missed commitments, interactive voice response complaints, queue times, hours of operation, etc.)

4. Potential cost-cutting opportunities (e.g., elimination of misdirects, repeat calls, lengthy contacts, billing errors, system deficiencies, online information deficits, etc.)

Identifying missed sales opportunities and account cancellations, coupled with the reasons that such events might have occurred, is one way in which the customer care environment can amplify its value to senior management: Too many customer care operations output daily reports that constitute a conglomeration of obscure market intelligence coupled with hundreds or thousands of account maintenance transactions. Another step is to succinctly capture customer problems or suggested enhancements to an existing product or service. This type of postsale support typifies the day-to-day operation of most call centers, but few seem to translate this knowledge into a competitive advantage. By gathering feedback from the customer on any contact from the company that may have given them cause for concern, reports from customer care can pinpoint opportunities for improvement in every facet of a company's business strategies. Many companies are incredulous about complaints emanating from customer care regarding telemarketing behaviors, for example, but properly designed management reports can be a powerful tool for assessing and rectifying market damage. Of particular interest to call center management, of course, are those reports that can pinpoint opportunities for cutting costs specific to operations in general. Again, this is an area in which many companies fall short due to poor design and implementation of reporting functions. Tracking and discouraging repeat callers, for example, and gauging the percentage of the customer base who are actually calling the toll-free number is a task that requires careful up-front planning and analysis.

It is worthwhile illustrating some of the requirements which might elaborate on the basic goals mentioned previously, thereby constituting the foundation of useful reporting structures within the customer care environment (see Table 13.1, Example of management report requirements).

Contact Categorization

From the management perspective, defining why customers contact the company is often as important as providing outstanding customer care. After all, the function of customer care is to eliminate as many of these costly contacts by acting as a conduit for information that details all necessary improvements to a particular product or service. Yet in most cases, definitions and explanations of why customers are contacting the company are obscured by inefficient categorizations and inconsistent or cryptic notations.

Most call centers, for example, require the agent to categorize the nature of a contact based on the initial inquiry or complaint as described by the customer. In some centers, this means selecting a category from a list of as many as three hundred options, or even typing in a three-digit code that correlates to a particular category.

TABLE 13.1.   Example of management report requirements.

#	Report Content	Business Need	Subelements Required	Recipient
1	Presales inquiries which did not result in a sale/postsale cancellations	Identify the reasons that a customer did not choose/retain the company's product or service and rectify as necessary	• Price issue • Features required • Branch/store location • Credit rejection • Preliminary inquiry only • Other	Executive committee
2	Business complaints by category	Identify areas of customer dissatisfaction and rectify as necessary	• Billing error • Marketing complaints • Price complaint • Quality Complaint	Billing Marketing Product management
3	Customer care complaints by category	Identify opportunities for improvement in the call center–customer interface	• Time in queue • IVR scripting/functions • Call center care level • Missed commitments	Call center management
4	Product/service problems by category	Identify opportunities for improvement in the design of products/services	• Specific problem type • Product/service suggestion	Product management
5	Missing or erroneous online information	Identify any information not immediately available to resolve a customer inquiry	• Missing, erroneous, or unclear procedures • Missing, erroneous, or unclear troubleshooting information	Content/knowledge engineers
6	Repeat calls, misdirects, missed commitments	Identify opportunities to reduce costs through the monitoring of unnecessary contacts with the customer care environment	• Agent suggestions • Repeat call tracking • Missed commitment tracking	Call center management
7	Billing inquiries other than complaints	Identify opportunities for improvement within the billing environment	• Bill format • Language facilitation • Rates notification • Special offer support	Billing

It is hardly surprising, therefore, that a large percentage of contacts are classified as "Other." One center, in an effort to force the agents to classify their calls correctly, took that culprit category out of the database, but did not support this action with any viable alternatives. Clearly it was a case of eliminating the effect, rather than identifying and remedying the cause. The busy agents then started selecting categories that had in many cases had the most obtuse relationship with the reason for the contact, resulting in reports that were less useful, and certainly more misleading, than when "Other" existed as an option.

This problem will continue to persist in environments in which agents are required to select a contact category from lists that are often counterintuitive and poorly maintained. Even in an optimal situation, where the lists are meticulously compiled based on customer contacts, and the agent is painstakingly careful in selecting a category, this is a tedious and time-consuming exercise that often does not give management the precise information needed to pinpoint product or service shortcomings. For this reason, notations made by the agent are often far more revealing than the call categorization, yet for various reasons lack the consistency necessary for interpretable management reports. The combination of rigid call categorizations and notations bordering on prose is virtually useless from a root cause analysis perspective. This entire scenario is one major reason customer care is rarely seen as a critical conduit for product and service feedback to other parts of the organization.

Yet there is a solution to this key issue that continues to gain prominence in the realm of customer care. The evolution of online support systems has paved the way for much more intuitive forms of contact classification and notations. By automatically gathering information pertinent to a particular customer contact, the customer care system can help the agent classify a call and identify a new or missing category, as well as generating an auto-notation. This approach assists tremendously in the root cause analysis process, as well as eliminating time-consuming after-call work. The caveat to all of this, of course, is that the agent must use the system, rather than providing an "off-the-cuff" answer to a customer. Customer care environments in which the first point of contact usage of online support systems is optional will almost always be prone to inconsistent and unreliable reports, as well as unnecessarily lengthy after-call work, unless the agents are exceptionally well-trained.

While the agent is always constrained by the categorical limitations of the system, the emergence of customer care on the World Wide Web means that the contact tracking system is bereft of human intervention, and must track and attempt to categorize contacts simply by analyzing customer activity. It is this paradigm more than any other that will necessitate the emergence of online system-augmented contact categorization.

System-assisted contact categorization is a useful asset in any customer care environment. The system will match the initial search string entered by the agent or customer against a database of known contact categories. This matching process will include synonyms for each contact category. Subsequent activity by the agent will result in the system's capturing notations, such as the title of a node of online documentation, thus ensuring consistency and ease-of-analysis in the management reporting process.

User Interface Considerations

One of the critical factors for success in any reporting environment is the user interface that is provided to agents for the purposes of inputting information pertaining to a particular customer contact. In many cases, "Reason for the customer call" type interfaces are cryptic and time-consuming, encouraging hard-pressed agents to do whatever is necessary to quickly rid themselves of this troublesome chore. This situation invariably leads to inaccurate management reports.

Apart from an intuitive human–computer interaction, the information being requested must inherently make sense to the agent in the context of the call just completed. For example, if the contact necessitated a callback commitment, the system response to that input should be to present a selectable list of logical reasons for the commitment (i.e., "Unable to locate information," "Requires higher approval," "Requires after-call work," "Not trained to handle," etc.).

Some companies provide reporting interfaces that require the agent to navigate through several contact identification input screens for every customer contact. Wherever possible, however, the system design should strive to eliminate convoluted user interaction and the need for the agent to painstakingly compose free-form text explanations of the circumstances surrounding a particular contact (see Figure 13.1, User interface considerations for reports). In one call center, for example, agents were observed to be taking up to five minutes to input a notation on a customer call. The agents complained that the system limited input to under three hundred characters, so they constantly had to revise their sentence structure to explain the entire context of the call. Such epitaphs may be useful to the next agent who handles that customer, but are virtually useless in terms of management reports (unless the company is experiencing extremely low call volumes or has dedicated root cause analysis resources available).

Typical elements of a user interface for inputting information relevant to management reports might include

- Contact type (call, fax, e-mail, Internet, U.S. Mail)
- Customer type (national, major, occasional)
- Status (resolved, escalated, transferred, callback)
- Contact classification (presales inquiry, order, postsales support, misdirect, other)

Certain elements will require additional input from the agent in order to further define the nature of the contact for reporting purposes. The property "Contact classification," for example, might contain the following elements:

- Presales Inquiry
  - Resulted in sale (yes/no)? If no:
    - Price issue
    - Features required
    - Branch/store location
    - Credit rejection
    - Preliminary inquiry only
    - Other
- Post-sales Support
  - Product/service problem
    - Specific problem type
    - Product/service suggestion
  - Business complaint
    - Billing error complaint

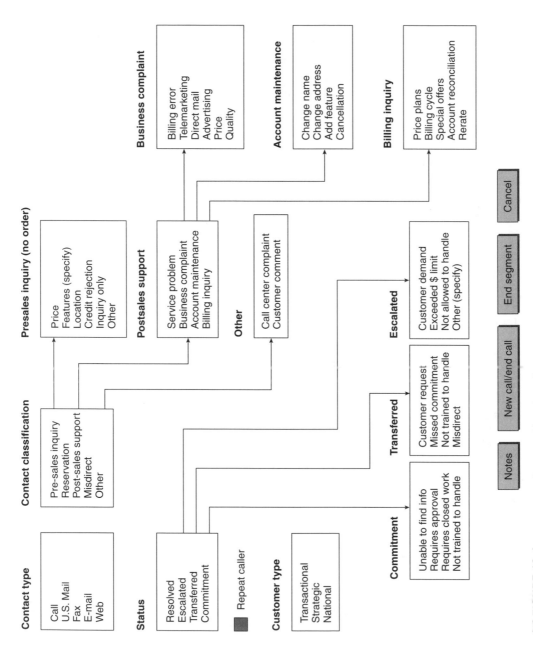

Contact type

Call
U.S. Mail
Fax
E-mail
Web

Contact classification

Pre-sales inquiry
Reservation
Post-sales support
Misdirect
Other

Presales inquiry (no order)

Price
Features (specify)
Location
Credit rejection
Inquiry only
Other

Business complaint

Billing error
Telemarketing
Direct mail
Advertising
Price
Quality

Status

Resolved
Escalated
Transferred
Commitment

■ Repeat caller

Postsales support

Service problem
Business complaint
Account maintenance
Billing inquiry

Account maintenance

Change name
Change address
Add feature
Cancellation

Other

Call center complaint
Customer comment

Billing inquiry

Price plans
Billing cycle
Special offers
Account reconciliation
Rerate

Customer type

Transactional
Strategic
National

Commitment

Unable to find info
Requires approval
Requires closed work
Not trained to handle

Transferred

Customer request
Missed commitment
Not trained to handle
Misdirect

Escalated

Customer demand
Exceeded $ limit
Not allowed to handle
Other (specify)

Notes   New call/end call   End segment   Cancel

FIGURE 13.1 User interface considerations for reports

242

- Marketing complaint (direct mail, telemarketing, advertising, etc.)
- Price complaint
- Quality complaint
  ◆ Account maintenance
    - Change name
    - Change address
    - Change billing cycle
    - Add feature (specify)
  ◆ Account cancellation (explain)
    - Did not meet needs (specify)
    - Competitive offer
    - Out of business, deceased, etc.
  ◆ Billing inquiry
    - Price plans
    - Special offers
    - Reconciliation
    - Rerates, etc.
- Misdirect
- Other
    - Call center complaint (e.g., missed commitment, interactive voice response, care level, care quality)
    - Other customer comment.

Contact status is another area that should be of critical interest to call center management. Reports generated regarding contact status should quantify issues that result in failure to resolve customer calls on the first point of contact. These include empowerment, training, and content issues, as well as quantifying those contacts that constantly require after-call work and callback commitments. Examples of elements that may belong to the "Status" property are as follows:

- Resolved
  ◆ Resolved on first contact
  ◆ Resolved following callback
- Escalated
  ◆ Customer demand
  ◆ Unable to locate information
  ◆ Exceeded $ limit (specify)
  ◆ Not permitted to handle
- Transferred
  ◆ Specific agent requested
  ◆ Not trained to handle
  ◆ Redirected contact (specify)
- Commitment
  ◆ Unable to locate information
  ◆ Requires higher approval
  ◆ Requires closed key work
  ◆ Not trained to handle

Other user interface considerations include "pushbutton" functions, such as "End segment" (i.e., giving the agent the ability to indicate that a particular customer contact involved more than one transaction, such as a billing inquiry followed by a question on how to operate a certain feature—each of which need to be stored separately for reporting purposes). "End call" pushbutton functionality will signal the system that the customer is no longer interacting with the agent. Normally, the "End call" pushbutton shares the dual function of reverting to a "New call" pushbutton as an intuitive means of interacting with the agent.

One of the most evasive tasks in customer care is systematically tracking those customers who repeatedly contact the company to complain about all aspects of a product or service (and in many cases request some form of reimbursement). A key metric in some call centers, for example, is the percentage of the customer base who are actually using the toll-free facility on a regular basis. In most cases, the company may simply take the total number of inbound calls and express it as a percentage of the number of sales of a product or subscribers to a service. In reality, of course, the percentage expressed may be significantly larger than actuality. One consumer products call center who estimated that up to 30 percent of the customer base were calling later discovered through intensive call monitoring that the actual figure was closer to 10 percent.

Tracking repeat callers is considered most important because it represents an opportunity to significantly reduce cost. Customers who constantly request billing adjustments, for example, should be identified and dissuaded according to company policy. Customers who call six or seven times regarding a commitment that is not due to be resolved until the following day can wreak havoc with call center service levels (some companies resolve this by having the customer enter a trouble ticket number via the interactive voice response unit, which through computer-telephony integration can automatically advise the customer of the status of the commitment).

Repeat calls are sometimes tracked using automatic number identification (ANI). This is particularly useful in a consumer market, where the majority of customers may be calling from their homes. It is not always enough to know that there are a large number of repeat calls, however. Taking it to a relative extreme, the cost to the company may need to be measured on an individual basis and a policy decision made as to the viability of continuing a relationship with a particular type of customer. One major service company involved in a highly competitive battle for customers discovered that a growing number of customers were constantly shifting loyalties from one company to another, picking up "reward" checks each time they returned. One such customer, for example, "earned" $300 in twelve months, despite the fact that their average bill for the service was just $2.56 each month.

In most cases, it is up to the agent to identify a repeat caller. A company may decide that, after a certain number of repeat calls, this customer must be transferred to a "special" queue staffed by agents trained to deal with such contacts, thereby not necessarily interfering with mainstream service levels. In any event, the user interface to the "Reason for the customer call" component should facilitate an intuitive way of identifying repeat callers, such as a check box.

In summary, therefore, the user interface that will be used to gather data for management reports must be intuitive, easy to use, responsive, and adaptable to change as dictated by the needs of the business. The content structure of the database must also be carefully designed, based on business requirements, in order to provide management with concise, meaningful reports that will position the customer care environment as a key component of the marketing process, and as a principal driver of product and service improvement.

Functional Design

A crucial step in the design process is to determine what information can automatically be provided by the system as opposed to that which must be input by the agent. Obviously, the more information that can be derived automatically, the more time the agent will have to interact with customers and the greater the likelihood of consistent verbiage being extracted for reporting purposes. In terms of the properties described previously (i.e., contact type, customer type, status and contact classification), most would normally require simple manual input. Companies who have implemented computer-telephony integration could feasibly automate certain information (e.g., selection of customer type). In many cases, however, this is an expensive proposition that is often considered less desirable than a few additional seconds of after-call work.

Some elements contain implied functions that should be handled automatically by the system. Automatic notations (i.e., the system makes notes in the customer's call history based on agent interactions, such as billing adjustments, troubleshooting scenarios, etc.) for example, are most useful for the next agent who deals with that customer, but are not always appropriate for reporting purposes. By considering the overall value of capturing each element, management should be able to create a functional requirements table for the capturing report data relevant to why the customer called. In other words, the system should be able to extract information from other applications used by the agent and/or the customer.

The examples listed in Table 13.2, Defining management reporting requirements, indicate only those functions that require system intervention in order to facilitate the agent's job of completing after-call work. In terms of actual report generation,

TABLE 13.2. Defining management reporting requirements.

Element	Goal	Source	Task	Report
Product/service problem: Specific problem type	Capture the type of problem the customer was experiencing	Troubleshooting system	System captures search criteria used to locate solution	Product/service problems by category
Escalation or commitment due to inability to find information	Identify areas of content that require revision/ training issues	Troubleshooting system/online documentation system	System captures search criteria used by the agent	Missing or erroneous online information
Billing error complaint	Capture the number of billing errors and total adjustments	Billing system	System captures reason for adjustment and total adjustment	Business complaints by category: Billing

however, there is a plethora of functional requirements that must be fully explored. In order to understand these requirements, it is first necessary to design the optimal "look and feel" of each report. While it is recognized that ad hoc reports are often considered ideal, failure to define exactly what management would most like to see in a report may result in a suboptimal system and database design. This should be achieved, therefore, in close collaboration with those managers who will be using the reports to improve business practices. The following section describes some of the management reports that might be generated from the properties described previously.

Reasons that customers did not choose/retain our product/service

Reason	Total	Contacts	%
Price issue			
Features/needs			
Branch/store location			
Credit rejection			
Preliminary inquiry only			
Competitive offers			
Other (list)			

Breakdown

Features/needs (list features and specific needs cited by customers)

Branch/store location (list customer zip codes)

Competitive offers (list competitive offers)

FIGURE 13.2   Report example—pre-sales inquiries that did not result in a sale/postsale cancellations

This report, illustrated in figure 13.2, indicates a need to systematically capture and even consolidate certain information entered by the agent and written to the database, such as presales inquiry elements coupled with account maintenance (account cancellation) elements and specific data entries pertinent to features/needs and competitive offers. In this example, the system also needs to extract zip codes of those customers who indicated that the branch/store location was a problem. In this case, it may be determined that the system needs to support the generation of such reports on a weekly, monthly, and yearly basis (see Table 13.3, Example of a call center monthly report).

Suggested Call Center Reports

1. The result of the calls and deviation from targets
2. Individual agent performance
3. Service level provided to incoming callers
4. Network performance

TABLE 13.3.   Example of a call center monthly report.

Measure	Target (e.g.)	Actual
Average Delay in Queue		
Strategic customers	x seconds	
Reservations	x seconds	
General inquiry	x seconds	
Billing inquiry	x seconds	
Collections	x seconds	
Percent abandoned (all queues)	5%	
Calls answered in 30 seconds	90%	
Service Level by Queue		
Strategic customers	98%	
Reservations	95%	
General inquiry	90%	
Billing inquiry	85%	
Collections	90%	
Cost per Call Answered by Queue		
Strategic customers	$x.xx	
Reservations	$x.xx	
General inquiry	$x.xx	
Billing inquiry	$x.xx	
Collections	$x.xx	
Total cost per call	$x.xx	
Average talk time (all queues)	x seconds	
After-call work (all queues)	x seconds	
Resolution on first contact	85%	
Percent of customer base calling	13%	
Percent occupied (all queues)	85%	

5. System performance (IVR, ACD, queue, routing, and system response time)
6. Measurement of customer satisfaction with the call center
7. Measurement of the accuracy of information delivered to the caller
8. The skill, attitude, and morale of call center employees.

Sources for These Reports

The relevant events making up call records and then the individual audit trail are

- Agent sign on/sign off times
- All event start and stop times
- Call disposition for all complete and incomplete call events
- Holds
- Transfers
- Three-way conference calls
- Agent identification
- Outbound calls.

Reports normally provided directly from the automatic call distributor:

- Service level (including abandonment)
- Talk time/after-call work
- Occupancy.

Maintenance/Change Management

Another common problem for customer care managers is that, when the development organization has completed the design for the reporting facility, it is more or less "set in stone" until such time as there is a need for a major system overhaul. This is particularly true in companies where an overworked systems development group is nevertheless unwilling to transfer responsibility for system and database maintenance to a dedicated call center resource. In such circumstances, even changing an element in the database can become a monumental task. As it is unlikely that those responsible for defining the business requirements thought of every required element in the first place, this often means that even the most wonderfully designed reports can be rendered obsolete. As discussed, agents who cannot intuitively find a relevant element will classify a particular contact as "Other." In one prominent company, it was noted that despite the existence of 115 call classifications, over 90 percent of all calls were being reported in this way. Of course, this was not purely a maintenance issue, but did indicate that the original design was in significant need of overhaul.

Root Cause Analysis

Many customer care environments perceive root cause analysis to be too costly and too much work to be worthwhile. This is the antithesis of the profit center mentality so often advocated for customer care endeavors. If root cause analysis were regarded as an investment instead of an expense, for example, with robust lines of communication between customer care and other organizational entities, its value would rapidly become apparent. In addition to allocating some form of resource to this important task, it is also necessary to identify sources of data that might be augmented by automation (e.g., automatic data gathering on information retrieved during the course of a customer contact). A methodology for rewarding customer care agents for gathering usable market intelligence data for root cause analysis during the course of a call should also be developed. The root cause analysis process (see Figure 13.3) depicts how the customer care analyst can augment both cross-organizational business process improvement as well as individual process owners in critical business functions, such as marketing, billing, sales, and product management. By sharing direct customer feedback in this manner, the customer care environment can become a significant contributor to new product and service realization, rather than a rather anonymous contributor to customer satisfaction.

World-class companies strive to identify customer problems after just ten calls, not ten thousand. A "rule of thumb" often used in the past was that if 80 percent of all calls were answered in 20 seconds or less, the majority of callers would be

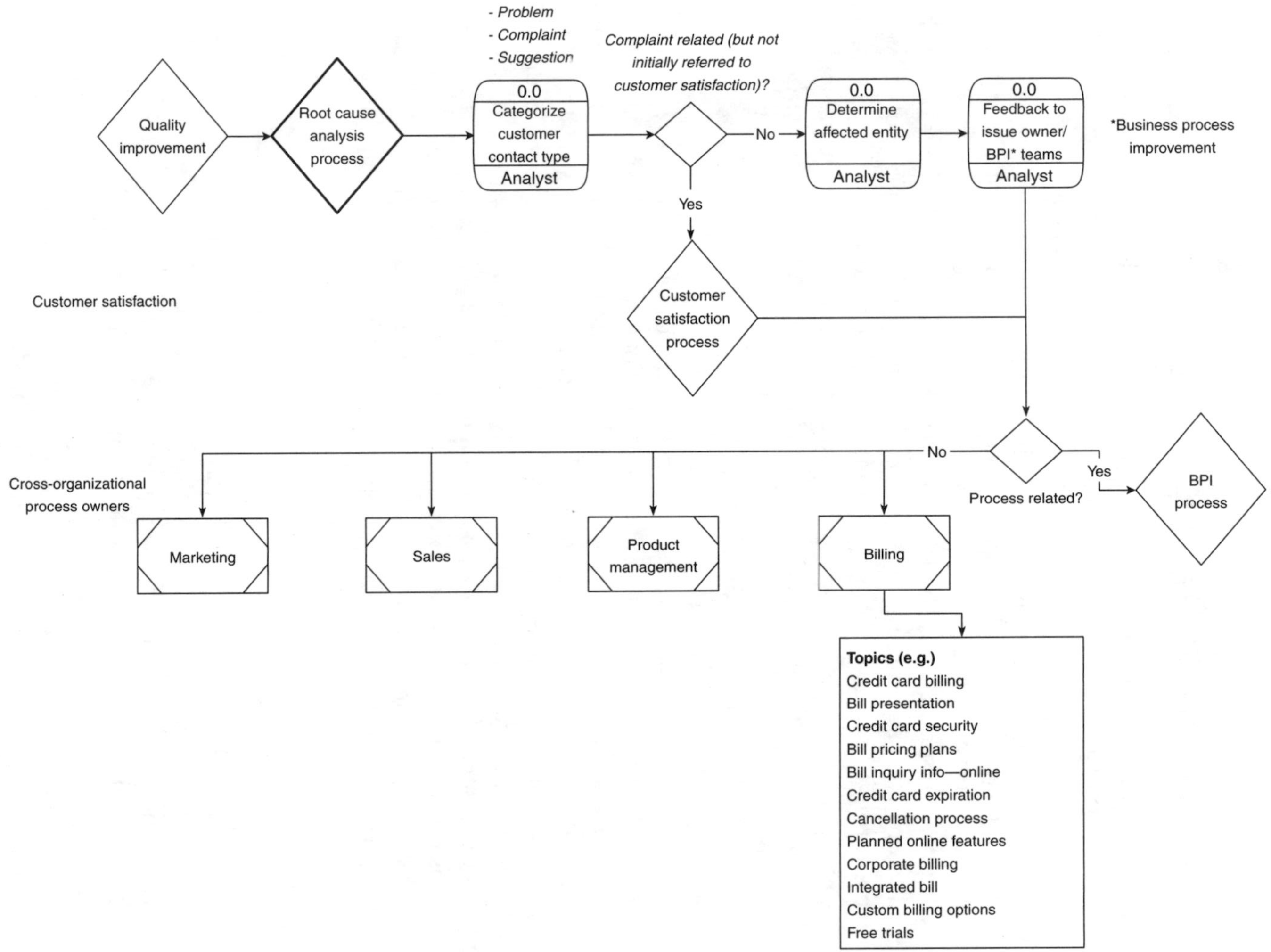

FIGURE 13.3 Root cause analysis process

satisfied. Yet customers differ in their expectations, especially in an era of increasing demand for immediate attention. Customers also represent differing levels of importance to a business. In other words, knowing who is calling and why can help a company assess the needs and expectations of particular customers.

Customer Satisfaction Tracking

It is not unusual for best in class companies to issue hundreds of thousands of customer satisfaction surveys per year. Returned surveys are normally processed within one or two business days, with the goal of generating reports on customer problems or perceived market trends, providing opportunities for improvement to senior management, and measuring the effectiveness of customer care in general. For example, a customer care survey might include questions about the perceived usefulness of the interactive voice response unit, the fax-on-demand feature, the customer care website, and so on. The same survey might explore the customer's perception of call center agents through ratings of courtesy, caring, comprehension, speed of response, ability to resolve on the first contact, adherence to callback commitments, and the like. The customer might also be asked to compare the customer care environment to competitive support offerings, as well as to answer questions concerning product or service loyalty and probability of retention.

While one of the call center manager's primary concerns is the level of customer satisfaction with regard to center accessibility and resolution on first contact, there is a larger issue with regard to product and service complaints. A complaint about a defective product, for example, may need to be rapidly evaluated by manufacturing. Similarly, a high-value customer complaint about a billing charge, the nonpayment of which has resulted in threatening letters from a collections agency, needs to be addressed immediately by an executive complaint desk. This type of damage control can be facilitated by a call center whose agents are cognizant of business policies relating to certain types of customer complaint. Failure to enact this process appropriately can result in a bottleneck at the call center, whereby a great deal of time is wasted, two or more call center staff become involved, and the customer relationship is seriously impaired.

Summary

The best means of demonstrating the power of customer care as a profitable enterprise is by providing management reports that enable a company to adjust and adapt its products and services to meet a customer's needs, while also gathering useful information about its customer base. Many companies, however, fail to take advantage of these opportunities. Instead, reports are often designed or generated in a manner that requires substantial back-end analysis in order to define viable opportunities for improvement. As a result, marketing and product management departments may be hard-pressed to recognize the innate value of postsale customer care, other than as a telephone answering facility for bothersome customers—a perception that obliterates any possibility that customer care might be recognized as an integral part of the marketing process.

By designing systems that either automatically gather usable data or enable agents to quickly capture customers' needs, a company can ensure that every customer call is viewed as a potential opportunity for improvement. Secondly, by conducting root cause analysis, a company can quickly identify product or service deficiencies and prevent market damage. Finally, by distributing relevant market intelligence to various entities within the company, the customer care environment can establish itself as a leader in the quest for competitive differentiation.

Glossary

After-call work (ACW) ACW refers to that work which the agent must accomplish in order to satisfactorily conclude the previous customer contact, such as a billing reconciliation, complex notation, correspondence, and the like.

Applications programming interface (API) An applications programming interface enables disparate computer applications to interact seamlessly by initiating functions and sending and receiving data.

Audiotex Audiotex enables call centers to provide prerecorded information to customers on a wide variety of subject areas, which are normally accessed through Touch-Tone selections.

Automated attendant Automated attendant delivers a prerecorded message, but also asks the caller to select his or her agent preference from a predefined list of choices.

Automated data gathering This term refers to the ability of a system to gather information relevant to a particular user transaction in a consistent and useful manner. For example, an integrated system might capture a billing transaction, while also gathering information regarding a product problem resolution without agent intervention.

Automatic call distributor (ACD) An ACD not only analyzes and distributes high volumes of inbound customer calls to agents, but also captures and stores extensive information relevant to those calls.

Automatic number identification (ANI) ANI is a telecommunications feature that enables the recipient to view the originating telephone number before accepting the call.

Average speed of answer (ASA) ASA usually refers to the time lapse between a call being received (or the caller selecting a prompt) and an agent accepting the call.

Average talk time (ATT) Average talk time refers to the average amount of time an agent or group of agents are taking between accepting and terminating a particular inbound call.

Case-based reasoning (CBR) Case-based reasoning is the term used to describe an "intelligent" system that attempts to match user inputs to a preexisting database of conditions, questions, answers, and remedies in order to achieve the highest probability of resolution to a particular problem.

Client-server Client-server relationships usually involve one powerful computer serving one or more client machines by efficiently sharing data access, presentation, and business logic across a local area network.

Common user access (CUA) Common user access principles were devised by IBM in order to create an industry standard approach to the properties and behavior of graphical user interface components, such as list boxes, push buttons, dialog boxes, and the like.

Computer-based training (CBT) CBT refers to the provisioning of online training scenarios that are designed to emulate the classroom, yet allow the user to learn at an individual pace and at the most convenient time available.

Computer-telephony integration (CTI) CTI refers to the marriage of computer functions with telecommunications in order to retrieve, process, and store information relevant to an inbound telephone call (such as automatically matching a customer contact record to an inbound number before the agent accepts the call).

Content improvement team (CIT) The goal of any customer care content improvement team is to ensure that relevant, accurate, and complete online information is available to users (agents and customers) in a timely manner.

Decision support systems This term most often refers to a software application that is designed to analyze user inputs and, using an "inference engine," to suggest potential solutions to problems within a narrow knowledge domain.

Dialed number identification service (DNIS) DNIS is a telephony function that enables inbound calls to be routed according to the number dialed. This is particularly useful for a call center with discrete toll-free numbers for different functions.

Fax-on-demand This automated facility enables inbound callers to select and receive information, such as technical specifications, via fax, without having to speak to an agent.

Frequently asked question (FAQ) FAQ is the term given to those questions and corresponding answers that are made available to customers online (usually via the World Wide Web) in an effort to reduce inbound call center volumes.

Help desk The help desk is the correlate to the call center in that its function is to resolve customer inquiries and problems. Unlike the call center, however, the help desk handles *internal* customer contacts, which typically involve technological issues.

Human factors engineer (HFE) Contemporary human factors engineers are most often utilized as part of the systems design process, whereby these individuals may represent the user population in order to provide input on screen design, functionality, and workflow.

Integrated services digital network (ISDN) ISDN enables digitized voice, data, fax, and even video to be carried over the same telephone line at high transmission speeds.

Intelligent troubleshooting system This term refers to any software application that uses some form of automated reasoning in order to diagnose a particular problem.

Interactive voice response (IVR) Interactive voice response describes computer software that is designed to enable customers to access certain types of information, via the telephone, without having to reach an agent (e.g., checking account balance, etc.).

Knowledge engineering (KE) Knowledge engineering originally referred to complex artificial intelligence programming. Today, it is often used to describe the task of construing solutions to user problems and inputting this information into an existing knowledge base "shell" for manipulation by an intelligent troubleshooting system.

Information retrieval system (IRS) Information retrieval systems are often a conglomerate of online documentation and intelligent troubleshooting systems whose primary function is to enable users to rapidly locate data that is relevant to a particular inquiry or problem.

Local area network (LAN) A local area network is usually comprised of a group of adjacent computers that share common resources, such as software applications.

Natural language (NL) Natural language is the term used to describe software that attempts to "understand" freeform text by parsing the input and using standard query language to interact with a database. Semantic complexities, however, continue to present a major obstacle to software developers.

Neural network A form of artificial intelligence software that is designed to "learn" from experience, ostensibly by creating logical associations between discrete pieces of information, akin to human thought.

Online Online refers to the use of computers in retrieving, processing, or storing information.

Predictive dialer Predictive dialers are most often used by outbound telemarketing centers in order to ensure that numbers automatically dialed from a (e.g., consumer) database reach a human before being transferred to an agent.

Quality improvement team (QIT) In the context of this book, the goal of a quality improvement team is to identify any contingency that may inhibit the efficient resolution of a customer contact, such as a process, system or content deficiency.

Resolution on first contact (ROFC) The primary goal of any customer care environment is to provide mechanisms that enable any relevant inbound contact to be satisfactorily resolved without need for any further interaction with the customer on that matter.

Service level A call center service level refers to the average number of inbound calls that are being accepted by agents within a given time frame. A traditional industry standard, for example, is the goal of answering "80 percent of calls within 20 seconds."

Skills-based routing Skills-based routing is an ACD feature that enables inbound calls to be routed to the agent best qualified to deal with the type of inquiry the caller has indicated (via prompts) he or she would like to make.

Speech recognition Speech recognition enables an inbound caller to respond to prompts using verbal, rather than keypad, responses.

Total quality management (TQM) An approach to management that evolved from W. Edwards Deming "Plan, Do, Check, Act" principles and was first used by the United States Department of Defense.

User Needs Analysis A systems design component that uses task analysis, rapid prototyping, and usability testing in order to ensure that the final product logically and intuitively supports users requirements.

Bibliography

Brooks, F. P. *The Mythical Man–Month*. Reading, MA: Addison-Wesley, 1995.

Camp, R. C. *Business Process Benchmarking*. Milwaukee, WI: Quality Press, 1995.

Connellan, T. K., and R. Zemke. *Sustaining Knock Your Socks Off Service*. New York: Amacom, 1993.

Cronin, M. J. *Doing Business on the Internet*. New York: Van Nostrand Reinhold, 1994.

Cusack, M. W. *Efforts to Simplify Human–Computer Communication*. Piscataway, New Jersey: IEEE Transactions on Professional Communication, March 1993.

Davenport, T. H. *Process Innovation. Boston:* Harvard Business School Press, 1993.

Dawson, K. *The Call Center Handbook*. New York: Flatiron Publishing, 1996.

Durr, W. *Building a World-Class Inbound Call Center*. Dobbs-Ferry, New York: TeleProfessional, 1996.

Feigenbaum, E., et al. *The Rise of the Expert Company*. New York: Vintage Books, 1989.

Garson, B. *The Electronic Sweatshop*. London: Penguin Books, 1989.

Hammer, M. *The Reengineering Revolution*. New York: HarperCollins Publishers, 1994.

Harmon, P., and B. Sawyer. *Creating Expert Systems*. New York: John Wiley & Sons, 1990.

Harrington, H. J. *Business Process Improvement*. New York: McGraw-Hill, 1991.

Hiltz, S. R., and M. Turoff. *The Network Nation*. Cambridge, MA: The MIT Press, 1993.

Laurel, B. *The Art of Human–Computer Interface Design*. Reading, MA: Addison-Wesley, 1990

Laurel, B. *Computers as Theatre*. Reading, MA: Addison-Wesley, 1991.

Lecht, C. *The Information Tsunami*. San Mateo, CA: IDG Books Worldwide, 1992.

Leebaurt, D. *Technology 2001*. Cambridge, MA: The MIT Press, 1991.

Meindl, J. *Brief Lessons in High Technology*. Stanford, CA: Stanford Alumni Association, 1991.

Morrison, I. *The Second Curve*. New York: Ballantine Books, 1996.

Negroponte, N. *Being Digital*. New York: Alfred A. Knopf, 1995.

Palfreman, J., and D. Swade. *The Dream Machine*. London: BBC Books, 1991.

Parsaye, K., and M. Chignell. *Expert Systems for Experts*. New York: John Wiley & Sons, 1988.

Ramaswamy, R. *Design and Management of Service Processes*. Reading, MA: Addison-Wesley, 1996.

Rheingold, H. *The Virtual Community*. Reading, MA: Addison-Wesley, 1993.

Riesbeck, C. K., and R. C. Schank. *Inside Case-Based Reasoning*. Hillsdale, NJ: Lawrence Erlbaum, 1989.

Rummler, G. A., and A. P. Brache. *Improving Performance*. San Francisco: Jossey-Bass Publishers, 1995.

Shafer, D. *Designing Intelligent Front Ends for Business Software*. New York: John Wiley & Sons, 1989.

Sterne, J. *Customer Service on the Internet*. New York: John Wiley & Sons, 1996.

TARP. *The Benefits of Tollfree Telephone Numbers and the Pitfalls of System Rollout*. Washington, DC, September 1993.

TARP. *The SOCAP/TARP 800 Number Survey*. Washington DC, June 1992.

Treacy, M., and F. Wiersema. The Discipline of Market Leaders. Reading, MA: Addison-Wesley, 1994.

Walton, M. *Deming Management at Work*. New York: Perigree Books, 1991.

Wang, C. B. *Techno Vision*. New York: McGraw-Hill, 1994.

Whiteley, R., and D. Hessan. *Customer Centered Growth*. Reading, MA: Addison-Wesley, 1996.

Zemke, R. *The Service Edge*. New York: Penguin Books, 1989.

Index